The Politics of Standard Setting

AF794008

European University Studies
Europäische Hochschulschriften
Publications Universitaires Européennes

Series V
Economics and Management

Reihe V Série V
Volks- und Betriebswirtschaft
Sciences économiques, gestion d'entreprise

Vol./Bd. 3401

PETER LANG
Frankfurt am Main · Berlin · Bern · Bruxelles · New York · Oxford · Wien

Ulf Michael Thomas Luthardt

The Politics of Standard Setting

Reflections on the Legitimacy of Accounting Procedures in Europe

PETER LANG
Internationaler Verlag der Wissenschaften

Bibliographic Information published by the Deutsche Nationalbibliothek
The Deutsche Nationalbibliothek lists this publication in the Deutsche Nationalbibliografie; detailed bibliographic data is available in the internet at http://dnb.d-nb.de.

Zugl.: Bremen, Univ., Diss., 2011

D 46
ISSN 0531-7339
ISBN 978-3-631-62126-4

© Peter Lang GmbH
Internationaler Verlag der Wissenschaften
Frankfurt am Main 2012
All rights reserved.

All parts of this publication are protected by copyright. Any utilisation outside the strict limits of the copyright law, without the permission of the publisher, is forbidden and liable to prosecution. This applies in particular to reproductions, translations, microfilming, and storage and processing in electronic retrieval systems.

www.peterlang.de

To my parents,
with thanks

To my parents,
with thanks

Table of Contents

List of Tables

List of Figures

List of Abbreviations

AICPA	American Institute of Certified Public Accountants
AISG	Accountants' International Study Group
ARC	Accounting Regulatory Committee
ARG	Analyst Representative Group
ASRB	Accounting Standards Review Board
BBA	British Bankers' Association
CEA	Comité Européen des Assurances (European Insurance Committee)
CESR	Committee of European Securities Regulators
CIS	Commonwealth of Independent States
CONSOB	Commissione Nazionale per le Società e la Borsa
CPA	Certified Public Accountant
DD	Discussion Document
DPOC	Due Process Oversight Committee
EC	European Commission (depending on context also European Council or European Community)
ECON	Committee on Economic and Monetary Affairs
ED	Exposure Drafts
EFRAG	European Financial Reporting Advisory Group
EP	European Parliament
EU	European Union
FASB	Financial Accounting Standards Board
FEE	Fédération des Experts Comptables Européens
GASB (US)	Governmental Accounting Standards Board
GPF	Global Preparers Forum
IASB	International Accounting Standards Board
IASC	International Accounting Standards Committee
IASCF	International Accounting Standards Committee Foundation
IFAC	International Federation of Accountants
IFRIC	International Financial Reporting Interpretation Committee
IFRS	International Financial Reporting Standards
IMF	International Monetary Fund
IOSCO	International Organization of Securities Commissions

ISVAP	Istituto per la vigilanza sulle assicurazioni private e di interesse collettivo
ITAC	Investors Technical Advisory Committee
JICPA	Japanese Institute of Certified Public Accountants
LIAJ	Life Insurance Association of Japan
MB	Monitoring Board (Group)
MoU	Memorandum of Understanding
IR	International Relations
OECD	Organisation for Economic Cooperation and Development
SAC	Standard Advisory Council
SARG	Standards Advice Review Group
SEC (US)	Securities and Exchange Commission
SIFMA	Securities Industry and Financial Markets Association
SME	Small and medium-sized enterprises
SOA (US)	Sarbanes-Oxley Act (Pub.L. 107-204, 116 Stat. 745)
SWP	Strategy Working Party
TAAG	Trustee Appointment Advisory Group
TEG	Technical Expert Group
US GAAP	United States Generally Accepted Accounting Principles

Foreword

The present study is the result of an arduous, but equally rewarding journey characterized by diverse avenues taken and temporal interruptions. Yet, wherever my curiosity took me, it was only due to the long lasting support of my PhD advisor Jochen Zimmermann that enabled me to proceed. I wish to express my sincere thanks for his constant encouragement during the preparation of my thesis.

Along the way, I had the privilege to study accounting from different perspectives involving distinct methodologies of science and logic, which, in turn, may be justified only in terms of their conduciveness to the ends of scientific discovery: the truth. Acknowledging the importance of probabilities it is, at least, equally important to understand on what the probability numbers are based: arguments. And in the substantive cases one wishes to comprehend, arguments are not evaluated by their probabilities but by critical thinking. It goes without saying that research in financial reporting is a complex field of scholarship and, given humans' fallibility in reasoning and judgment, no one should claim to have privileged access to the resolution of scientific problems. To comprehend accounting as an interdisciplinary subject and studying it accordingly is the lesson I have learned. I thoroughly enjoyed writing this thesis.

1 Introduction

„Die Politik ist keine exakte Wissenschaft.
Die Politik ist die Kunst des Möglichen."
Otto von Bismarck (1 April 1815 – 30 July 1898)

1.1 Problem definition and objectives

The annual report of the International Accounting Standards Committee Foundation (IASCF) of 2009 showed that, since 2001, nearly 120 countries have approved the use of International Financial Reporting Standards (IFRS).[1] In Europe, the regulation (EC) No. 1606/2002[2] (henceforth IAS Regulation) compels all listed European companies to prepare and disclose their consolidated financial statements in accordance with IFRS. These standards are developed by the International Accounting Standards Board (IASB), a privately organized body. Nowadays, they are universally regarded as the foundation of internationally accepted accounting rules. The US Securities and Exchange Commission's decision to eliminate accounting reconciliation requirements for foreign registrants using IFRS and to propose the use of IFRS by all publicly listed companies in the US marks a further step on the path to the global recognition of IFRS.[3] The growing application of IFRS increases their importance for international financial stability. The IASB's rise to worldwide influence also means that today the IASB is peerless when it comes to setting international accounting rules.

As a consequence, the IASB finds itself subject to much more political pressure from competing interests regarding financial reporting issues. Not only accounting standards are subject to special interest demands: the organizational set-

1 International Accounting Standards Committee Foundation (2009). Annual Report, p. 3.

2 Council of the European Communities (2002). *Regulation (EC) No 1606/2002 of the European Parliament and of the Council of 19 July 2002 on the application of international accounting standards.*

3 U.S. Securities and Exchange Commission (2008). *SEC Proposes Roadmap Toward Global Accounting Standards to Help Investors Compare Financial Information More Easily.* Press Release, Washington, D.C., Available at: http://www.sec.gov/news/press/2008/2008-184.htm. A decision whether to adopt IFRS in the US is expected in 2011 by the US Securities and Exchange Commission (SEC).

up is also being challenged by diverse stakeholder groups. In 2001 the International Accounting Standards Committee's (IASC) organizational structure and processes were allegedly not keeping pace with the demands that accompanied its increasing recognition. The voiced objections resulted in broad organizational restructuring; following a major reform, the IASC, which was founded in 1973, became the IASB. Organizational, in particular governance issues of the IASB received new attention by the Group of Twenty (G-20) Finance Ministers and Central Bank Governors' declarations at the April 2009 summit. These included that the IASC Foundation:

> "[...] within the framework of the independent accounting standard-setting process, should improve involvement of stakeholders, including prudential regulators and emerging markets, through the IASB's constitutional review."[4]

Similar concerns pertaining to the governance structure of the IASC Foundation have been voiced at European level. The report on IFRS and the governance of the IASB, issued by the Committee on Economic and Monetary Affairs (ECON) in 2008, observed that:

> "[...] the IASCF/IASB lack transparency, legitimacy, accountability and are not under the control of any democratically elected parliament or government, without the EU institutions having established the accompanying procedures and practices of consultation and democratic decision-making that are usual in its own legislative procedures [...]."[5]

At the core of this criticism lies a fundamental problem of accounting regulation in its organizational and social context: how collectively binding decisions should be made in the face of reasonable disagreement. Previously, accounting regulation was often localized within the nation-state and concepts of authority, democracy and legitimacy ensured agreement and acceptance for legislation even by those whose primary interests were not satisfied. These concepts are of particular importance because the functioning and effectiveness of any social order presupposes a high level of compliance with its rules which, in turn, are based on legitimate decision-making structures. The emergence of global governance dealing with policy issues beyond the nation-state, however, altered the institutional and organizational context of national rule making profoundly, concomitantly contesting the validity of the underlying views of the state, territorialism and sovereignty. From this observation follows that "[...] the concept of

4 The Group of Twenty (G-20) (2009). *Declaration on strengthening the financial system – London summit, 2 April, 2009*. Available at: http://g20london.wordpress.com/2009/04/02/g20-london-summit-declaration.

5 Radwan, Alexander (2008). Report on International Financial Reporting Standards (IFRS) and the Governance of the International Accounting Standards Board (IASB), Committee on Economic and Monetary Affairs. European Parliament. 1-23, p. 4.

legitimate political power or authority has to be separated from its exclusive traditional association with states and fixed national borders [and that] the meaning and nature of power, authority and accountability have to be re-examined."[6]

Bismarck's view that politics cannot be an exact science, but is rather the 'art of the possible' has important implications for this study. Politics implies the possibility of choice. This opportunity does not only include the substantive body of laws or regulations but also the organizational structure of governments or regulatory bodies, which is by no means predetermined. To make that kind of decision, any particular normative theory, which means how things should or ought to be, offers a criterion for distinguishing between better and worse forms of government. In the context of this study, concepts of legitimacy can be used to assess the acceptance of the accounting standard-setting processes and their resulting norms in the absence of a coherent social choice theory.[7] Therefore, the first objective of this study is to show how transnational governance modes comprising non-state regulatory organizations can be linked to a democratic conception of legitimate political authority. If a procedural account of legitimate authority succeeds, it allows the avoidance of potential questions about which independent standard should be used to judge outcomes. The normative ideals of institutional arrangements can subsequently be contrasted with the descriptive-empirical world, which is the second objective of this study.

Building on the work of Zimmermann *et al.* who analyze different governance modes ('state', community' and 'market') and how the respective roles of these actors changed in disclosure and enforcement regulation, this study explores what constitutes 'good' (legitimate) governance. An 'actor-centered' view on governance issues provides a consistent analytical framework of both works.[8]

1.2 Course of investigation

I address the objectives of this study from a philosophical, political science, economic as well as psychological perspective. Specifically, I wish to include topics from related but different research areas. It goes without saying that the interdisciplinary approach of this study inevitably poses questions with regard to con-

6 Held, David (1995). *Democracy and the global order: from the modern state to cosmopolitan governance*. Cambridge: Polity, p. 22.

7 Scharpf, Fritz W. (2004). *Legitimationskonzepte jenseits des Nationalstaats*. MPIfG Working Paper. (4):6. 1-31, p. 23.

8 Zimmermann, Jochen, Werner, Jörg R. and Volmer, Philipp B. (2008). *Global governance in accounting: rebalancing public power and private commitment*. Basingstoke: Palgrave Macmillan, p. 185.

tent. As a result, some parts of the analysis will seem superficial: The political scientist will find the treatment of authority and models of democracy unsophisticated, whereas the economist would like to see a stronger emphasis on the principle of methodological individualism. Nevertheless, I hope the careful selection of different aspects taken from diverse fields of scholarship provides some enlightening elements of analysis.

Initially, *chapter 2* highlights the political dimensions of accounting standards as well as the institutions responsible for developing these standards. The observation that accounting regulation is embedded within a political environment is a precondition for the use of political concepts to this study. Against this background, the historical development and institutional changes that accompanied the harmonization of accounting regulation in Europe are illustrated. The changing institutional landscape involves a shift of legislative competence from member states to the European Commission (EC) and subsequently to the privately organized body, the IASB. Chapter 2 stresses the importance of clearly identifying the extent (or location within the overall regulatory framework) of delegated private authority and emphasizes that it is *only* the legislative process which is delegated and subject of this study. The final decision to adopt the standards promulgated by the IASB still rests within the European Commission.[9] Chapter 2 closes with a discussion of where and how public authority is being challenged. This discussion helps, in turn, to clarify the 'legitimacy-demand' posed by transnational governance structures as compared to national/public rule making. In contrast, chapter 2 does not provide a discussion of whether there is a need for accounting regulation, a subject which is covered by different theories of regulation.[10] Based on the assumption that accounting regulation is warranted,

9 A clear understanding of the shift in actor involvement has important implications for the legitimacy assessment because too "[...] often [people] assume the erosion of state power in the face of globalizing pressures and fail to recognize the enduring capacity of the state apparatus to shape the direction of domestic and international politics." Held, David (1995). *Democracy and the global order: from the modern state to cosmopolitan governance*. Cambridge: Polity, p. 96.

10 Two distinct theories discuss the need for accounting regulation: the public interest theory and the interest group theory. Scott, William R. (2009). *Financial accounting theory*. Toronto: Pearson Prentice Hall, chapter 13. For example, Healy and Palepu argue that "[...] accounting information can be viewed as a public good since existing stockholders implicitly pay for its production but cannot charge potential investors for their use of the information [...]" which, according to Laughlin and Puxty results in the fact that "[...] the great majority of writers on regulation assume that it is necessary, justifying the need on the basis of economic disequilibrium arguments." Healy, Paul M. and Palepu, Krishna G. (2001). *Information asymmetry, corporate disclosure, and the capital markets: A review of the empirical disclosure literature*.

chapter 2 asks which factors create 'legitimacy-demands' on its organizational structure. To rephrase and reiterate, the question is not if there is a general need for accounting regulation, but how it should be regulated: the governance mode and its desirable characteristics.

Chapter 3 develops the analytical framework, which will be subsequently used to assess the legitimacy of the contemporary regulatory structures in Europe. Political philosophy as a normative science guides the ideas developed in chapter 3 as a starting point of how things ought to or should be. Before turning to the normative criteria employed, the natural point of origin to re-examine contemporary governance systems is the concept of political authority and its distinct justifications. As David Miller points out "[...] these very basic questions need to be resolved before we can move on [...] to ask how best to constitute the form of government and what limits should be set to its authority."[11] The normative dimension of authority relates to questions of how authority is justified, who or what gives legitimacy, and why the authority of someone is accepted as such. An inter-subjective belief in the legitimacy of an institution (authority), in turn, "[...] is a precondition to the effectiveness of authorities [...] since the purpose of creating laws and empowering legal authorities is to establish and maintain social order by regulating public behavior."[12] Legitimate authority can be based on democratic processes for decision-making, but what characterizes democratic procedures? Definitions, in general, can involve scalar concepts: they identify certain characteristics. Therefore, democracy as a scalar concept means to say that political systems can have certain properties, for example the degree of inclusiveness.[13] Based on different models of democracy, chapter 3 develops procedural characteristics that allow the establishment of legitimate (legislative) decision-making beyond the nation-state.

Chapter 4 contrasts the normative ideals of institutional arrangements set out in chapter 3, with the descriptive-empirical 'world' based on the fundamental fact

---

Journal of Accounting and Economics. (31):1-3. 405-440, pp. 411-412 and Laughlin, Richard C. and Puxty, Anthony G. (1983). *Accounting regulation: An alternative perspective*. Journal of Business Finance & Accounting. (10):3. 451-479, p. 453.

11 Miller, David (2003). *Political philosophy a very short introduction*. Oxford: Oxford University Press, p. 20.

12 Tyler, Tom R. (2006). *Why people obey the law*. Princeton: Princeton University Press, p. 5 and p. 269. See also Easton, David (1975). *A Re-Assessment of the Concept of Political Support*. British Journal of Political Science. (5):4. 435-457, p. 447.

13 In contrast, sortal concepts designate a class. See Hyland, James L. (1995). *Democratic theory: the philosophical foundations*. Manchester: Manchester University Press, pp. 49-50.

that there are "[...] no general reasons stemming from the findings of empirical political science to rule out a wide range of institutional democratic forms."[14] Firstly, chapter 4 highlights the current organizational arrangements (actors and processes) surrounding the private standard setting (legislation). In doing so, chapter 4 also contrasts the constitutional reforms that took place during 2008 – 2010 with the analytical framework developed in chapter 3 in order to identify adjustments made by the IASB with the aim of mitigating organizational (governance) shortcomings. This investigation includes a content analysis of comment letters from the IASC Foundation's constituents, which had the opportunity to discuss the IASC Foundations future organizational structure. The legislative step along the regulatory process is followed by the policy implementation step. Accordingly, the EU-implementation procedures (actors and processes) are illustrated.

Secondly, the overall regulatory landscape in Europe, a hybrid mix of private and public actors, is evaluated against the normative model of procedural legitimacy developed in chapter 3. Legitimacy defined in terms of democratic procedures is based on a composite of principles, which are complementary, but not equally applicable.[15] For example, to be accountable implies a genuine control of how one acted. The structural analysis, however, reveals that the IASB itself has no authority to make the adoption of IFRS binding, nor has it control over the EU procedures and their final outcome. In contrast, deliberation brings forth competing views, although it does not necessarily lead to sensible action.[16] Control mechanisms are therefore needed. As a result, the focus for assessing the private setting of accounting standards should predominantly be placed on representation (descriptive/substantive) and public debate, whereas public rule making should be assessed more in terms of accountability.

Finally, *chapter 5* summarizes and provides a discussion of the majority of the results obtained from this study. It further draws attention to potential limitations of the study and suggests future research directions.

---

14 Weale, Albert (2007). *Democracy.* Basingstoke: Palgrave Macmillan, pp. 13-14.

15 Luthardt, Ulf and Zimmermann, Jochen (2009). *A European view on the legitimacy of accounting procedures: Towards a deliberative-accountability framework for analysis.* Research in Accounting Regulation. (21):2. 79-88, p. 80.

16 Pink, Thomas (2004). *Free will: a very short introduction.* Oxford: Oxford Univerity Press, p. 36.

1.3 Paths not taken

This study develops an analytical framework for assessing regulatory governance structures in general. Along these lines, it seems reasonable to assume that, for example, participatory mechanisms that are fair and transparent result in norms that are accepted even in the face of disagreement. However, using economic phraseology, this constitutes only the institutional 'supply-side' and as Mattli and Wood appropriately observe "[...] common interest regulation is not assured unless key demand-side conditions are satisfied."[17] Likewise, Denise Vitale argues that democracy is "[...] exercise, practice and process, its success depends on how it is exercised and practiced [...]."[18] However, the focus of this study is normative in character and highlights the institutional features instead of the behavioral dimensions of political practice. Nevertheless, to comprehend transnational governance modes "[...] we [also] must understand the role of humankind – the citizens, stakeholders, and public administrators who are the tool makers and tool users."[19] A behavioral analysis of demand-side conditions would focus upon how people act within institutional constraints and possibilities.[20] It would thus help to explain, for example, whether "[...] a lack of participation and accountability may be caused not just by exclusion or non-transparent procedures, but also by ignorance, information deficits, erroneous beliefs, or collective action dilemmas."[21] Likewise, it is argued that "[...] legitimacy depends crucially upon not only the epistemic virtues of the institution itself but also on the activities of external epistemic actors. [...] Institutional legitimacy, then, is not simply a

---

17 Mattli and Wood further argue that "[...] proper institutional supply needs to be met by robust societal demand (from the public and private sectors alike) for common interest regulation to emerge. [...] In the absence of broad societal demand, industry and other concentrated groups targeted for regulation may be the most frequent users of due process channels – because of their organizational capacity, resources, and expertise – and thus may succeed in influencing the fine details of regulation to benefit themselves." Mattli, Walter and Woods, Ngaire (2009). *The politics of global regulation*. Princeton: Princeton University Press, pp. 3-4.

18 Vitale, Denise (2006). *Between deliberative and participatory democracy: A contribution on Habermas*. Philosophy & Social Criticism. (32):6. 739-766, p. 752.

19 Bingham, Lisa Blomgren, Nabatchi, Tina and O'Leary, Rosemary (2005). *The New Governance: Practices and Processes for Stakeholder and Citizen Participation in the Work of Government*. Public Administration Review. (65):5. 547-558, p. 548.

20 A behavioral study would also ask "[...] whether citizens at large avail themselves of the institutional possibilities open to them to influence public policy, or whether decision making in practice is largely concentrated in the hands of a few people." Weale, Albert (2007). *Democracy*. Basingstoke: Palgrave Macmillan, pp. 27-28.

21 Mattli, Walter and Buethe, Tim (2005). *Global Private Governance: Lessons from a National Model of Setting Standards in Accounting*. Law and Contemporary Problems. (68):3/4. 225-262, p. 226.

function of the institution's characteristics; it also depends upon the broader institutional environment in which the particular institution exists."[22] In short, a behavioral account shifts attention away from the institutional structures of government to the actions of individuals and groups within those structures. However, this is beyond the scope of this study. It is rather argued that the natural starting point of analysis should be the supply-side of institutional legitimacy. Only if appropriate structures are in place can people make use of them. Building upon an in-depth analysis of institutional features would subsequently facilitate an analysis of how observable and measurable variations in institutional arrangements affect governance performance. Likewise, this study is not about alternative modes of standard setting (private, public or hybrid) but focuses on institutional characteristics. For a similar approach, see Reginald Wallace who "[…] separates out the IASC from its standards or actual activity so as to explain why and how it continues to survive."[23] But again, an analysis of how the institutional design of accounting regulation affects outcomes (accounting rules) is beyond the scope of this study.

---

22 Buchanan, Allen and Keohane, Robert O. (2006). *The Legitimacy of Global Governance Institutions*. Ethics & International Affairs. (20):4. 405-437, p. 432.

23 Wallace, Reginald Sylvanus Olusegun (1990). *Survival Strategies of a Global Organization: The Case of the International Accounting Standards Committee*. Accounting Horizons. (4):2. 1-22, p. 1.

2 A Political Perspective on Accounting Regulation

2.1 Political dimensions of accounting regulation

Accounting standards are supposed to resolve measurement, valuation and reporting problems arising from business transactions. More generally, accountability and accounting "[...] reflect a general societal discourse about firms: what is to be expected from them and by whom."[24] The institutional framework as well as the development of accounting standards has been described as political for many years. In 1977, Marshall S. Armstrong, the former chairman of the Financial Accounting Standards Board (FASB), announced "[...] in my view, accounting, like law, is an art whose rules are a convention supported only by general acceptance, [...] perceptions among individuals vary widely; so broad, in fact, is this diversity in perception that, in my view, true consensus is impossible."[25] In support of this view, Dale Gerboth argued that "[...] the fundamental question of accounting inquiry is not 'what is income and wealth?' or even 'how shall we compute income and wealth?' Instead, the fundamental question is 'How shall we go about deciding rules for computing income and wealth?' [...]

---

24 Jochen Zimmermann shortly adds "[t]his extended concept of accountability thus makes accounting not only a matter of market efficiency, but also a policy field in its own right." Zimmermann, Jochen (2010). *EU Federalism and the Governance of Financial Reporting.* Publius: The Journal of Federalism. (40):1. 200-225, p. 206. This view is supported by various authors, e.g. May, Robert G. and Sundem, Gary L. (1976). *Research for Accounting Policy: An Overview.* Accounting Review. (51):4. 747-763, Solomons, David (1983). *The Political Implications of Accounting and Accounting Standard Setting.* Accounting & Business Research. (13):50. 107-118, Mattli, Walter and Buethe, Tim (2005). *Accountability in Accounting? The Politics of Private Rule-Making in the Public Interest.* Governance. (18):3. 399-429.

25 This is an excerpt of a speech by Marshall S. Armstrong before the Third Annual Securities Regulation Institute, on January 16, 1976. Armstrong, Marshall S. (1977). *The politics of establishing accounting standards.* Journal of Accountancy. (143):2. 76-79 (pp. 76-77). Georgia Saemann provides ample evidence that indeed users, preparers and auditors have different (opposing) views regarding financial reporting. Saemann, Georgia (1999). *An Examination of Comment Letters Filed in the U.S. Financial Accounting Standard-Setting Process by Institutional Interest Groups.* Abacus. (35):1. 1-28, p. 6. The differences in perception accentuate in situations where accounting policies require value/qualitative judgments in contrast to mere technical considerations. Solomons, David (1983). *The Political Implications of Accounting and Accounting Standard Setting.* Accounting & Business Research. (13):50. 107-118, p. 109-112.

an accounting rule-making body will not succeed on its technical competence but rather on its political competence."[26]

Building on Kenneth Arrow's social choice considerations[27], Joel Demski demonstrated that "[...] no set of standards [...] exist that will always rank accounting alternatives in relation to consistent individual preferences and beliefs."[28] To rephrase, there is no way of proving that one constituent's value judgment is superior in achieving the common good compared to others. Nevertheless, the wealth of both users and preparers of financial information can be affected by changes in regulation which, in combination with Joel Demski's analysis, renders the development of a universally acceptable accounting standard improbable.[29] This pessimistic view was further elaborated to show that the selection of financial reporting alternatives "[...] ultimately must entail trading off one person's gain for another [...]"[30] and that the resolution of financial reporting alternatives will require "[...] value or ethical judgments as to whose well-being will be traded off – and in what dimensions for whose."[31]

Barry Cushin synthesizes both views and argues that "[...] an accounting policy maker's [...] attempts to use standards apparently will be fruitless, that optimal accounting principles apparently do not exist and that s/he must reconcile himself or herself to a political role of trading off conflicting objectives of financial statement user groups."[32] That said, the essence of a political situation becomes apparent: it is disagreement caused by diversity of condition and opinion.[33] Against this background, Brennen and Hamlin suggest that "[...] the delicate trade-offs and compromises between opposing interests and values are what

---

26 Gerboth, Dale L. (1973). *Research, Intuition, and Politics in Accounting Inquiry*. The Accounting Review. (48):3. 475-482, p. 479.

27 Arrow, Kenneth Joseph (1970). *Social choice and individual values*. New Haven: Yale U. P.

28 Demski, Joel S. (1973). *The General Impossibility of Normative Accounting Standards*. Accounting Review. (48):4. 718-723, p. 721.

29 That the choice of accounting standards has economic consequences is illustrated in Holthausen, Robert W. and Leftwich, Richard W. (1983). *The Economic Consequences of Accounting Choice*. Journal of Accounting and Economics. (5):2. 77-117, Watts, Ross L. and Zimmerman, Jerold L. (1986). *Positive accounting theory*. Englewood Cliffs, New Jersey: Prentice-Hall, Fields, Thomas D., Lys, Thomas Z. and Vincent, Linda (2001). *Empirical research on accounting choice*. Journal of Accounting and Economics. (31):1-3. 255-307.

30 Demski, Joel S. (1974). *Choice among Financial Reporting Alternatives*. The Accounting Review. (49):2. 221-232, p. 232.

31 Beaver, William H. and Demski, Joel S. (1974). *The Nature of Financial Accounting Objectives: A Summary and Synthesis*. Journal of Accounting Research. (12):170-187, p. 175.

32 Cushing, Barry E. (1977). *On the Possibility of Optimal Accounting Principles*. The Accounting Review. (52):2. 308-321, p. 311.

33 Miller, J. D. B. (1962). *The nature of politics*. London: Duckworth, pp. 14-16.

political process is all about."[34] Yet, collective decisions have to be made in the face of mutually exclusive courses of action by procedures that accommodate these differences. For example, William Scott argues that

> "[...] while decision usefulness and reduction of information asymmetry are necessary for any standard, [...] much more is needed. Specifically, the standard must be acceptable to its various constituents. This requires a careful attention to due process by the standard setter."[35]

With respect to the governance mode (organizational or procedural design), Ronen and Schiff highlight the early debate in the US of who should set accounting standards: the private or public sector.[36] Jonathan Wolff sharpens the picture of a political environment by commenting that there are in essence two central questions in political theory: 'who gets what?' and 'says who?' meaning the distribution of wealth and who should have the right to command others.[37] Finally, the possibility of choice regarding accounting policies and institutional design allows the 'system performance' to be judged in terms of content or procedural specific characteristics.[38] For example, Johnson and Solomons evaluate the institutional legitimacy of the FASB[39] whereas Matthias Schmidt focuses on the legitimacy of accounting procedures by privately organized institutions in Germany and Europe.[40] Likewise, Bruce Committe investigates the legitimacy of the US Congress' decision to delegate, in the first place, accounting rule making to the SEC and the SEC's subsequent delegation to the FASB.[41] Most recently, Gerhard Kurz analyzes the IASB's standard-setting activities with respect to lobbying and special interest demands,[42] whereas Richardson and Eberlein,

34 Brennan, Geoffrey and Hamlin, Alan (1999). *On Political Representation.* British Journal of Political Science. (29):1. 109-127, p. 113.

35 Scott, William R. (2009). *Financial accounting theory.* Toronto: Pearson Prentice Hall, p. 484.

36 Ronen, Joshua and Schiff, Michael (1978). *The setting of financial standards – private or public?* Journal of Accountancy. (145):3. 66-73, p. 66. See also Horngreen, Charles T. (1972). *Accounting principles: Private or public sector?* Journal of Accountancy. 37-41.

37 Wolff, Jonathan (2006). *An introduction to political philosophy.* Oxford: Oxford University Press, p.1.

38 See, for example, Alicia, Adsera (2003). *Are You Being Served? Political Accountability and Quality of Government.* Journal of Law Economics & Organization. (19):2. 445-490.

39 Johnson, Steven B. and Solomons, David (1984). *Institutional Legitimacy and the FASB.* Journal of Accounting & Public Policy. (3):3. 165-183.

40 Schmidt, Matthias (2002). *On the legitimacy of accounting standard setting by privately organised institutions in Germany and Europe.* Schmalenbach Business Review (SBR). (54):2. 171-193.

41 Committe, Bruce Edward (1990). *The delegation and privatization of financial accounting rulemaking authority in the United States of America.* Critical Perspectives on Accounting. (1):2. 145-166.

42 Kurz, Gerhard (2009). *Das IASB und die Regulierung der Rechnungslegung in der EU: eine Analyse von Legitimation und Lobbying.* Frankfurt: Peter Lang.

building on the work of Luthardt and Zimmermann,[43] assess the legitimacy of transnational standard setting.[44]

In Europe, the strategy to harmonize accounting regulation across its member states emphasized the underlying political nature. Politics is about disagreement caused by diversity of condition and opinion. Many different opinions regarding financial reporting exist across Europe. The differences mainly stem from differing purposes: tax, financial or managerial. This, in turn, makes it impossible for accounting to "[...] be the same for all purposes [...] rather to the contrary, the accounting rules change with purpose."[45] Political activity results in change or the protection of the status quo by using some form of government and it has been said that the process towards accounting harmonization in Europe caused over 2 million companies in Europe to amend or extend existing regulation.[46] The situation becomes even more problematic since minimizing differences in a single society is already a formidable exercise, but raising this task to questions of global reach involving multiple actors with diverse and conflicting needs seems intractable. On top of that, it is nowadays a privately organized institution, the IASB, that develops these standards through an international system of due process. William Bratton notes that private sector involvement "[...] can trigger legitimate objections grounded in public values [;] standard setters are accused of being secretive, industry dominated, and unrepresentative of all interested parties."[47] Observing the harmonization process of accounting regulation, Chua and Taylor therefore argue that "[...] the move towards a single set of standards under the auspices of a private sector international issuing organization independent of state-sponsored national bodies [...] is as much, if not more about the politics of setting accounting standards."[48]

---

43 Luthardt, Ulf and Zimmermann, Jochen (2009). *A European view on the legitimacy of accounting procedures: Towards a deliberative-accountability framework for analysis.* Research in Accounting Regulation. (21):2. 79-88.

44 Richardson, Alan and Eberlein, Burkard (2011). *Legitimating Transnational Standard-Setting: The Case of the International Accounting Standards Board.* Journal of Business Ethics. (98):2. 217-245.

45 Zimmermann, Jochen, Werner, Jörg R. and Volmer, Philipp B. (2008). *Global governance in accounting: rebalancing public power and private commitment.* Basingstoke: Palgrave Macmillan, p. 6.

46 Haller, Axel (2002). *Financial accounting developments in the European Union: past events and future prospects.* European Accounting Review. (11):1. 153-190, pp. 156-159.

47 Bratton, William (2007). *Private standards, public governance: a new look at the Financial Accounting Standard Board.* Boston College Law Review. (48):1. 5-53, p. 6.

48 Chua, Wai Fong and Taylor, Stephen L. (2008). *The rise and rise of IFRS: An examination of IFRS diffusion.* Journal of Accounting and Public Policy. (27):6. 462-473, p. 463.

In sum, the process towards greater harmonization of accounting regulation in Europe not only touched the content of financial statements but also the institutional framework; from national standard setting to private-public transnational governance.[49] These developments prompted the EU Commissioner for Internal Market and Services, Charlie McCreevy to remark "Accounting is [...] a hot political topic [and] far too important to be left solely to accountants!"[50] The following chapter illustrates the changing landscape of accounting regulation in Europe in more detail.

2.2 Accounting regulation in Europe

The need for transnational governance emerges from "[...] issues that spill across national borders and the need to manage the interdependence [...]" to accommodate collective problems.[51] Governance refers to a close cooperation between public and private organizations jointly confronting problems needing solution.[52] Nowadays nation-states operate in complex networks of international cooperation in which authority is at least shared or at most surrendered to privately organized bodies. Indeed, the regulatory patterns now observed range from regulation-by-non-regulation, through formal self-regulation, hybrid private-private regulation, hybrid public-private regulation, network governance by state officials, and inter-governmental organizations with significant (indirect or direct) regulatory powers.[53]

---

49 Chiapello, Eve and Medjad, Karim (2009). *An unprecedented privatisation of mandatory standard-setting: The case of European accounting policy*. Critical Perspectives on Accounting. (20):4. 448-468, p. 449-450.

50 McCreevy, Charlie (2009). *Keynote Address*. Financial Reporting in a Changing World, Brussels In a similar spirit Alexander Schaub argues that the impact accounting standards can have on the economy is simply too important to be left to the standard-setter alone. Schaub, Alexander (2005). *The Use of International Accounting Standards in the European Union*. Northwestern Journal of International Law & Business. (25):3. 609-629.

51 Esty, Daniel C. (2006). *Good Governance at the Supranational Scale: Globalizing Administrative Law*. Yale Law Journal. (115):7. 1490-1562, p. 1500.

52 In contrast to government, "[...] governance refers to the creation, execution, and implementation of activities backed by the shared goals of citizens and organizations, who may or may not have formal authority and policing power." Bingham, Lisa Blomgren, Nabatchi, Tina and O'Leary, Rosemary (2005). *The New Governance: Practices and Processes for Stakeholder and Citizen Participation in the Work of Government*. Public Administration Review. (65):5. 547-558, p. 548.

53 Kingsbury, Benedict , Krisch, Nico, Stewart, Richard B. and Wiener, Jonathan B. (2005). *Global Governance as Administration – National and Transnational Approaches to Global Administrative Law*. Law and Contemporary Problems. (68):3/4. 1-13, p. 2.

Any form of governance that gives a third party control over the decision-making process involves – to varying degrees – some form of delegation. Accordingly, Bradley and Kelly define international delegation as "[…] a grant of authority by two or more states to an international body to make decisions or take actions."[54] The emergence of private authority in transnational governance along the regulatory process has been documented for diverse political environments.[55] With respect to accounting standard-setting bodies, Richardson and Eberlein observe that "[…] these bodies establish rules and make decisions that are recognized as authoritative, even if they are technically voluntary and not legally binding."[56]

A shift in the governance mode of accounting regulation (actor involvement or forum choice) can be observed for Europe as well.[57] The changing regulatory pattern of European accounting regulation can be illustrated using the concept of international delegation. The contemporary institutional setting was developed along the way towards greater harmonization in two main stages as follows.

Stage 1: Delegation to the European level

A fundamental objective of the European Union (EU) is the establishment of an integrated economic and financial market which, in turn, provides a strong impetus for accounting harmonization.[58] In general, the benefits of increased accounting harmonization are derived from network externalities; positive network externalities exist if the benefits are an increasing function of the number of

---

54 Bradley, Curtis A. and Kelley, Judith G. (2008). *The Concept of International Delegation*. Law and Contemporary Problems. (71):1. 1-36, p. 3. On the benefits of delegation see Reinicke, Wolfgang H. (1998). *Global public policy: governing without government?* Washington, D.C.: Brookings Institution Press, p. 89-90 or Porter, Tony (2005). *Private Authority, Technical Authority, and the Globalization of Accounting Standards*. Business & Politics. (7):3. 1-30, p. 3. The costs of delegation or challenges to democratic thought are discussed in chapter 2.4.

55 Hall, Rodney Bruce and Biersteker, Thomas J. (2002). *The emergence of private authority in global governance*. Cambridge: Cambridge University Press, Mattli, Walter and Woods, Ngaire (2009). *The politics of global regulation*. Princeton: Princeton University Press.

56 Richardson, Alan and Eberlein, Burkard (2011). *Legitimating Transnational Standard-Setting: The Case of the International Accounting Standards Board*. Journal of Business Ethics. (98):2. 217-245.

57 Zimmermann, Jochen (2008). *The Role of the Nation State in the Internationalization of Accounting Regimes. Transforming the Golden-Age Nation State*. Leibfried, Stephan, Martens, Kerstin and Mayer, Peter. Basingstoke: Palgrave Macmillan, p. 188.

58 Hopwood, Anthony G. (1994). *Some reflections on 'The harmonization of accounting within the EU'*. European Accounting Review. (3):2. 241-254, p. 241. See also Haller, Axel (2002). *Financial accounting developments in the European Union: past events and future prospects*. European Accounting Review. (11):1. 153-190, p. 155.

other users.[59] To many, financial reporting as an integral part of the broader market infrastructure seemed to be in need of harmonization to achieve free mobility of capital, labor and trade.[60] Accounting diversity, in contrast, has been considered as a barrier to the provision of accounting services or cross-border capital flows. Additionally, the use of different accounting systems is supposed to impede the comparability of financial information across firms in different jurisdictions.[61]

Initially, the instruments to achieve accounting harmonization were the Fourth[62] and Seventh[63] EC Directives. Directives, as legal instruments, are adopted by the Council of Ministers after a proposal by the European Commission, and subsequently transposed into national law by its member states.[64] Stage 1 (see also Figure 1 below) therefore reflects only the first step of a 'delegation-chain' whereby European member states coordinated their activities within supra-national institutions. At this stage and in contrast to subsequent developments, the former European Commissioner Karel van Hulle emphasized that "[...] accounting standards are not set by the accounting profession."[65]

---

59 Katz, Michael L. and Shapiro, Carl (1985). *Network Externalities, Competition, and Compatibility*. American Economic Review. (75):3. 424-440, Dye, Ronald A. and Sunder, Shyam (2001). *Why Not Allow FASB and IASB Standards to Compete in the U.S.?* Accounting Horizons. (15):3. 257-271.

60 Thorell, Per and Whittington, Geoffrey (1994). *The harmonization of accounting within the EU -- Problems, perspectives and strategies*. European Accounting Review. (3):2. 215-240, p. 216.

61 For a general discussion of the benefits of harmonization (albeit from a user perspective) see Ball, Ray (2006). *International Financial Reporting Standards (IFRS): pros and cons for investors*. Accounting & Business Research. (36):5-27. For a critical perspective, see Chua and Taylor who find no evidence that comparability as an attribute of financial reporting is supported by empirical studies. Chua, Wai Fong and Taylor, Stephen L. *The rise and rise of IFRS: An examination of IFRS diffusion*. Journal of Accounting and Public Policy. (27):6. 462-473, p. 467.

62 Council of the European Communities (1978). *Fourth Council Directive 78/660/EEC of 25 July 1978 based on Article 54 (3) (g) of the Treaty on the annual accounts of certain types of companies.*

63 Council of the European Communities (1983). *Seventh Council Directive 83/349/EEC of 13 June 1983 based on the Article 54 (3) (g) of the Treaty on consolidated accounts.*

64 Haller, Axel (2002). *Financial accounting developments in the European Union: past events and future prospects*. European Accounting Review. (11):1. 153-190, p. 155. and van Hulle, Karel (1992). *Harmonization of accounting standards: A view from the European community*. European Accounting Review. (1):1. 161-172, p. 389.

65 In his capacity as European Commissioner Karel van Hulle served as Head of Unit for Accounting Standards and for Financial Reporting and Company Law. See van Hulle, Karel (1992). *Harmonization of accounting standards: A view from the European community*. European Accounting Review. (1):1. 161-172, p. 166.

The political goal of establishing a single market accompanied by a shared set of accounting standards stands, however, in contrast to the notion that the development of accounting standards was (still is) embedded within the specific socio-economic environment of a country. Socio-economic factors influencing the development of accounting regulation and concurrently constituting obstacles towards convergence are discussed among scholars of accounting classification research.[66] Stephen Zeff identifies four areas that could impede international harmonization: the business and financial culture, the accounting culture, the auditing culture, and the regulatory culture.[67] Against this background, it was not surprising that most member states were not willing to make major concessions to narrow the diversity of accounting practice across Europe.[68] Consequently, the harmonization strategy was one of mutual recognition that took account of local peculiarities. It was believed that options "[...] are perfectly acceptable as long as they can be considered equivalent and are supplemented by appropriate disclosure in the notes."[69] As a result, harmonization in Europe was only achieved through compromise in the form of numerous options rather than true consensus.[70]

To sum up, although the efforts in stage 1 (delegation to the European level) were a large step toward harmonization, the results fell short of expectations. The

---

66 Representatives are: Doupnik, Timothy S. (1987). *Evidence of International Harmonization of Financial Reporting*. International Journal of Accounting. (23):1. 47-67, D'Arcy, Anne (2001). *Accounting classification and the international harmonisation debate--an empirical investigation*. Accounting, Organizations & Society. (26):4/5. 327-349, Larson, Robert K. and Street, Donna L. (2004). *Convergence with IFRS in an expanding Europe: progress and obstacles identified by large accounting firms' survey*. Journal of International Accounting, Auditing and Taxation. (13):2. 89-119, Nobes, Christopher (2004). *On accounting classification and the international harmonisation debate*. Accounting, Organizations & Society. (29):2. 189-200.

67 Zeff, Stephen A. (2007). *Some obstacles to global financial reporting comparability and convergence at a high level of quality*. The British Accounting Review. (39):4. 290-302, p. 291-296. See also Nobes, Christopher and Parker, Robert (2008). *Comparative international accounting*. Harlow: Financial Times/Prentice Hall, pp. 16-30.

68 Haller, Axel (2002). *Financial accounting developments in the European Union: past events and future prospects*. European Accounting Review. (11):1. 153-190, p. 156.

69 van Hulle, Karel (1993). *Harmonization of accounting standards in the EC – Is it the beginning or is it the end?* European Accounting Review. (2):2. 387-396, p. 387.

70 With respect to the Fourth Directive a total number of 76 options have been mentioned. See Haller, Axel (2002). *Financial accounting developments in the European Union: past events and future prospects*. European Accounting Review. (11):1. 153-190, p. 157. And with reference to the Seventh Directive, Diggle and Nobes observe that the British accounting profession was able to introduce changes in 14 out of 19 main features in the draft of the Seventh Directive to protect their preferred status quo. See Diggle, Graham and Nobes, Christopher (1994). *European Rule-making in The Seventh Directive as a Case Study*. Accounting & Business Research. (24):96. 319-333, p. 328.

reasons were the sheer diversity of legal and institutional frameworks which existed across different countries that had to be taken into account while, at the same time, member states acted as safeguards to protect their status quo. Accordingly, the Fourth Directive resulted in a compromise that did not increase harmonization but led to window-dressing of existing practice[71] with the result that "[s]ubstantial differences in accounting remained; the goal of achieving comparative statements all over Europe was not fully achieved."[72] The situation became even more problematic due to the implementation process by the member states, which was characterized by an extensive time gap between the approval and transformation of the Directives into national law coupled with doubts of "[...] whether the directives have been correctly implemented."[73] Taken together, the harmonization effort with the Fourth and Seventh Directives as its main instruments missed its intended targets. Furthermore, the strategy to use Directives as legal instruments revealed that the discussions never focused on a common way to develop accounting standards.[74]

Stage 2: Re-delegation to a private body

Given the lack of progress at national or European level, the European Commission realized that it was necessary to revise its strategy regarding the harmonization of accounting policy. A revision seemed also to be necessary because of demands from firms that needed to finance their business by tapping foreign capital markets, and the resulting information needs of investors in different countries outside Europe. At that time, one of the most important strategic questions facing the EU was whether it should focus on harmonization within or beyond Europe if it wanted "[...] to keep itself in the game of taking future influence in international accounting harmonization [...]"[75] Within the Commission there was a growing realization that "[...] the existing accounting rules based on

71 Thorell, Per and Whittington, Geoffrey (1994). *The harmonization of accounting within the EU -- Problems, perspectives and strategies*. European Accounting Review. (3):2. 215-240, p. 216-217.

72 Zimmermann, Jochen (2010). *EU Federalism and the Governance of Financial Reporting*. Publius: The Journal of Federalism. (40):1. 200-225, p. 206.

73 van Hulle, Karel (1993). *Harmonization of accounting standards in the EC – Is it the beginning or is it the end?* European Accounting Review. (2):2. 387-396, p. 391-392.

74 Haller, Axel (2002). *Financial accounting developments in the European Union: past events and future prospects*. European Accounting Review. (11):1. 153-190, p. 176.

75 Thorell, Per and Whittington, Geoffrey (1994). *The harmonization of accounting within the EU -- Problems, perspectives and strategies*. European Accounting Review. (3):2. 215-240, p. 228. and van Hulle, Karel (1993). *Harmonization of accounting standards in the EC – Is it the beginning or is it the end?* European Accounting Review. (2):2. 387-396.

the directives did not meet the challenges preparers, users of accounts and standard setters had to face."[76]

A potential strategy was to achieve mutual recognition of European and United States Generally Accepted Accounting Principles (US GAAP) to address the demands from firms wanting to tap the US capital market and investors' information needs.[77] For Europe, this would have left the opportunity to further its harmonization program while giving its member states the possibility to diversify their financing base. However, during the late 1980s and early 1990s "[...] the Commission did not see any realistic chance to export its concept of accounting harmonization [...] to the US and to obtain the acceptance of European financial statements without reconciliation."[78] In a communication, the European Commission disclosed that it "[...] attempted to initiate such discussions, but has found little interest on the American side."[79] An alternative way to circumvent the existing problems was to support and cooperate with the IASC in order to exert influence on the outcome of its work. The establishment of a 'European Standard Setting Body' seemed impractical given the disillusioning experience of the Fourth and Seventh Directives. Moreover, the European Commission simply lacked the capacity or ambition "[...] to take over the role of an active standard setter in the accounting field."[80] Bernstein and Cashore argue that it is exactly the absence of effective national and intergovernmental regulation (capacity gaps) to solve transnational coordination problems that caused private alternatives to emerge.[81] The shift towards a greater recognition of the IASB was beneficial in two ways: international reporting standards were already available

76 Haller, Axel (2002). *Financial accounting developments in the European Union: past events and future prospects.* European Accounting Review. (11):1. 153-190, p. 165.

77 Mattli, Walter and Buethe, Tim (2005). *Accountability in Accounting? The Politics of Private Rule-Making in the Public Interest.* Governance. (18):3. 399-429, p. 228. and Thorell, Per and Whittington, Geoffrey (1994). *The harmonization of accounting within the EU -- Problems, perspectives and strategies.* European Accounting Review. (3):2. 215-240, p. 216.

78 van Hulle, Karel (1993). *Harmonization of accounting standards in the EC – Is it the beginning or is it the end?* European Accounting Review. (2):2. 387-396, p. 395.

79 European Commission (1995). *Accounting Harmonisation: A new strategy vis-a-vis international harmonisation*, p. 5.

80 van Hulle, Karel (1993). *Harmonization of accounting standards in the EC – Is it the beginning or is it the end?* European Accounting Review. (2):2. 387-396, p. 396.

81 Bernstein and Cashore argue that private alternatives substitute or compensate capacity gaps at the state level. See Bernstein, Steven and Cashore, Benjamin (2007). *Can non-state global governance be legitimate? An analytical framework.* Regulation & Governance. (1):4. 347-371, p. 347.

and these standards also possessed international credibility due to the endorsement by the International Organization of Securities Commissions (IOSCO).[82]

As a result, from mid-1995 onward, accounting regulation in Europe progressively developed toward the use of International Accounting Standards (IAS) for listed companies.[83] This is a fundamental departure not only in the content and scope of accounting regulation; it also constitutes a significant shift in forum choice for decision-making given the previous announcement of the European Commission that "[...] leaving everything to the IASC is not an option."[84] In effect, the European Commission proposed the aligning of the European Union's and the IASC's harmonization efforts, with the aim to "[...] establish a set of standards which will be accepted in capital markets world-wide."[85] In this new context, member states could allow companies to report under IASs as long as these were compatible with the European Directives.

In 2000, the strategic goal of establishing an efficient and integrated financial market by 2005 was re-formulated by the Lisbon Extraordinary European Council: "In order to accelerate the completion of a single securities market, urgent action in the field of financial reporting is required to enhance comparability of financial statements, as requested by the European Council in Lisbon."[86] In response to the Lisbon conclusions, the European Council presented a proposal, a 'landmark decision',[87] requiring all listed European companies to prepare their consolidated accounts in accordance with IAS developed by the IASB: "In order to contribute to a better functioning of the internal market, publicly traded companies must be required to apply a single set of high quality international accounting standards for the preparation of their consolidated financial statements."[88] The IAS Regulation entered into force in July 2002 and, since 2005, all

---

82 Whittington, Geoffrey (2005). *The adoption of International Accounting Standards in the European Union.* European Accounting Review. (14):1. 127-153, p. 129. See also European Commission (2000). *EU Financial Reporting Strategy: the way forward*, p. 5.

83 Haller, Axel (2002). *Financial accounting developments in the European Union: past events and future prospects.* European Accounting Review. (11):1. 153-190, p. 164-165. IFRS refer to the new numbered series of pronouncements that the IASB is issuing as distinct from the International Accounting Standards (IASs) series issued by its predecessor. IAS and IFRS are used interchangeably in this study.

84 van Hulle, Karel (1993). *Harmonization of accounting standards in the EC – Is it the beginning or is it the end?* European Accounting Review. (2):2. 387-396, p. 394.

85 European Commission (1995). *Accounting Harmonisation: A new strategy vis-a-vis international harmonisation*, p. 2.

86 European Commission (2000). *EU Financial Reporting Strategy: the way forward*, p. 2.

87 Haller, Axel (2002). *Financial accounting developments in the European Union: past events and future prospects.* European Accounting Review. (11):1. 153-190, p. 165.

88 European Commission (2000). *EU Financial Reporting Strategy: the way forward*, p. 2.

listed European companies have to prepare their consolidated financial statements in accordance with IAS/IFRS.[89] The main reason for adopting IAS was that the EC Directives could not "[...] ensure the high level of transparency and comparability of financial reporting from all publicly traded [...]."[90]

From a European perspective, it is important to note that the institutional framework at stage 2 does not imply "[...] *a conditional grant of authority from a principal to an agent that empowers the latter to act on behalf of the former*", a definition often adopted in political science literature on the basis of principal-agent theory. While the application of principal-agent theory seems appropriate for the institutional framework in the US with regard to the SEC-FASB relationship,[91] the IASCF/IASB regards itself as a global standard setter with Europe as one of its main constituents but *prima facie* it does not act in Europe's interest. The controversy around the development of IAS 39 (financial instruments) or IFRS 8 (segment reporting) illustrates that fact.[92]

At stage 1 (delegation to the European level), the harmonization strategy was to use legally binding directives. At stage 2 (re-delegation to a private body), which represents the current state of affairs, the European Commission re-delegated legislative authority to another entity but with the crucial difference that the standards promulgated by the IASB do not become automatically legally binding in the EU.

---

89 Council of the European Communities (2002). *Regulation (EC) No 1606/2002 of the European Parliament and of the Council of 19 July 2002 on the application of international accounting standards.*

90 European Commission ([EC] 2002). *Regulation on the application of international accounting standards*, p. 1.

91 See Mattli, Walter and Buethe, Tim (2005). *Accountability in Accounting? The Politics of Private Rule-Making in the Public Interest.* Governance. (18):3. 399-429 For a recent analysis of this relationship see Palmon, Dan, Peytcheva, Marietta and Yezegel, Ari (2011). *The Accounting Standards Setting Process in the U.S.: Examination of the SEC–FASB Relationship.* Group Decision and Negotiation. (20):2. 165-183.

92 Evidence for the case of IAS 39 is provided by Schaub, Alexander (2005). *The Use of International Accounting Standards in the European Union.* Northwestern Journal of International Law & Business. (25):3. 609-629 The controversy around IFRS 8 is described in Brackney, Kennard S. and Witmer, Philip R. (2005). *The European Union's Role in International Standards Setting – Will Bumps in the Road to Convergence affect the SEC's Plans?* CPA Journal. (75):11. 18-27.

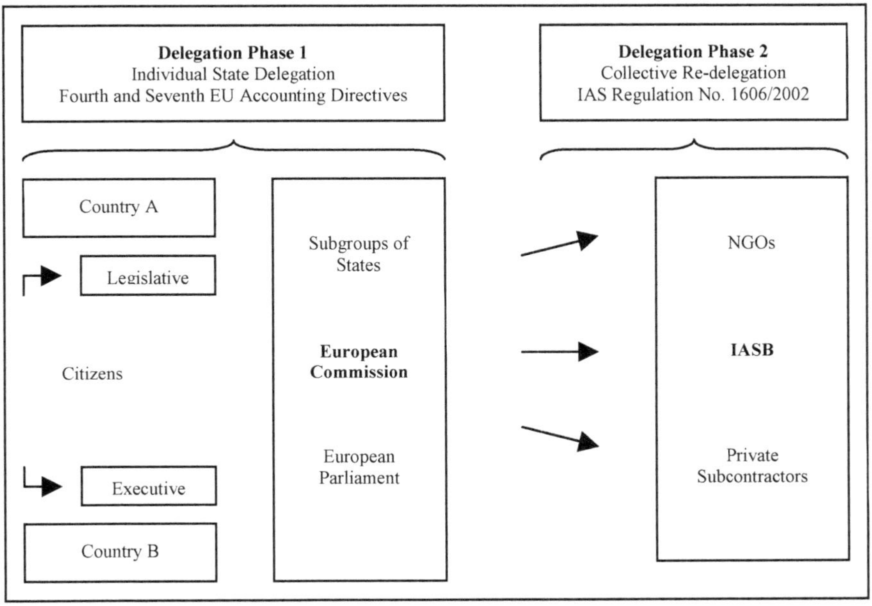

Figure 1: Harmonization of accounting regulation in Europe – the 'delegation chain'[93]

To summarize, the structural and economic changes across Europe led to an increased demand for international accounting rules.[94] Against this background, nation-states firstly delegated legislative competencies to the European level. Following the disillusioning experience of the first European harmonization wave, the European Commission decided to re-delegate rule-making authority to a non-governmental body, the IASB. Accounting regulation changed from government-to-government negotiations to the point where nation-states agreed, not on specific substantive outcomes, but rather on decision-processes, essentially creating "[...] mechanisms of global policymaking or supranational governance."[95] However, global regulation "[...] does not necessarily imply a shift of the whole regulatory process to the global level. In some instances specific tasks are moved beyond the borders of the nation-state where public and private actors

93 Bradley, Curtis A. and Kelley, Judith G. (2008). *The Concept of International Delegation*. Law and Contemporary Problems. (71):1. 1-36, p. 6.

94 Whittington, Geoffrey (2005). *The adoption of International Accounting Standards in the European Union*. European Accounting Review. (14):1. 127-153, p. 128.

95 Esty, Daniel C. (2006). *Good Governance at the Supranational Scale: Globalizing Administrative Law*. Yale Law Journal. (115):7. 1490-1562, p. 1499.

cooperate while other stages of regulation remain at the national level."[96] The emergence, legitimacy and effectiveness of private authority in governance systems, however, can only be assessed by appreciating the tasks private or public actors are assumed to perform and by their localization within the overall regulatory process. Insufficient context awareness could lead to misleading generalizations and superficial analysis. Therefore, it is essential to set the emergence of transnational governance in the context of a financial regulatory framework, which will be done in the next chapter.

2.3 Financial reporting regulation: The overall picture

In order to evaluate the changing landscape of financial reporting regulation it is helpful to conceptualize the different stages of the political process and its actors' involvement along these stages. This approach seems appropriate since Hurrelmann *et al.*, based on David Beetham's theory of legitimacy[97], conclude that "[...] in making normative judgments about the legitimacy of governance arrangements, [social scientists] have to take a look at political processes [...]."[98] Abbott and Snidal describe the regulatory process as comprising five main stages: placing an issue on the regulatory agenda; negotiation, drafting and promulgating regulatory standards (negotiation); implementing standards within the operations of firms (implementation); monitoring compliance; and promoting compliance and responding to noncompliance (enforcement).[99] This broadly reflects the various tasks which can be delegated: legislative; adjudicative; regulatory; monitoring and enforcement; agenda-setting; research and advice; policy implementation; and re-delegation.[100] The specific task of the delegated regulatory process and its legal effect are important features of delegation and consequential to the extent of the authority endowed. For example, delegating the

---

96 Mattli, Walter and Woods, Ngaire (2009). *The politics of global regulation*. Princeton: Princeton University Press, p. 3.

97 Beetham, David (2002). *The Legitimation of Power*. Basingstoke: Palgrave Macmillan.

98 Hurrelmann, Achim, Schneider, Steffen and Steffek, Jens (2007). *Legitimacy in an age of global politics* Palgrave Macmillan, p. 9.

99 Abbott, W. Kenneth and Snidal, Duncan (2009). *The Governance Triangle: Regulatory Standards Institutions and the Shadow of the State. The Politics of Global Regulation*. Mattli, Walter and Woods, Ngaire. Princeton: Princeton University Press, p. 63.

100 Bradley, Curtis A. and Kelley, Judith G. (2008). *The Concept of International Delegation*. Law and Contemporary Problems. (71):1. 1-36, pp. 10-17. Although Bradley and Kelly speak of different authorities that can be delegated it seems more appropriate to speak about tasks. See chapter 3.1 on the meaning of authority.

creation of legally binding obligations is more extensive than delegations of only an advisory or agenda-setting character. But even when the decisions are legally binding, their effect will also depend on the locus of the relevant enforcement authority. A related factor pertains to the opportunities that member states have to influence the independence of the international body by, for example, control mechanisms or representation on the body.[101]

In delegating authority to the European level, which subsequently led to the involvement of the IASB and the use of its standards, member states have recognized the risk of being faced with policy outcomes that could differ from their favored policy choice. To cope with this, they have created comitology procedures to assist, oversee and monitor the activities of the European Commission which is ultimately responsible for the implementation of new accounting policies in Europe. Consequently, each individual standard developed by the IASB has to be endorsed into European law by the Commission in accordance with a specific committee procedure[102] to ensure that the standards meet the needs of European listed companies.[103] The procedure implies an opportunity to amend or change any standard promulgated by the IASB. Consequently, European companies are obliged to use an IASB standard only if it has been endorsed by the European Union and published in the European Union's Official Journal.

That said, it becomes apparent that the tasks of agenda-setting, negotiation and, to a greater extent, policy formation have been delegated while implementation and enforcement have remained the responsibility of the European Commission or its member states. One obvious benefit of adopting a hybrid (private-public) governance mode is that individual member states can retain their influence on the private sector while taking advantage of the private-sector expertise. Porter confirms this assertion by arguing that the case of accounting harmonization involves a functional differentiation "[...] in which public, private, and technical authority are brought together in a way that preserves their autonomy from one another to a significant degree."[104]

In sum, while the delegation of policy-formation is ostensibly of primary concern it may very well appear to be circumscribed by oversight mechanisms if the

101 Ibid., p. 17-19.

102 Council of the European Communities (2002). *Regulation (EC) No 1606/2002 of the European Parliament and of the Council of 19 July 2002 on the application of international accounting standards*, Article 6.

103 Ibid., *Article 2 (2).*

104 Porter, Tony (2005). *Private Authority, Technical Authority, and the Globalization of Accounting Standards*. Business & Politics. (7):3. 1-30, p. 7-8.

overall regulatory picture is taken into account.[105] The role and emergence of private authority in governance structures therefore depends on the larger institutional framework and needs to be evaluated accordingly. As Claire Cutler observes "[...] one of the important analytical goals in studying private international regimes is to understand the degree to which the private actors in a regime are independent of the public ones."[106] Failing to appreciate this assertion leads to diffuse concerns about the legitimacy of public-private regimes and potential strategies to establish a well-functioning international order.[107] Accordingly, Michael Livermoore argues that a functional differentiation of tasks can be a "[...] promising mechanism to promote the legitimacy and effectiveness of international regimes in the future."[108] For example, as long as nation-states remain involved in the enforcement of accounting policies, they can relocalize or reterritorialize the authority delegated for policy-formation to counterbalance an often voiced concern of 'loss of state sovereignty' in the context of transnational governance.[109] In a similar spirit, Cooper and Robson point out that "[...] it is important to avoid adopting the myth that national systems of regulation, or the nation state, are obsolete [...]" if the increasing role of global and international systems are analyzed.[110]

---

105 Louis Pauly aptly illustrates "[...] if residual rights of control continue to reside in states as agents of legitimate public authority, we should expect them to reassert their regulatory power. However, if authority has truly been transferred, or worse, relinquished without the establishment of a new legitimate basis of authority upon which the global financial system rests, markets collapse." Pauly, Louis W., Ed. (2002). *Global finance, political authority, and the problem of legitimation.* Cambridge: Cambridge University Press, p. 87.

106 Cutler, Claire A., Ed. (2002). *Private international regimes and interfirm cooperation.* Cambridge: Cambridge University Press, p. 29.

107 David Held emphasizes that some global restructuring did indeed take place whereby states delegated authority but that these states subsequently gained and extended their influence in other areas. Held, David (1995). *Democracy and the global order: from the modern state to cosmopolitan governance.* Cambridge: Polity, p. 136.

108 Livermore, Michael A. (2006). *Authority and Legitimacy in Global Governance: Deliberation, Institutional Differentiation, and the Codex Alimentarius.* New York University Law Review. (81):Available at: http://ssrn.com/abstract=903408. 766-801, p. 797.

109 Hamlin, Alan P. and Pettit, Philip (1989). *The Good polity: normative analysis of the state.* Oxford: Basil Blackwell, p. 4.

110 Cooper, David J. and Robson, Keith (2006). *Accounting, professions and regulation: Locating the sites of professionalization.* Accounting, Organizations and Society. (31):4-5. 415-444, p. 430.

2.4 Regulatory shift: Challenges to democratic thought

A fundamental problem of social organization relates to the question of how collectively binding decisions should be made in the face of reasonable disagreement. Concepts of authority, democracy and legitimacy originally developed for the nation-state try to address this question. The emergence of global governance dealing with policy issues beyond the nation-state, however, altered the institutional and organizational context of national rule making profoundly, contesting the validity of the underlying views of the state, territorialism and sovereignty.[111] However, the functioning and effectiveness of any social order presupposes a high level of compliance with rules that, in turn, are based on legitimate decision-making structures. Accordingly, David Held argues that the emergence of global governance involving private actors necessitates that "[...] the concept of legitimate political power or authority has to be separated from its exclusive traditional association with states and fixed national borders" and that "the meaning and nature of power, authority and accountability have to be reexamined."[112]

Historically, rule making within the nation-state was embedded in "[...] a system of institutionalized procedural and substantive norms [...]" closely connected to state sovereignty.[113] For example, Zimmermann *et al.* assert that "[...] governance was generally localized at the national level, and this was also true for the localization of disclosure and enforcement."[114] Equally, Cooper and Robson point out that "[...] the state in Anglo-American countries has had a longstanding involvement with the development of accounting rules, practices and what constitutes a profession."[115] Against this background, the relevant political community was clearly identified by national boundaries as lines of demarcation

111 David Esty points out that "[...] the emergence of private authority has affected the operational meaning of state sovereignty [and] distrust of international organizations is a hallmark of [...] sovereignist thinking." Esty, Daniel C. (2006). *Good Governance at the Supranational Scale: Globalizing Administrative Law*. Yale Law Journal. (115):7. 1490-1562, p. 1493.

112 Held, David (1995). *Democracy and the global order: from the modern state to cosmopolitan governance*. Cambridge: Polity, p. 22.

113 Mattli, Walter and Buethe, Tim (2005). *Global Private Governance: Lessons from a National Model of Setting Standards in Accounting*. Law and Contemporary Problems. (68):3/4. 225-262, pp. 225-226.

114 Zimmermann, Jochen, Werner, Jörg R. and Volmer, Philipp B. (2008). *Global governance in accounting: rebalancing public power and private commitment*. Basingstoke: Palgrave Macmillan, p. 19.

115 Cooper, David J. and Robson, Keith (2006). *Accounting, professions and regulation: Locating the sites of professionalization*. Accounting, Organizations and Society. (31):4-5. 415-444, p. 425.

(concept of territorialism) and electoral mechanisms served to authorize representatives. With regard to the delegation-chain, national policy making conversely has a 'chain of responsiveness' and it is argued that "[...] democratic legitimation can only be established and sustained through an uninterrupted chain of legitimacy between the governmental body and the citizenry."[116] In this light, Albert Weale defines democracy "[...] as a political system in which there is a formal connection between public opinion and the content of laws and policies."[117] International Relations (IR) literature also identifies the state as "[...] both the source, and the exclusive location of legitimate, public authority. [...] The authority they [states] exercise over their subjects in the domestic realm conveys to them a legitimacy and agency to interact with other states in the international society of states."[118] Against this background, concepts of political authority formerly developed for the nation-state are missing a "[...] counterpart at the international level [...]"[119] and consequently call into question the understanding of legitimate rule. Grant and Keohane observe that "[...] many of the chief sources of legitimacy at the domestic level, such as constitutional mandates, electoral processes, legality, and tradition, are not available to transnational organizations [...]."[120]

Legitimacy is typically evaluated by employing criteria of democratic theories, which stipulate that the right of rulers to set binding rules depends on their direct accountability through representative democratic means, especially elections and party competition. If political authority is to be constituted legitimately in the transnational arena, two fundamental questions need to be addressed: who makes the rules at the systematic level? And whose interests are most effectively served?[121]

116 Powell, G. Bingham (2004). *The Chain of Responsiveness*. Journal of Democracy. (15):4. , pp. 91-92 and Nullmeier, Frank and Pritzlaff, Tanja (2010). *The Great Chain of legitimacy. Justifying Transnational Democracy*. TranState Working Papers. (No. 123):Bremen: Sfb 597 "Staatlichkeit im Wandel". 1-17, p. 1.

117 Weale, Albert (2007). *Democracy*. Basingstoke: Palgrave Macmillan, p. 140.

118 Hall, Rodney Bruce and Biersteker, Thomas J. (2002). *The emergence of private authority in the international system. The Emergence of Private Authority in Global Governance*. Hall, Rodney Bruce and Biersteker, Thomas J. Cambridge: Cambridge University Press, p. 3.

119 Mattli, Walter and Buethe, Tim (2005). *Global Private Governance: Lessons from a National Model of Setting Standards in Accounting*. Law and Contemporary Problems. (68):3/4. 225-262, pp. 225-226.

120 Grant, Ruth W. and Keohane, Robert O. (2005). *Accountability and Abuses of Power in World Politics*. The American Political Science Review. (99):1. 29-43, p. 35.

121 Pauly, Louis W., Ed. (2002). *Global finance, political authority, and the problem of legitimation*. Cambridge: Cambridge University Press, p. 76.

At least three dimensions underlie the two questions which, in turn, increase the demand for legitimate rule-making structures:

(1) The localization of authority.
(2) The legal extent of policy proposals (their binding character).
(3) The political value of policy proposals (the nature of disagreement).

Figure 2 is a simplified overview to keep track of the possible combinations. Moving north-east will lead to an increasing demand for legitimate decision-making institutions and processes.[122]

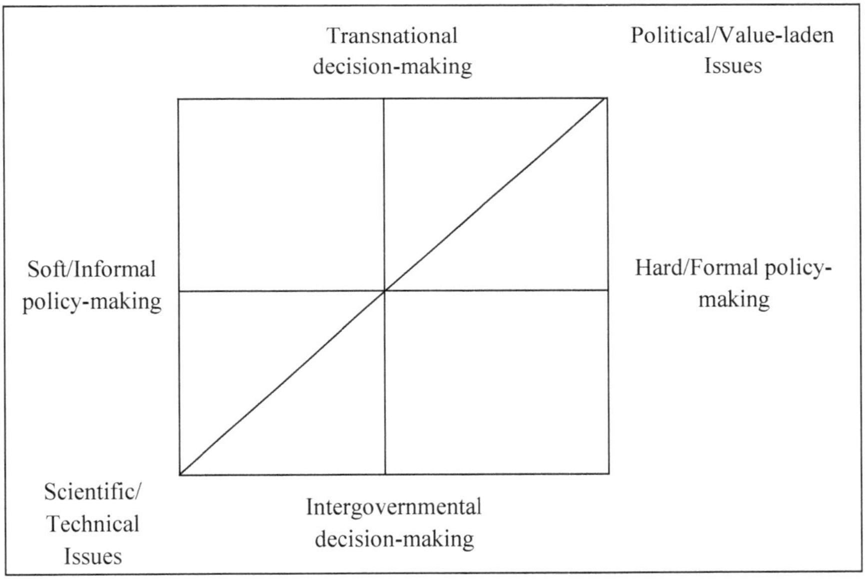

Figure 2: Determinants of demand on legitimacy[123]

The north-south dimension of Figure 2 deals with the localization of the decision-making authority. If one moves from intergovernmental decision-making northward to transnational decision-making the distance from the decision-maker

122 Klaus Dingwerth assumes that transnational rulemaking processes require different degrees of democratic legitimacy according to the normative context in which they operate. He defines four contextual factors to determine legitimacy requirements: authorization, affectedness, quality of rule(s) and subsidiarity. Dingwerth, Klaus (2007). *The new transnationalism: transnational governance and democratic legitimacy* Palgrave Macmillan, pp. 32-36.

123 Adopted from Esty, Daniel C. (2006). *Good Governance at the Supranational Scale: Globalizing Administrative Law*. Yale Law Journal. (115):7. 1490-1562, p. 1509.

and its constituents increases, which, in turn, "[…] create[s] serious legitimacy issues [because] international bodies will be unaccountable, prone to mistakes, subject to manipulation by special interests, or guided by voting provisions that do not reflect the realities of power."[124] In a similar vein, Urbinati and Warren argue that "[…] policy-driven networks […] lack formal legitimacy and clear accountability to those affected by decisions."[125] Implicitly, legitimacy is solely defined in terms of electoral representation, which, in turn, "[…] provides an ultimate reference for state power."[126] While this is a general problem of transnational governance, the Radwan Report notes that "[…] the IASCF is a private self-regulatory body which has been given the role of lawmaker for the EU by Regulation (EC) No 1606/2002; [underlining] that the IASCF/IASB lack transparency, legitimacy, accountability and are not under the control of any democratically elected parliament or government […]."[127] Observing a general tendency towards greater privatization of regulation, Hall and Biersteker predict "[…] less democracy and accountability around the world."[128] Thomas Risse concludes that "[…] democratic governance beyond the nation-state faces serious hurdles. […] The main problem of transnational governance concerns the lack of congruence between those who are being governed and those to whom the governing bodies are accountable."[129] In addition, rules arising from complex interactions of private and public actors characterized by polycentric decision-making authorities might also obscure the lines of responsibility, and therefore, the accountability of nation-states themselves.[130]

Seeing accountability and the lack of election as the core criticism of global governance is, at least, a limited perspective. Within the concept of representation (which implies the question of where political authority is located) this constitutes only a formalistic (as opposed to substantive) view of representation and

124 Ibid., p. 1503.

125 Urbinati, Nadia and Warren, Mark E. (2008). *The Concept of Representation in Contemporary Democratic Theory*. Annual Review of Political Science. (11):387-412, p. 390.

126 Ibid., p. 390.

127 Radwan, Alexander (2008). Report on International Financial Reporting Standards (IFRS) and the Governance of the International Accounting Standards Board (IASB), Committee on Economic and Monetary Affairs. European Parliament. 1-23, p. 4.

128 Hall, Rodney Bruce and Biersteker, Thomas J. (2002). *The emergence of private authority in global governance*. Cambridge: Cambridge University Press, p. 211.

129 Risse, Thomas (2006). *Transnational Governance and Legitimacy, in: Governance and democracy: comparing national, European and international experiences*. London: Routledge, p. 180.

130 Held, David (1995). *Democracy and the global order: from the modern state to cosmopolitan governance*. Cambridge: Polity, p. 135.

grossly overstates the effect of elections.[131] For example, Brennen and Hamlin argue that a citizen can merely choose "[...] what or who they vote for: what they can't choose is the electoral outcome."[132] Urbinati and Warren further point out that "[...] votes in themselves are information-poor. Elected representatives are left to rely on other means [...] to guess what voters intend them to represent, over what spectrum of issues, in what proportion, and with what intensity."[133] While, on the one hand, it is fair to say that "[...] the scope of authority lodged with unelected international officials might inappropriately diminish the authority of those democratically elected at the national level who would otherwise exercise this power [...]",[134] it is, on the other hand, imprecise if the overall regulatory structure is not taken fully into account. For example, in Europe the IASB itself has no authority to make the adoption of IFRS binding, nor does it have control over the EU procedures and their final outcome.[135] However, if the EU-comitology procedures are used to change standards that were initially developed by the IASB, then calls for greater accountability of the IASB are an absurdity because accountability implies that one had genuine control over one's actions.[136]

The east-west dimension of Figure 2 pertains to the legal extent of policy proposals (their binding character) issued in the transnational realm. What is contested is how much reliance should be placed on international officials and entities, particularly when exercising political judgment as autonomous decision-makers.[137] Therefore, the second dimension can either heighten the problems relating to accountability or mitigate them if legislative decision-making authority is delegated but the application of the resulting rules is only voluntary. In either

131 See chapter 3.2.3 on the concept of representation and chapter 3.3.4 for different mechanisms to ensure accountability.

132 Brennan, Geoffrey and Hamlin, Alan (1999). *On Political Representation*. British Journal of Political Science. (29):1. 109-127, p. 118.

133 Urbinati, Nadia and Warren, Mark E. (2008). *The Concept of Representation in Contemporary Democratic Theory*. Annual Review of Political Science. (11):387-412, p. 403.

134 Esty, Daniel C. (2006). *Good Governance at the Supranational Scale: Globalizing Administrative Law*. Yale Law Journal. (115):7. 1490-1562, pp. 1503-1504.

135 As Andreas Fleckner clearly points out: "[...] in the European Union, standards set by the IASB are given no authority unless the European Commission expressly adopts them." Fleckner, Andreas M. (2008). *FASB and IASB: Dependence Despite Independence*. Virginia Law & Business Review. (3):275-309, p. 291.

136 Pink, Thomas (2004). *Free will: a very short introduction*. Oxford: Oxford Univerity Press, p. 36.

137 Esty, Daniel C. (2006). *Good Governance at the Supranational Scale: Globalizing Administrative Law*. Yale Law Journal. (115):7. 1490-1562, p. 1495.

case, the costs of delegation constitute a "[...] reduction in state autonomy through displacement of its decision-making or control."[138]

Finally, the near-far dimension of Figure 2 pertains to the issue under consideration, more precisely the nature of disagreement. Needless to say, this is not solely of concern to international governance, but to collective decision-making in general. However, elevating decision-making to an international forum accentuates national differences in standard setting, and rivalries between interest groups conflict. In contrast to national rule making it seems reasonable to assume a steady increase in the potential for inter-group conflict. Besides, if a policy proposal is merely a question of scientific truth, or technical in nature, legitimacy concerns are not likely to evolve. However, as political questions become more and more value laden (normatively charged), delegation to transnational organizations "[...] becomes increasingly problematic [...]."[139] For example, Chiapello and Medjad argue that "[...] the very length – and diversity – of the list of stakeholders concerned by the standardisation of accounting practices make accounting rules a matter of public interest. What is a profit or a loss is a convention, not a fact [and] accounting standards answer this question [...]."[140]

In sum, the developments in accounting regulation have led to a profound change in the character of the decision-making structure: from intergovernmental to transnational decision-making structures, nowadays involving private as well as public actors. In addition, the character of the standard-setting body changed greatly from one issuing entirely 'soft' regulations to a body with the ability to promulgate standards with 'hard' consequences as they are nowadays, quasi-binding legal standards in Europe. As a result, the decision-making forum progressively moved towards the north-east quadrant in Figure 2, accentuating the problems relating to accountability, sovereignty and loss of state control.[141]

---

138 Bradley, Curtis A. and Kelley, Judith G. (2008). *The Concept of International Delegation.* Law and Contemporary Problems. (71):1. 1-36, p. 27-29.

139 Esty, Daniel C. (2006). *Good Governance at the Supranational Scale: Globalizing Administrative Law.* Yale Law Journal. (115):7. 1490-1562, p. 1512.

140 Chiapello, Eve and Medjad, Karim (2009). *An unprecedented privatisation of mandatory standard-setting: The case of European accounting policy.* Critical Perspectives on Accounting. (20):4. 448-468, p. 449.

141 In addition, Richard and Eberlein argue that the macro-political context also shapes the "[...] demands on legitimacy: the post-Enron context of financial reporting in the US, for example, had the effect of de-legitimating private-sector mechanisms [...]." Richardson, Alan and Eberlein, Burkard (2011). *Legitimating Transnational Standard-Setting: The Case of the International Accounting Standards Board.* Journal of Business Ethics. (98):2. 217-245, p. 223. However, whether public sector regulation would have prevented the 'Enron-case' is, at least, ambiguous. See Zimmermann, Jochen (2002). *Ordnungspolitische Fragen zur Unternehmenspublizität nach der Enron-Insolvenz.* Wirtschaftsdienst. (82):5. 303-312, p. 307 and p. 310.

2.5 Chapter summary

Chapter 2 highlights that the content and the mode of rule setting are closely intertwined.[142] Observing the emerging structures of accounting regulation in and for Europe, it becomes apparent that the institutions and their decision-making procedures have to be explored in an international context that transcends national boundaries. The challenge ahead is no longer purely a "[...] quest to better adapt the democratic idea, originally suited to populations of several thousand in a Greek city-state, to populations of many millions in a modern megastate."[143] Assuming that democracy is the "[...] leading standard of political legitimacy [...]",[144] the relevant question is how the democratic conception of legitimate political authority should be constituted beyond the nation-state. This is not only important because the "[...] problems of legitimacy raised by this shift of power and authority to extra-state processes and norms are graphic and unresolved [...]." The challenge ahead lies also in establishing "[...] suitable democracy-respecting but functionally effective relationships between national institutions [and] private institutions of global governance."[145] While the overall regime might seem to be broadly accepted "[...] the substantive and procedural standards remain an issue of ongoing struggles and contestation among the actors involved."[146]

---

142 See also Cooper and Robson who argue that "[...] the institutions and locations where regulation takes place affect both the outcome of the regulatory process and the legitimacy of the rules and practices produced. Changes in regulatory processes affect opportunities for democratic control and legitimacy." Cooper, David J. and Robson, Keith (2006). *Accounting, professions and regulation: Locating the sites of professionalization*. Accounting, Organizations and Society. (31):4-5. 415-444.

143 Fishkin, James S. (1991). *Democracy and deliberation: new directions for democratic reform*. New Haven; London: Yale University Press, p. 1.

144 Held, David (2006). *Models of democracy*. Cambridge: Polity, preface. Davis Held further elaborates that "[...] democracy bestows an aura of legitimacy on modern political life: laws, rules, and policies appear justified when they are democratic." Held, David (1995). *Democracy and the global order: from the modern state to cosmopolitan governance*. Cambridge: Polity, p. 1. Likewise, Hurrelmann *et al.* observe that "[...] democracy has experienced a formidable triumph in recent decades, and there is a conspicuous lack of normatively plausible alternatives to it." Hurrelmann, Achim, Schneider, Steffen and Steffek, Jens (2007). *Legitimacy in an age of global politics* Palgrave Macmillan, p. xi. For a general discussion of why democratic principles should be supported in governance structures, see Dahl, Robert Alan (1998). *On democracy*. New Haven; London: Yale University Press, in particular chapter 5 – Why Democracy?

145 Kingsbury, Benedict , Krisch, Nico, Stewart, Richard B. and Wiener, Jonathan B. (2005). *Global Governance as Administration – National and Transnational Approaches to Global Administrative Law*. Law and Contemporary Problems. (68):3/4. 1-13, p. 3.

146 Quack, Sigrid (2010). *Law, expertise and legitimacy in transnational economic governance: an introduction*. Socio-Economic Review. (8):1. 3-16, p. 9.

The first task of chapter 2 was to demonstrate the political nature of accounting standard setting. Disagreement caused by diversity in opinion and condition, and the absence of unanimous decision-making, are at the heart of accounting policy formation. The political process intends to bring about or resist change at the substantive or procedural level by some form of government. In Europe, the process of harmonizing accounting regulation illustrated how the form of government – from national rule making to transnational governance modes – as well as the substantive character of accounting rules changed profoundly. These institutional developments, in turn, pose challenges to concepts of authority, democracy, its institutions and rules. However, at first it is important to conceptualize the institutional structure; which tasks are delegated and truly transcend national boundaries to address these challenges. In the regulatory setting of accounting procedures, European member states delegated legislative capacities to European supra-national and subsequently to a private institution. Ratification, implementation and enforcement of accounting rules still remain the responsibility of each individual member state. At the end, all these considerations take us back to the initial question: how should decisions that are collectively binding be made in the face of reasonable disagreement within an international governance regime? The next chapter attempts to frame an answer by exploring the concepts of authority, legitimacy and a discussion of the models of democracy.

3 Democratic Authority: A Framework

3.1 Legitimate authority

Authority: Its meaning and prerequisites

The term authority is used in various contexts, and its meaning can only be understood by its specific usage. On the one hand, authority can be possessed (i.e. to have authority). Authority used in this *de jure* sense means that someone has the right to make decisions and assumes some method of entitlement.[147] Accordingly, Raz argues that to have authority implies "[...] to have a right (created by a permission) to do something; it is also to have the right to grant such permissions [...]."[148] On the other hand, the statement that a person has authority is also used in a *de facto* sense, "[...] to indicate that a person is quite capable of eliciting a distinctive kind of obedience, allegiance, to be 'an authority'."[149] This kind of authority relation is based on a belief that a person is entitled to rule (the source of the authoritative utterance) and the belief in the correctness of his commands or utterances (content).[150] This means that in order to have authority, a person must have special attributes which, in turn, provide the link between the exercise of authority and the possession of authority. Authority in this sense is additionally charged with a moral dimension.

The concept of authority is closely connected to conceptions of legitimacy and power. Therefore, authority is sometimes defined as "[...] power that is legitimized [...]"[151], illustrating the authority relationship as a distinctive mode of influence.[152] However, to explain the meaning of authority by the concept of power

---

147 Cassinelli, C. W. (1961). *Political Authority: Its Exercise and Possession.* The Western Political Quarterly. (14):3. 635-646, p. 60.

148 Raz, Joseph (1990). *Authority and Justification. Authority.* Raz, Joseph. New York: New York University Press, p. 2.

149 Friedman, R. B. (1990). *On the concept of Authority in Political Philosophy. Authority.* Raz, Joseph. New York: New York University Press, p. 61, p. 63.

150 Ibid., pp. 68-69.

151 Ibid., p. 56.

152 According to Anthony Birch political authority is "[...] best defined as a combination of political power and legitimacy, where power is the ability to get things done." Birch, Anthony Harold (1993). *The concepts and theories of modern democracy.* London: Routledge, p. 32.

is misleading because there is a crucial difference between the two: power constitutes an ability to do or achieve various things and to enforce obedience whereas authority means to have the right to rule. For example, an armed man may compel others to do as he wants, but he would be unable to impose a moral obligation to comply. In contrast, the normative notion of authority explicitly excludes coercion; it argues that "[...] where force is used, authority itself has failed."[153] The gunman is not exercising authority in this situation; rather authority has broken down. The term authority used here achieves compliance not because of the threat of punishment or the offer of reward. Rather, the attitudes individuals attach to the source of authoritative utterances are decisive to achieve compliance. Against this background, authority is closely connected to legitimacy.[154]

Before addressing the question of how the authority relationship should be (legitimately) constituted, the question of whether authority is actually required needs to be addressed. The need for authority rests on the assumption that social order is impossible in the absence of authority as illustrated in Thomas Hobbes's *Leviathan*, where he describes a situation in which political authority is absent (the 'natural condition of human mankind'):

> "In such a condition [Hobbes argues], there is no place for Industry; because the fruit thereof is uncertain: and consequently no Culture of the Earth; no Navigation, nor use of the commodities that may be imported by Sea, no commodious Building; no Instruments of moving, and removing such things as require much force; no Knowledge of the face of Earth; no account of Time; no Arts; no Letters; no Society; and which is worst of all, continuall feare, and danger of violent death; And the life of man, solitary, poore, nasty, brutish, and short."[155]

In a similar spirit to Hobbes, John Finnis points out that because of typical human traits like "[...] stupidity, incompetence, selfishness and malice [...]" the establishment of authority seems reasonable.[156] To rephrase and reiterate, coordination among individuals requires the making of choices on collective outcomes, which sometimes results in selection between alternative and mutually exclusive courses of action.

153 Arendt, Hannah (2006). *Between past and future: eight exercises in political thought.* New York; London: Penguin Books, p. 92. Hannah Arendt further points out that "[...] if authority is defined at all, then, it must be in contradiction to both coercion by force and persuasion through arguments." (p. 93).

154 Authority based on a moral right to rule is often called legitimacy and "[...] it is no doubt the most important variety of political authority." Cassinelli, C. W. (1961). *Political Authority: Its Exercise and Possession.* The Western Political Quarterly. (14):3. 635-646, p. 645.

155 Tuck, Richard (1997). *Hobbes, Thomas: Leviathan. Cambridge texts in the history of political thought.* Cambridge: Cambridge University Press, p. 89.

156 Finnis, John M. (1990). *Authority. Authority.* Raz, Joseph. New York: New York University Press, p. 174.

In such a choice situation there are only two ways of making a decision: unanimity or authority.[157] Friedman further elaborates that a necessary condition for the establishment of authority premises that "[...] it must be sufficiently unlikely or even impossible for consensus to be brought about at the substantive level [...]."[158] In general, unanimity or true consensus often seems beyond the bounds of practical possibility; not only in the setting of accounting standards (see also chapter 2.1). If this is the case for the development of national accounting standards it is even more likely to hold true in a transnational context where the diversity of constituents and conflicts are not only the result of sectional but also regional interests. This diversity in accounting regulation is a fundamental characteristic stemming from the large amount of comparative international accounting research.[159] Conversely, if decision making cannot be achieved on consensual grounds, an account of authority needs to be developed that is both justified and legitimate; even if one accepts the claim that authority is warranted. For example, Buchanan and Keohane observe that "[...] it is not enough that the relevant actors agree that some institution is needed; they must agree that this institution is worthy of support."[160]

Justification: consent and its reconstructions

The ambivalence of the authority relationship is based on the fact that an institution claims the right to rule another individual though everyone is assumed to have an equal right to freedom.[161] From this liberal tradition, it follows that no one may be subordinated to anyone else's commands by nature. Yet, the concept of authority and its effectiveness presupposes a minimum level of compliance to its commands which, in turn, implies an abdication of autonomy. Joseph Raz makes it abundantly clear that an authoritative directive "[...] pre-empts one's

157 Ibid., p. 175.

158 Friedman, R. B. (1990). *On the concept of Authority in Political Philosophy. Authority.* Raz, Joseph. New York: New York University Press, p. 78.

159 For a general discussion on the diversity of accounting practice and regulation see Werner, Jörg Richard and Zimmermann, Jochen (2009). *Internationaler Vergleich von Rechnungslegungssystemen.* Die Betriebswirtschaft. (61):1. 85-106.

160 Buchanan, Allen and Keohane, Robert O. (2006). *The Legitimacy of Global Governance Institutions.* Ethics & International Affairs. (20):4. 405-437, p. 408.

161 In the words of Edward Harris: "The assumptions of human equality, individualism, and autonomy mean that no person has natural authority over another." Harris, Edward A. (1992). *From Social Contract to Hypothetical Agreement: Consent and the Obligation to Obey the Law.* Columbia Law Review. (92):3. 651-683, p. 657.

own judgment – one should comply with them whether or not one agrees with them."[162] However, what can justify the claim of political authority?

Rousseau, Hobbes and Locke placed the idea of the social contract at the center of the justification of political authority. In the first place, the social contract provides a stable political and social arrangement; and secondly, it incorporates the principle of consent to justify *de jure* authority and political obligation.[163] Consent theory states that the "[...] claim that no man is obligated to support or comply with any political power [is undisputed] unless he has personally consented to its authority [to authorize someone to act in someone else's name]."[164] In this respect, the consent of each one of the governed is used as a contrivance to preserve one's autonomy.

The act of consenting has, in turn, three important characteristics for creating an obligation to comply. Firstly, to consent implies a moral duty one would otherwise not have; secondly, the liabilities created by the act of consenting are impossible to know in detail at the time consent is given; and thirdly, consenting implies a permission to sanction the consenter's failure.[165] Here again, in contrast to the concept of political power, authority based on consent has a normative appeal. For consent theory to create political obligations, consent must be given voluntarily and, more importantly, intentionally, which is often called express consent.[166] Accordingly, Edward Harris defines the expression of consent as "[...] a voluntary declaration of the individual's intentions to renounce her natural right and liberty, to become a member of the state, and to be subject to its laws [...] in return for the secured protection of her person and property."[167]

However, basing the justification of authority and political obligation on the idea of consent has several weaknesses. At the outset, critics argue that "[...] even if there had been such a contract, it would hardly explain the political obli-

---

162 Raz, Joseph (1990). *Introduction. Authority*. Raz, Joseph. New York: New York University Press, p. 4.

163 Harris, Edward A. (1992). *From Social Contract to Hypothetical Agreement: Consent and the Obligation to Obey the Law*. Columbia Law Review. (92):3. 651-683, pp. 655-657.

164 Simmons, A. John (1976). *Tacit Consent and Political Obligation*. Philosophy and Public Affairs. (5):3. 274-291, p. 274. See also Julian Franklin who argues that "[...] all political obligation arises from consent [...]" Franklin, Julian H. (1996). *Allegiance and Jurisdiction in Locke's Doctrine of Tacit Consent*. Political Theory. (24):3. 407-422, p. 407.

165 Edmundson, William A. (2008). *Consent and its Counterfeits*. Available at: http://papers.ssrn.com/sol3/papers.cfm?abstract_id=1222922. 1-33, pp. 5-7.

166 Lewis, Thomas J. (1989). *On Using the Concept of Hypothetical Consent*. Canadian Journal of Political Science / Revue canadienne de science politique. (22):4. 793-807, p. 801.

167 Harris, Edward A. (1992). *From Social Contract to Hypothetical Agreement: Consent and the Obligation to Obey the Law*. Columbia Law Review. (92):3. 651-683, pp. 658-659.

gation of existing citizens who presumably have no real choice to consent."[168] Moreover, the social contract conception requires broad participation in creating the collective outcomes so that natural freedom transmutes into moral obligation.[169] For better or for worse, this means that governance systems need to be truly participatory systems in order to create political obligations. John Simmons consolidates the discussion about express/explicit consent to justify political obligations with the words "[...] since the earliest consent theories, it has been recognized that 'express consent' is not a suitable general ground for political obligation [and] the real battleground for consent theory is generally admitted to be the notion of tacit consent."[170]

Consent is called tacit when it is given by remaining silent or inactive and is inferred rather than observed.[171] Signs from which it may be valid to infer consent are typically assumed to be: residence in the state and/or the acceptance of benefits from the state.[172] In the first place, if consent is given to a specific authority (government) which, in turn, is based on a territorial concept, it seems reasonable to infer that "[...] everyone who is in the territory of such a government has consented to the power of that government."[173] But, in the second place, the difficulty is to show why someone should be obligated to obey the laws s/he does not benefit from. In general, tacit consent theory is only applicable if, firstly, dissent can be reasonably easily (cheaply) performed and, secondly, the consequences of dissent cannot be extremely detrimental (costly) to the potential consenter.[174] David Hume aptly pointed out that residence cannot be interpreted as tacit consent:

> "Can we seriously say that a poor peasant or artisan has a free choice to leave his country, when he knows no foreign language or manners, and lives from day to day by the small wages he acquires? We may as well assert that a man, by remaining in a vessel, freely consents to the

---

168 Wolff, Jonathan (2006). *An introduction to political philosophy.* Oxford: Oxford University Press, pp. 40-41.

169 Weale, Albert (2007). *Democracy.* Basingstoke: Palgrave Macmillan, p. 36.

170 Simmons, A. John (1976). *Tacit Consent and Political Obligation.* Philosophy and Public Affairs. (5):3. 274-291, p. 278.

171 Harris, Edward A. (1992). *From Social Contract to Hypothetical Agreement: Consent and the Obligation to Obey the Law.* Columbia Law Review. (92):3. 651-683, p. 660.

172 Wolff, Jonathan (2006). *An introduction to political philosophy.* Oxford: Oxford University Press, p. 42 and Harris, Edward A. (1992). *From Social Contract to Hypothetical Agreement: Consent and the Obligation to Obey the Law.* Columbia Law Review. (92):3. 651-683, p. 665.

173 Bennett, John G. (1979). *A Note on Locke's Theory of Tacit Consent.* The Philosophical Review. (88):2. 224-234, p. 227.

174 Simmons, A. John (1976). *Tacit Consent and Political Obligation.* Philosophy and Public Affairs. (5):3. 274-291, p. 280.

dominion of the master: though he was carried on Board while asleep, and must leap into the ocean, and perish, the moment he leaves her."[175]

Conversely, to conclude that residence within a territory governed by an invidious dictator constitutes consent seems quite unreasonable. Inhabitancy can qualify as a possible candidate for tacit consent "[…] only in those states that the individual can freely leave and only for those individuals for whom continued residence is a genuine alternative."[176] This mirrors the aforementioned criteria posed by John Simmons that there must be a real choice that can be performed at reasonable cost. From a more practical perspective, if residence already seemed inappropriate as a basis for tacit consent at the time David Hume lived, it seems particularly far beyond the bounds of contemporary politics and the background of this study. The IASB defined its organizational objective as one of becoming a world standard setter, and most of its constituents share the goal of having world-wide uniform accounting standards. Moreover, it is not conceivable that a national standard setter or an organization comparable to the IASB will emerge that could challenge its work and provide some form of competing standards. As a result, national as well as international corporations find themselves in a situation which can be described as the 'end of geography'. There is no real choice to select between competing accounting doctrines. In this context, global standards by definition leave no room to escape which would afford a real possibility of non-consent. Similarly, Richardson and Eberlein argue that "[…] state consent to IFRS […] is a blunt instrument for legitimating these standards […]. Once standards have reached a certain level of 'global authority', having being adopted by major jurisdictions, it becomes difficult for other jurisdictions not to opt in, for reasons of competitiveness, access to capital markets, or simply because other international organizations (IMF, World Bank) may require endorsement of IFRS as a condition for participating in their programs."[177] To conclude with Hannah Pitkin's words "[…] it appears to be extremely difficult to formulate a notion of tacit consent strong enough to create the required obligation, yet not so strong as to destroy the very substance and meaning of consent."[178]

---

175 Miller, Eugene F. (1987). *Hume, David: Essays: moral, political, and literary. Liberty classics.* New York: Liberty Fund, p. 485.

176 Harris, Edward A. (1992). *From Social Contract to Hypothetical Agreement: Consent and the Obligation to Obey the Law.* Columbia Law Review. (92):3. 651-683, p. 661.

177 Richardson, Alan and Eberlein, Burkard (2011). *Legitimating Transnational Standard-Setting: The Case of the International Accounting Standards Board.* Journal of Business Ethics. (98):2. 217-245, p. 221.

178 Pitkin, Hanna (1965). *Obligation and Consent--I.* The American Political Science Review. (59):4. 990-999, p. 994.

In contrast, the second variation of consent – hypothetical consent – assumes that the social contract is purely hypothetical – an idealized choice situation: out of reflection on how life would look like in the 'state of nature', one comes to realize that consent is in one's best interest.[179] Jonathan Wolff describes this situation "[...] an as-yet-unexpressed attitude of consent [and shortly adds that an] unexpressed even unacknowledged [...] form of consent cannot create a moral obligation to comply."[180] In the same way, John Simmons argues "[...] that binding consent can be given unintentionally is a patent absurdity [...]"[181] and John Bennett concludes that "[...] the attempt to make consent central to the justification of government [...] is doomed to fail."[182] Somewhat less pessimistic, Edward Harris concludes that "[...] only explicit consent is an adequate consensual source of political obligation, but so few people perform acts of explicit consent that it is practically insignificant as the basis of an account of political obligation even in the contemporary liberal democratic society."[183] Against this background, Hannah Pitkin provides a different perspective on consent theory. She argues that the crucial question should be "[...] to what have you consented when you live in a country and use its highways?" which then leads to a situation in which the obligation to obey rests on "[...] certain characteristics of the government [...]."[184] In contrast to a general obligation arising from the act of consenting one is "[...] obligated to consent, if the government is just [...]."[185] As a result, the perspective shifts from the idea of consent as a justification of political authority to the nature of government. Stated differently, the subsequent analysis needs to focus on what constitutes, or how to establish, legitimate authority.

---

179 Edward Harris suggests that "[...] instead of entering into a social contract by voluntary signs of express or tacit consent, the individual is led through a theoretical exercise that culminates in hypothetical agreement." Harris, Edward A. (1992). *From Social Contract to Hypothetical Agreement: Consent and the Obligation to Obey the Law*. Columbia Law Review. (92):3. 651-683, p. 679.

180 Wolff, Jonathan (2006). *An introduction to political philosophy*. Oxford: Oxford University Press, p. 44-45 or Stark, Cynthia A. (2000). *Hypothetical Consent and Justification*. The Journal of Philosophy. (97):6. 313-334, p. 314-316.

181 Simmons, A. John (1976). *Tacit Consent and Political Obligation*. Philosophy and Public Affairs. (5):3. 274-291, p. 282.

182 Bennett, John G. (1979). *A Note on Locke's Theory of Tacit Consent*. The Philosophical Review. (88):2. 224-234, p. 224.

183 Harris, Edward A. (1992). *From Social Contract to Hypothetical Agreement: Consent and the Obligation to Obey the Law*. Columbia Law Review. (92):3. 651-683, pp. 654-655.

184 Pitkin, Hanna (1965). *Obligation and Consent--I*. The American Political Science Review. (59):4. 990-999, pp. 995-996.

185 Pitkin, Hanna (1966). *Obligation and Consent--II*. The American Political Science Review. (60):1. 39-52, p. 39.

Social organization based on authority can only be effective as long as the commands issued also guide public behavior. Two distinct explanations exist that try to elucidate why people follow the law: the instrumental and the normative (legitimate) perspective.

The instrumental approach to securing compliance gained particular momentum with the emergence of public choice literature in politics. Public choice can be defined as "[...] the economic study of nonmarket decision-making, or simply the application of economics to political science."[186] Building its assumptions for decision-making on expected utility,[187] public choice theory argues that "[...] people will break rules when they feel that the likelihood that they will gain from doing so outweighs the potential costs of being caught and punished."[188] This postulation reflects the basic behavioral assumption of public choice: "[...] man is an egoistic, rational, utility maximizer."[189] If accounting disclosure is viewed as a public good[190], it follows that the impossibility of exclusion provides an incentive for non-cooperative, individualistic behavior and raises the likelihood that purely voluntary schemes for providing a public good will break down. As a result, equilibrium solutions can only be achieved by punishment (or threat thereof) of the non-cooperative behavior of any player. From this follows that compliance is achieved by altering the costs of law breaking, which means the likelihood and level of punishment.

Authority relationships are always hierarchical; therefore, the instrumental view can also be analyzed from a bottom-up perspective. This bottom-up view is closely linked to the 'concept of support', more precisely – specific support.[191] The contentment individuals will feel from the perceived output (policy deci-

---

186 Mueller, Dennis C. (1976). *Public Choice: A Survey*. Journal of Economic Literature. (14):2. 395-433, p. 395.

187 Expected utility theory as a major device for decision-making is discussed by Schoemaker, Paul J. H. (1982). *The Expected Utility Model: Its Variants, Purposes, Evidence and Limitations*. Journal of Economic Literature. (20):2. 529-563.

188 Tyler, Tom R. (2006). *Why people obey the law*. Princeton: Princeton University Press, p. 22.

189 Mueller, Dennis C. (1991). *Public choice II: a revised edition of Public Choice* Cambridge Univ. Press, pp. 1-2.

190 Healy and Palepu argue that "[...] accounting information can be viewed as a public good since existing stockholders implicitly pay for its production but cannot charge potential investors for their use of the information [...]."Healy, Paul M. and Palepu, Krishna G. (2001). *Information asymmetry, corporate disclosure, and the capital markets: A review of the empirical disclosure literature*. Journal of Accounting and Economics. (31):1-3. 405-440, pp. 411-412.

191 Easton, David (1975). *A Re-Assessment of the Concept of Political Support*. British Journal of Political Science. (5):4. 435-457, p. 436.

sions) and general performance of political authorities provides the basis for specific support and stability of the social order.[192] In sum, the instrumental perspective (either bottom-up or top-down) achieves compliance by coercion (punishment) or self-interest (reward). This instrumental research tradition partly reflects the definition suggested by Peter Stillman who asserts that "[...] a government is legitimate if and only if the results of governmental output are compatible with the value pattern of the society."[193]

Yet, those (enforcement) mechanisms are costly and often inadequate because people may tolerate any form of government as long as these help them to obtain favorable policies and conditions. It goes without saying that this kind of support varies with perceived benefits and as soon as these decline, support will do likewise.[194] This deterioration of the social order is, however, exactly what will happen in an environment of limited resources in which policy expectations that benefit everyone cannot be satisfied. The result will be a situation described by Habermas as a legitimation crisis, allowing for massive non-compliance[195] because a society is faced with a government that "[...] will be legitimate authority for some of its subjects but naked illegitimate powers to others."[196]

Hibbing and Theiss-Morse conclude "[...] that policy satisfaction is an important factor in the public's relationship with government, but previous research suggests that a great deal of variation in this relationship remains to be explained."[197] With respect to accounting regulation and policy outcomes, Richardson and Eberlein also emphasize that "[...] technical competence is indeed a *necessary* condition to establish legitimacy with constituencies. However, this may not be *sufficient* to sustain legitimacy."[198]

---

192 Ibid., pp. 436-437.

193 Stillman, Peter G. (1974). *The Concept of Legitimacy*. Polity. (7):1. 32-56, p. 39.

194 Easton, David (1975). *A Re-Assessment of the Concept of Political Support*. British Journal of Political Science. (5):4. 435-457, pp. 438-439.

195 Wolfe, Joel D. (1985). *A Defense of Participatory Democracy*. The Review of Politics. (47):3. 370-389, p. 383.

196 Pitkin, Hanna (1965). *Obligation and Consent--I*. The American Political Science Review. (59):4. 990-999, p. 992.

197 Hibbing, John R. and Theiss-Morse, Elizabeth (2001). *Process Preferences and American Politics: What the People Want Government to Be*. The American Political Science Review. (95):1. 145-153, p. 146. For a general discussion on the difficulties of effective governance via only instrumental approaches, see Green, Donald P. and Shapiro, Ian (1994). *Pathologies of rational choice theory: a critique of applications in political science*. New Haven; London: Yale University Press.

198 Richardson, Alan and Eberlein, Burkard (2011). *Legitimating Transnational Standard-Setting: The Case of the International Accounting Standards Board*. Journal of Business Ethics. (98):2. 217-245, p. 222.

In contrast, the normative (legitimacy) perspective "[...] focuses on the values that lead people to comply voluntarily with legal rules and the decisions of legal authorities. [...] To say that an institution is legitimate implies that it has the right to rule even if it does not act in accordance with the rational self-interest of everyone who is subject to its rule."[199] The voluntary aspect of this legitimacy perspective is of particular relevance to this study. Even if universal agreement were to exist with regard to international accounting standards, the IASCF/IASB would have no power to enforce them; therefore compliance with IFRS is voluntary.[200] According to a normative perspective, "[...] people will be concerned with whether they receive fair outcomes, arrived at by a fair procedure, rather than with the favorability of the outcomes."[201] Conversely, acting only in accordance with favorable policy evaluations can be "[...] dismissed as a basis of legitimacy, because in this instance the norm or authority is accepted, not out of a feeling of rightness, but out of the rational calculation that submission is in the interests of the concerned party."[202] Against this background, Bernstein and Cashore, for example, develop a framework to evaluate different governance modes based on a 'logic of appropriateness' rather than a 'logic of consequences'.[203] From a bottom-up perspective it becomes clear that legitimacy is the most stable base for a social order because "[...] it rests on a conception of obligation to obey any commands an authority issues so long as that authority is acting in appropriate limits. [...] [C]itizens who accept the legitimacy of the legal system and its officials are expected to comply with their dictates even when the dictates conflict with their self-interest."[204] Max Weber compares the instrumental and normative perspective and concludes that "All order which is adhered to from motives of pure expediency is generally much less stable than one up-

199 Buchanan, Allen and Keohane, Robert O. (2006). *The Legitimacy of Global Governance Institutions*. Ethics & International Affairs. (20):4. 405-437, pp. 409-410. Buchanan and Keohane further argue that "[...] the concept of legitimacy allows various actors to coordinate their support for institutions by appealing to their common capacity to be moved by what might be called *normative reasons*, as distinct from purely strategic or exclusively self-interested reasons, under conditions in which there is serious and persisting normative disagreement." (p. 409).

200 Botzem, Sebastian and Quack, Sigrid (2008). *Contested rules and shifting boundaries: International standard-setting in accounting. Transnational governance: institutional dynamics of regulation.* Djelic, Marie-Laure and Sahlin-Andersson, KerstinCambridge University Press, p. 266.

201 Tyler, Tom R. (2006). *Why people obey the law*. Princeton: Princeton University Press, p. 5.

202 Spencer, Martin E. (1970). *Weber on Legitimate Norms and Authority*. The British Journal of Sociology. (21):2. 123-134, pp. 126-127.

203 Bernstein, Steven and Cashore, Benjamin (2007). *Can non-state global governance be legitimate? An analytical framework.* Regulation & Governance. (1):4. 347-371, p. 347.

204 Tyler, Tom R. (2006). *Why people obey the law*. Princeton: Princeton University Press, p. 26.

held on a purely customary basis [...]. But even this type of order is, in turn, much less stable than an order which enjoys the prestige of being considered binding, or, as it may be expressed, of 'legitimacy'."[205] In contrast, outputs and beneficial performance may rise and fall while this support, in the form of a generalized attachment, continues.[206] It reflects "[...] a more general support for a regime [or governance institution], which makes subjects willing to substitute the regime's decisions for their own evaluation of a situation."[207] Consequently, Julia Black argues that a precondition for successful (continued) cooporation between a transnational standard setter and its diverse stakeholders is responding to their legitimacy claims.[208] This broadly reflects Kenny Larson's definition of organizational legitimacy: "[...] acceptance of an organization by its institutional environment [which] it is frequently viewed as vital for an organization's survival and success."[209]

The normative concept of legitimate authority may be based on fair procedures (input and throughput legitimacy) usually associated with procedural characteristics derived from democratic theory.[210] Against this background, the purpose of authority is to "[...] achieve agreement on the procedural level in the face of disagreement at the substantive level."[211] As mentioned earlier, consensus seems to be unattainable under the conditions of accounting diversity however; the idea here is that individuals do not have to agree on a specific outcome but only on those principles that apply to the basic structure of decision-making. While disagreement on policy issues might persist, Tom Tyler showed that "[...] within the context of a particular type of problem or dispute, different types of

---

205 Weber, Max (1947). *The theory of social and economic organization*. New York: Oxford University Press, p. 125.

206 Easton, David (1975). *A Re-Assessment of the Concept of Political Support*. British Journal of Political Science. (5):4. 435-457, pp. 444-445.

207 Bodansky, Daniel (1999). *The Legitimacy of International Governance: A Coming Challenge for International Environmental Law?* The American Journal of International Law. (93):3. 596-624, p. 602.

208 Black, Julia (2008). *Constructing and contesting legitimacy and accountability in polycentric regulatory regimes*. Regulation & Governance. (2):2. 137-164, p. 157.

209 Larson, Robert K. (2002). *The IASC's search for legitimacy: An analysis of the IASC's standing interpretations committee*. Advances in International Accounting. (15):79-120, p. 81.

210 Although much of the work that follows is informed by administrative law as well, Mattli and Buethe correctly observe that "[...] many of these core principles of administrative law seem to be grounded in democratic theory." Mattli, Walter and Buethe, Tim (2005). *Global Private Governance: Lessons from a National Model of Setting Standards in Accounting*. Law and Contemporary Problems. (68):3/4. 225-262, p. 226.

211 Friedman, R. B. (1990). *On the concept of Authority in Political Philosophy. Authority*. Raz, Joseph. New York: New York University Press, p. 78.

people generally agree about the criteria that should be used to judge the fairness of the procedure."[212]

To rephrase and reiterate, the final decision is not decisive for securing compliance because the establishment of authority exactly aims to "[...] dissociate the claim to obedience from the question of the merits of the particular decision one is being asked to accept."[213] In this respect, proceduralism "[...] seeks an account of the reasonableness of accepting the procedures it counts as fair in the characteristics of the procedures themselves, rather than in considerations about the merits of the decisions they are likely to yield."[214] Based on the idea of procedural fairness, Mark Suchman defines organizational legitimacy in terms of procedural legitimacy (as a part of moral legitimacy). According to this definition, organizations can achieve moral legitimacy "[...] by embracing socially accepted techniques and procedures [...]. Such procedural legitimacy becomes most significant in the absence of clear outcome measures [further reference], when 'sound practices' may serve to demonstrate that the organization is making a good faith effort to achieve valued, albeit invisible, ends."[215]

Social psychologists use perception of legitimacy to study the impact of people's evaluations of decision-making processes; a construct that "[...] translates nicely into evaluations of the legitimacy of the lawmaking process."[216] Empirical support for the relevance of this perspective is provided, for example, by Hibbing and Theiss-Morse who find that process matters "[...] even with all the other controls included, particularly those for policy outcomes and policy outputs, a process that matches a person's preferences for how the process should work increases approval of government."[217] Further, Hartner *el al.* used a procedural justice model to analyze tax compliance and showed that "[...] when people feel treated in a procedurally fair manner motivational postures of deference increase whereas motivational postures of defiance decrease."[218] The importance

212 Tyler, Tom R. (2006). *Why people obey the law*. Princeton: Princeton University Press, p. 165.

213 Friedman, R. B. (1990). *On the concept of Authority in Political Philosophy. Authority*. Raz, Joseph. New York: New York University Press, p. 80.

214 Beitz, Charles R. (1989). *Political equality: an essay in democratic theory*. Princeton: Princeton University Press, p. 77.

215 Suchman, Mark C. (1995). *Managing legitimacy: Strategic and institutional approaches*. Academy of Management Review. (20):3. 571-610, p. 580.

216 Gangl, Amy (2003). *Procedural Justice Theory and Evaluations of the Lawmaking Process*. Political Behavior. (25):2. 119-149, p. 120.

217 Hibbing, John R. and Theiss-Morse, Elizabeth (2001). *Process Preferences and American Politics: What the People Want Government to Be*. The American Political Science Review. (95):1. 145-153, pp. 147-150.

218 Hartner, Martina, Rechberger, Silvia, Kirchler, Erich and Schabmann, Alfred (2008). *Procedural Fairness and Tax Compliance*. Economic Analysis & Policy. (38):1. 137-152, p. 150.

of procedural fairness considerations in the evaluation of organizational decisions and commitment is also shown in various other contexts: job performance, payment distribution, layoff procedures, work and labor disputes, drug testing programs, acceptance of task assignments and work goals.[219]

The first objective of this study is therefore to show how legitimate authority, defined in procedural terms, should be constituted at the transnational level. As a starting point, chapter 3.2 provides a discussion of models of democracy as potential sources of legitimacy. In particular, democracies' underlying generic properties subsequently pave the way for the procedural characteristics developed in chapter 3.3. Conversely, the discussion surrounding the models of democracy is not intended to serve as a general discourse about theories of the state but to illuminate the desirable characteristics to construct a legitimate account of collective decision-making.

3.2 Models of democracy

3.2.1 Participatory democracy

The idea of direct or participatory models of democracy can be traced back to ancient Greek city-states and Italian city-republics but it was Rousseau who formulated today's idea that citizens themselves should be the source of the rules which govern their lives.[220] This concept is based on the proposition that citizens are naturally free and any political obedience must be self-willed. Henceforth, in participatory models of democracy, citizens assemble and decide collectively on the content of public policies. The idea that only a few individuals rule a society is therefore excluded as "[...] no person could represent another's interest in general."[221] From this follows that any legislation is the result of the "[...] participatory process, and it is the law, not men, that governs individual action."[222] If this is the case, compliance with law actually means that "[...] each person is in

219 Lind, E. Allan, Kulik, Carol T., Ambrose, Maureen and Park, Maria V. de Vera (1993). *Individual and Corporate Dispute Resolution: Using Procedural Fairness as a Decision Heuristic*. Administrative Science Quarterly. (38):2. 224-251, p. 224.

220 Held, David (2006). *Models of democracy*. Cambridge: Polity, p. 27.

221 Wolfe, Joel D. (1985). *A Defense of Participatory Democracy*. The Review of Politics. (47):3. 370-389, p. 372.

222 Pateman, Carole (1970). *Participation and democratic theory*. Cambridge: University Press, pp. 23-24.

fact merely obeying himself [...]"[223] and "[...] liberty [...] is attained by participating in the generation and enactment of the general will, which establishes equality among citizens in that they can all enjoy the same rights."[224]

First and foremost, participatory theorists argue that this form of democracy is intrinsically valuable. For example, Lane Davis argues that through political participation the "[...] horizons of the participating individual would be widened, his knowledge extended, his sympathies made less parochial, his practical intelligence developed [thus serving] as vital means of intellectual, emotional, and moral education leading toward the full development of the capacities of individual human beings [...] to transcend the narrow bounds of their private affairs."[225] This 'ideal citizen' will help to prevent a divided society caused by factionalism.[226] From this follows that all individuals are equally dependent on each other and equally subject to the law which, in turn, facilitates the acceptance of collective decisions. That said, the central function of participatory action is an 'educative one' in order to develop responsible citizens.[227] It is in the process of participation that the individual preferences become less important and each citizen has to take into account wider matters in order to achieve cooperation with others. Mark Warren generally agrees that political activity can result in democratic efficacy (self-transformation thesis), however due to "psychodynamic blockages [...] democratic organizations [need to] have 'therapeutic' as well as discursive dimensions."[228]

---

223 Manin, Bernard, Stein, Elly and Mansbridge, Jane (1987). *On Legitimacy and Political Deliberation.* Political Theory. (15):3. 338-368, p. 343.

224 Rousseau, Jean-Jacques (2004). *The Social Contract.* London: Penguin; Revised Edition, p. 76.

225 Davis, Lane (1964). *The Cost of Realism: Contemporary Restatements of Democracy.* The Western Political Quarterly. (17):1. 37-46, p. 40. Carole Pateman emphasizes this argument in Rousseau's theory and further elaborates that "[...] participation has a psychological effect on the participants, ensuring that there is a continuing interrelationship between the working of institutions and the psychological qualities and attitudes of individuals interacting with them." Pateman, Carole (1970). *Participation and democratic theory.* Cambridge: University Press, pp. 24-26.

226 Held, David (2006). *Models of democracy.* Cambridge: Polity, p. 35.

227 Davis, Lane (1964). *The Cost of Realism: Contemporary Restatements of Democracy.* The Western Political Quarterly. (17):1. 37-46, p. 40 and p. 43. See also John Stuart Mill who argues that "[...] the most important point of excellence which any form of government can possess is to promote the virtue and intelligence of the people themselves. Mill, John Stuart (1861). *Considerations on representative government. On liberty and other essays.* Gray (ed.), John. Oxford: Oxford University Press, 2008, p. 226, p. 226.

228 Warren, Mark E. (1993). *Can Participatory Democracy Produce Better Selves? Psychological Dimensions of Habermas's Discursive Model of Democracy.* Political Psychology. (14):2. 209-234, p. 211.

Beyond the development of civic virtue, the individual's participatory right ensures a certain degree of control over policy outcomes. This is labeled the protective function of participation because policy outcomes are self-determined. To put it into economic phraseology "[...] as the number of participations (access points) in an administrative process is expanded at the various levels of decision-making, the amount of monopoly rents powerful interest groups may be able to extract will decrease."[229] These two principles: educative and protective, emphasize on the one hand "[...] the intrinsic value of political participation for the development of citizens as human beings, while [on the other hand] protective theorists stress its instrumental importance for the protection of citizens' aims and objectives."[230] Finally, participation is supposed to have an integrative function. By participation in collective decision making, individuals will feel "[...] that they 'belong' in their community and the experience that the individual attaches to his society facilitates the establishment of a true community."[231] As a result, a sense of community spirit provides both the source of, and motivation for, participation in collective action.[232]

To put the idea of participatory models into practice, however, "[...] requires the active and creative participation of the citizen in collective self-government and the pursuit of the common good."[233] Furthermore, the participatory system envisaged by Rousseau can attain its objective only in a society of roughly economic and political equality.[234] In Jean-Jacques Rousseau's words: "[...] when particular interests begin to make themselves felt and sectional societies begin to exert influence over the greater society, the common interest becomes corrupted and meets opposition; voting is no longer unanimous; the general will is no longer the will of all; contradictions and disputes arise; and even the best opinion is not allowed to prevail unchallenged."[235]

Barriers to political and economic equality, however, are numerous. Robert Dahl lists at least five major obstacles towards greater equality which extend not

---

229 Rossi, Jim (1997). *Participation run amok: The costs of mass participation for deliberative agency decision-making.* Northwestern University Law Review. (92):1. 174-250, p. 213.

230 Held, David (2006). *Models of democracy.* Cambridge: Polity, p. 35.

231 Pateman, Carole (1970). *Participation and democratic theory.* Cambridge: University Press, p. 30, p. 27.

232 Wolfe, Joel D. (1985). *A Defense of Participatory Democracy.* The Review of Politics. (47):3. 370-389, p. 376.

233 Davis, Lane (1964). *The Cost of Realism: Contemporary Restatements of Democracy.* The Western Political Quarterly. (17):1. 37-46, p. 45.

234 Pateman, Carole (1970). *Participation and democratic theory.* Cambridge: University Press, p. 22.

235 Rousseau, Jean-Jacques (2004). *The Social Contract.* London: Penguin; Revised Edition, p. 123.

merely to income and wealth but, indirectly and directly, to information, status, education, and access to political elites.[236] Yet, only against the background of equality can individuals assemble as equals; and the autonomous wills can merge into the general, as opposed to the sum of all wills. Against this background, James Madison contested that even if "[…] enlightened statesmen could radically reduce the unequal possession and distribution of property […] human beings always recreate patterns of inequality – homogeneity of interests would not follow. […] The formation of factions is inescapable […]."[237] Therefore, it seems doubtful whether it is reasonable to assume that individual and community preferences will collapse.

In addition, Schumpeter's critique casts doubts upon the idealized view of the individual because "[…] everyone would have to know definitely what he wants to stand for [,] a clear and prompt conclusion as to particular issues would have to be derived according to the rules of logical inference [,] all this the model citizen would have to perform for himself and independently of pressure groups and propaganda."[238] He further argues that as soon as ordinary man gets involved in political activity "[…] the sense of reality is […] completely lost and he [the individual] drops to a lower level of mental performance as soon as he enters the political field."[239] Against this background, it has also been argued that "[…] an increase in political participation by present non-participants could upset the stability of the democratic system."[240]

More practical problems of widespread citizen participation are related to the size and complexity of industrialized societies. At the origins of classical Greek democracy, barriers to political participation were not yet of considerable magnitude.[241] Later on, Montesquieu, however, aptly illustrated the problems related to size when he argued that:

> "[…] it is in the nature of a republic to have only a small territory; otherwise it can scarcely continue to exist. […] In a large republic, the common good is sacrificed to a thousand considerations […] it depends on accidents, [whereas] in a small one, the public good is better

---

236 The barriers are: the distribution of political resources, skills and incentives, irreducible limits on time, the size of political systems, and the prevalence of market economies. Dahl, Robert Alan (2006). *On political equality*. New Haven; London: Yale University Press, pp. 50-67.

237 Hamilton, Alexander and Fairfield, Roy P. (1966). *The Federalist papers: a collection of essays written in support of the Constitution of the United States*. Garden City, N.Y.,: Anchor Books, p. 52.

238 Schumpeter, Joseph Alois (1954). *Capitalism, socialism, and democracy*. London: Allen & Unwin, pp. 253-254.

239 Ibid., p. 255.

240 Pateman, Carole (1970). *Participation and democratic theory*. Cambridge: University Press, p. 3.

241 Held, David (2006). *Models of democracy*. Cambridge: Polity, p. 12.

felt, better known, lies nearer to each citizen; abuses are less extensive there and consequently less protected."[242]

David Held further points out that the classical participatory model which emerged from small city-states in conjunction with social exclusion cannot be "[...] adapted to stretch across space and time."[243] Without institutional adjustments, the decision-making structures of such a system in contemporary politics would be extraordinarily costly. Albert Weale summarizes the critique related to participatory models of democracy by stating that the conception of democracy envisaged by Rousseau "[...] is both an ideal and an idealization [because] it incorporated the value of moral autonomy, and it is an idealization in the sense that it does not describe any particular functioning democracy [...]."[244] Defending the idea of participatory democracy Lane Davis, instead, argues that at its origins "[...] the theory was not created to describe any existing democratic polity of any considerable size [but rather] as an essay in prescription [...] for a worthwhile polity which should be thought after [...] or a point of departure for criticism of existing politics and society."[245] From this observation follows that an analysis about the desirable properties of participatory models should not be excluded from a more general discussion of how to constitute legitimate governance structures at the transnational level. In constructing legitimate transnational governance modes it is important to bear in mind the intrinsic (desirable) properties of participatory systems: educative, protective and integrative.

Participation and the idea of deliberation are inextricably linked. If participation is not reduced to mere voting it requires communication. In this way, issues of participation lead into issues of deliberation.

3.2.2 Deliberative democracy

Theorists on deliberative democracy emphasize the quality of democratic reasoning that provides the basis for governing disagreement within society.[246] De-

---

242 Cited in Fishkin, James S. (1991). *Democracy and deliberation: new directions for democratic reform*. New Haven; London: Yale University Press, pp. 15-16. See also Pateman, Carole (1970). *Participation and democratic theory*. Cambridge: University Press, p. 2.

243 Held, David (1995). *Democracy and the global order: from the modern state to cosmopolitan governance*. Cambridge: Polity, p. 14.

244 Weale, Albert (2007). *Democracy*. Basingstoke: Palgrave Macmillan, p. 36, p. 87.

245 Davis, Lane (1964). *The Cost of Realism: Contemporary Restatements of Democracy*. The Western Political Quarterly. (17):1. 37-46, p. 39.

246 Vitale, Denise (2006). *Between deliberative and participatory democracy: A contribution on Habermas*. Philosophy & Social Criticism. (32):6. 739-766, p. 751 and p. 753.

liberative theorists argue that the substantive character of democracies is not just about the aggregation of preferences. It rather "[...] involves processes of discussion and the exchange of information through which preferences are formed."[247] Similarly, to Manin and Stein deliberation means "[...] the process of the formation of the will, the particular moment that precedes choice, and in which the individual ponders different solutions before settling for one of them."[248] It is generally assumed that "[...] the force of the better argument is able to persuade those who hold differing perspectives"[249] because the "[...] power of reason is less directly tied to the existing distribution of power."[250] On the contrary, Gutmann and Thompson argue that "[...] deliberative democracy itself exposes the exclusionary biases in democratic practice that undermine the conditions of civic equality."[251] If this is the case, public reasoning has the potential to challenge it.

Gutmann and Thompson define deliberative democracy "[...] as a form of government in which free and equal citizens (and their representatives), justify decisions in a process in which they give one another reasons that are mutually acceptable and generally accessible, with the aim of reaching conclusions that are binding in the present for all citizens but open to challenge in the future."[252] Equally, Joshua Cohen's account on deliberative democracy is characterized by citizens' "[...] commitment to the resolution of problems of collective choice through public reasoning [and institutions are seen as legitimate] insofar as they establish the framework for free public deliberation."[253]

Both definitions reflect four distinct characteristics that belong to this understanding of deliberative democracy. Firstly, deliberative democracy (in representative systems) requires leaders to provide reasons for their decisions which "[...] are meant both to produce a justifiable decision and to express the value of mutual respect."[254] Similarly, John Stuart Mill defends the deliberative function of parliament on the grounds that "[...] those whose opinion is overruled, feel satisfied that it is heard, and set aside not by a mere act of will, but for what are

---

247 Weale, Albert (2007). *Democracy*. Basingstoke: Palgrave Macmillan, p. 82.

248 Manin, Bernard, Stein, Elly and Mansbridge, Jane (1987). *On Legitimacy and Political Deliberation*. Political Theory. (15):3. 338-368, p. 345.

249 Rossi, Jim (1997). *Participation run amok: The costs of mass participation for deliberative agency decision-making*. Northwestern University Law Review. (92):1. 174-250, p. 213.

250 Gutmann, Amy and Thompson, Dennis (2004). *Why deliberative democracy?* Princeton, N.J.; Oxford: Princeton University Press, pp. 42-43.

251 Ibid., p. 48.

252 Ibid., p. 7.

253 Cohen, Joshua (1989). *Deliberation and Democratic Legitimacy. The good polity: Normative analysis of the state*. Hamlin, Alan P. Oxford: Blackwell, p. 21.

254 Gutmann, Amy and Thompson, Dennis (2004). *Why deliberative democracy?* Princeton, N.J.; Oxford: Princeton University Press, pp. 3-4.

thought superior reasons [...]."[255] Justifying political decisions also promotes civic freedom because it "[...] entails the effective liberty to affirm or deny the reasoning of one's representatives. Citizens cannot exercise this liberty unless officials justify their actions, and respond to criticism."[256] Furthermore, political decisions involving value judgments are said to be neither true nor false "[...] but what excludes the possibility of arbitrariness is its justification."[257] Conversely, if information (reasons that guided the decision-making process) on policy outcomes is kept secret, Buchanan and Keohane argue that there is "[...] good reason to believe the institution is not satisfying the substantive criteria for legitimacy."[258] Secondly, the reasons provided by deliberators should, in principle, be comprehensible to all citizens. If citizens cannot understand the content of policy proposals, a justificatory process cannot evolve.[259] For a deliberative theory it is then crucial that the interests and reasons are contested in a public forum. If deliberation is based on reasoning, reciprocity and publicity to further the common interest has the potential to bring disparate groups together and mitigates subjectivism. It can thus result, in principle, in the acceptance of norms to everyone participating in the process of deliberation.

Similarly to the conditions of participatory democracy, if deliberation is to attain its goals "[...] participants must be willing to consider the arguments offered on their merits [which] presuppose a relatively reasonable audience, multiplicity of points of view, individuals to listen to arguments formulated by others."[260] More than that, participants are required to take the perspectives of others "[...] as a starting point in shaping dialogue and moving towards consensus."[261] Thirdly, deliberative theorists acknowledge that at some point in time "[...] the

---

255 Gray, John, Ed. (1991). *Mill, John Stuart: On liberty and other essays. The world's classics.* Oxford: Oxford Univerity Press, p. 282.

256 Gutmann, Amy and Thompson, Dennis (2004). *Why deliberative democracy?* Princeton, N.J.; Oxford: Princeton University Press, p. 45. Manin, Bernard, Stein, Elly and Mansbridge, Jane (1987). *On Legitimacy and Political Deliberation.* Political Theory. (15):3. 338-368, pp. 355-357.

257 Manin, Bernard, Stein, Elly and Mansbridge, Jane (1987). *On Legitimacy and Political Deliberation.* Political Theory. (15):3. 338-368, p. 354.

258 Buchanan, Allen and Keohane, Robert O. (2006). *The Legitimacy of Global Governance Institutions.* Ethics & International Affairs. (20):4. 405-437, pp. 429-430.

259 Gutmann, Amy and Thompson, Dennis (2004). *Why deliberative democracy?* Princeton, N.J.; Oxford: Princeton University Press, p. 4.

260 Fishkin, James S. (1991). *Democracy and deliberation: new directions for democratic reform.* New Haven; London: Yale University Press, p. 37.

261 Rossi, Jim (1997). *Participation run amok: The costs of mass participation for deliberative agency decision-making.* Northwestern University Law Review. (92):1. 174-250, p. 205.

deliberation temporarily ceases, and the leaders make a decision."[262] While the deliberative process aims to minimize differences, it does so without the necessity of arriving at consensus. According to this proposition, the requirement is not one of actual consensus, but rather a reasonable consensus grounded in the requirements of fairness.[263] On issues where disagreement persists, "[...] voting and other aggregative methods will continue to be necessary."[264] The fourth characteristic of deliberative democracy relates to the nature of the process itself. Once a decision is made, it might be reverted in the light of new evidence. Reversibility seems indispensable, given that decision-making processes are imperfect since they depend upon incomplete human understandings and fallibility.

The character of deliberation can be further illustrated if contrasted with bargaining activities. Indeed, Joshua Cohen's criteria of deliberative democracy are not simply used to define an ideal deliberative procedure, but also to distinguish collective, deliberative decision making from "[...] bargaining, contracting and other market-type interactions [...]."[265] If citizens take the deliberative process seriously, they are supposed to "[...] expand their knowledge, including both their self-understanding and their collective understanding of what will best serve their fellow citizens."[266] In contrast, aggregative conceptions take the expressed preferences not just as raw material but also as the only input for democratic decision making. Preferences as such do not need to be justified or challenged.[267] The assumption underlying aggregative decision-making structures is that individuals already know what they want, which, in light of the complexity of social life, is at least questionable. Accounting regulation (standards) does not constitute an exception from this. As Andreas Fleckner observes "[...] hardly anyone except professional accountants understand it, and it would be naïve to assume that government officials or members of parliament could draft, discuss, and enact accounting rules. Most of the people involved would not even have a cursory understanding of the relevant issues [...]."[268] Therefore, deliberative theorists argue that the "[...] source of legitimacy is not the predetermined will

262 Gutmann, Amy and Thompson, Dennis (2004). *Why deliberative democracy?* Princeton, N.J.; Oxford: Princeton University Press, p. 5.

263 Weale, Albert (2007). *Democracy*. Basingstoke: Palgrave Macmillan, p. 80.

264 Manin, Bernard, Stein, Elly and Mansbridge, Jane (1987). *On Legitimacy and Political Deliberation*. Political Theory. (15):3. 338-368, p. 341.

265 Cohen, Joshua (1989). *Deliberation and Democratic Legitimacy. The good polity: Normative analysis of the state*. Hamlin, Alan P. Oxford: Blackwell, p. 17.

266 Gutmann, Amy and Thompson, Dennis (2004). *Why deliberative democracy?* Princeton, N.J.; Oxford: Princeton University Press, pp. 10-12.

267 Ibid., p. 16.

268 Fleckner, Andreas M. (2008). *FASB and IASB: Dependence Despite Independence*. Virginia Law & Business Review. (3):275-309, p. 277.

of all, but rather the process of its formation, that is, deliberation itself."[269] Albert Weale smoothly closes the 'aggregate-deliberative' controversy by introducing a time dimension in the sequence of political decision making arguing that "[...] if we allow deliberation at the pre-decision stage and aggregation at the decision stage, we do not have a contest between the two models of democracy, but merely different aspects of a not very complex story."[270]

If deliberative democracy can be regarded as a normative concept, it follows that there must be criteria that allow discrimination between good or bad deliberation; what are the criteria for successful deliberation? Some deliberative theorists defend the claim that procedural ideals, rather than outcomes, constitute the decisive parameters for democratic legitimacy.[271] Others emphasize that deliberation either constructs or discovers the common good. Deliberative policy studies applying a procedural approach investigate the design of institutions and venues for developing policy.[272] In this sense, "[...] the success of deliberative politics depends not on a collectively acting citizenry but on the institutionalization of the corresponding procedures and conditions of communication, as well as on the interplay of institutionalized deliberative processes with informally developed public opinions."[273] One step further, David Estlund stresses that democratic legitimacy, unlike pure proceduralist accounts of democracy which are often decoupled from its substantive character, "[...] requires that the procedure can be held, in terms acceptable to all qualified points of view, to be epistemically the best (or close to it) among those that are better than random."[274] His account of legitimate authority in terms of epistemic proceduralism relies, therefore, "[...] on the epistemic value of the procedure rather than on [merely] some non-epistemic virtue of a procedure such as its fairness to participants or to their points of view."[275] Again, participation and deliberation are intertwined at this point. Deliberative processes require a minimum amount of participation (people who are interested in the political process), whereas participation *per se* does not

269 Manin, Bernard, Stein, Elly and Mansbridge, Jane (1987). *On Legitimacy and Political Deliberation.* Political Theory. (15):3. 338-368, pp. 351-352.

270 Weale, Albert (2007). *Democracy.* Basingstoke: Palgrave Macmillan, p. 80.

271 See, for example, Joshua Cohen arguing for deliberative democracy in terms of an ideal deliberative procedure. Cohen, Joshua (1989). *Deliberation and Democratic Legitimacy. The good polity: Normative analysis of the state.* Hamlin, Alan P. Oxford: Blackwell, p. 17.

272 For further references on how to study the character of deliberation see Ryfe, David M. (2005). *Does deliberative democracy work?* Annual Review of Political Science. (8):1. 49-71.

273 Habermas, Jürgen (1996). *Between facts and norms: contributions to a discourse theory of law and democracy.* Cambridge, Mass: MIT Press, p. 298.

274 Estlund, David M. (2008). *Democratic authority: a philosophical framework* Princeton, N.J.; Oxford: Princeton University Press, p. 98.

275 Ibid., p. 116.

result in epistemically valuable procedures. The requirements of reasoning and justification are central in achieving collective decisions that are acceptable to all.

3.2.3 Representational democracy

The theory of representational or indirect democracy can be seen as an attempt to adapt democratic political theory to the needs of contemporary economic and political realities. John Stuart Mill points in this direction:

> "[...] any participation, even in the smallest function, is useful; that the participation should everywhere be as great as the general degree of improvement of the community will allow; but since all cannot, in a community exceeding a single small town participate personally in any but some minor portions of the public business, it follows that the ideal type of a perfect government must be representative."[276]

In this respect, David Plotke suggests that "[...] representation is not an unfortunate compromise between an ideal of direct democracy and messy modern realities [but rather] crucial in constituting democratic practices."[277] In contrast to participatory models of democracy, citizens are not directly the source of politics (procedures and outcomes); rather, representatives are supposed to make political choices and act in the interests of their constituents.[278] The fundamental question faced by liberal democrats then is how to connect the sovereign state with the sovereign people "[...] who were recognized as the legitimate source of the state powers?"[279] In liberal theories of democracies the focus thus became less a "[...] sense of public or political liberty, 'the right of the people to share in the government', and more a sense of personal or private liberty, 'the protection of rights against all governmental encroachments, particularly by the legislature."[280] If one accepts the claim that direct models of democracy are beyond the bounds of practical possibility, a theory of representation needs to be developed.

---

276 Gray, John, Ed. (1991). *Mill, John Stuart: On liberty and other essays. The world's classics.* Oxford: Oxford Univerity Press, p. 256.

277 Plotke, David (1997). *Representation is Democracy.* Constellations. (4):1. 19-34, p. 19. See also Brennan and Hamlin who argue that "[...] direct democracy is the relevant ideal, and representation simply a useful device to render democracy less costly." Brennan, Geoffrey and Hamlin, Alan (1999). *On Political Representation.* British Journal of Political Science. (29):1. 109-127, p. 126.

278 Brennan, Geoffrey and Hamlin, Alan (1999). *On Political Representation.* British Journal of Political Science. (29):1. 109-127, p. 109.

279 Held, David (2006). *Models of democracy.* Cambridge: Polity, p. 59.

280 Ibid., p. 55.

Hannah Pitkin identifies five different perspectives on how to conceptualize representation: authorization, accountability, substantive representation, descriptive, and symbolic representation.[281] The formalistic view of representation pictures the representative as "[...] someone who has been authorized to act. [H]e has been given a right to act which he did not have before."[282] Authorization of a representative takes place at the 'pre-representation stage' and elections confer authority initially possessed by the voter to the representative. In general, delegating authority to another person or institution also provides an opportunity for abusing this power; that is why people need to make inference about the nature of their relationship with an authority. This is the main problem that arises from the delegation of authority to public or private agents: accountability.[283] In this formalistic context, elections also play a major role at the 'post-representation stage' because they provide a control mechanism for faithful representation. Against the background of periodic elections, "[...] representatives have their interests bound to those of their constituents."[284] Conversely, accountability theorists argue that, without electoral mechanisms, representatives are prone to ignoble behavior. John Stuart Mill's considerations on representative government aptly point out that:

> "[o]ne of the greatest dangers, therefore, of democracy, as of all other forms of government, lies in the sinister interest of the holders of power: it is the danger of class legislation; of government intended for (whether really effecting it or not) the immediate benefit of the dominant class, to the lasting detriment of the whole. And one of the most important questions demanding consideration, in determining the best constitution of a representative government, is how to provide efficacious securities against this evil."[285]

Retrospective accountability, therefore, is the possibility "[...] to impose sanctions – to attach costs to the failure to meet the standards" initially agreed upon.[286] The formalistic view of representation reflects, for example, Joseph Schumpter's understanding of democracy as a method of "[...] institutional ar-

---

281 Pitkin, Hanna Fenichel (1972). *The concept of representation*. Berkeley: University of California Press.

282 Ibid., pp. 38-39.

283 Scott, Colin (2000). *Accountability in the Regulatory State*. Journal of Law and Society. (27):1. 38-60, p. 39.

284 Rogowski, Ronald (1981). *Representation in Political Theory and in Law*. Ethics. (91):3. 395-430, p. 402.

285 Gray, John, Ed. (1991). *Mill, John Stuart: On liberty and other essays. The world's classics*. Oxford: Oxford Univerity Press, p. 299.

286 Buchanan, Allen and Keohane, Robert O. (2006). *The Legitimacy of Global Governance Institutions*. Ethics & International Affairs. (20):4. 405-437, p. 426. See also Fishkin, James S. (1991). *Democracy and deliberation: new directions for democratic reform*. New Haven; London: Yale University Press, p. 18.

rangements for arriving at political decisions in which individuals acquire the power to decide by means of a competitive struggle for the people's vote."[287] To summarize, democratic theory in this sense is mainly concerned with the choice of, and control over, leaders. An influence over the content of specific policy proposals is assumed only indirectly.

The descriptive view of representation emphasizes the composition of the decision-making forum, which is supposed to be a portrait or mirror image of the society. It is not decisive what a representative does, but rather their specific characteristics.[288] The descriptive view of representation follows the argument that "[…] the best people to express an opinion are those who actually share the social characteristics of those who are being represented."[289] Proportionalist theorists, for example, favor this dimension of representation, advocating a randomized process of selecting decision makers. Successful representation is judged against the standard "[…] the more accurate the better."[290] Albert Weale further argues that representation of specific groups is as much related to concerns about diversity as it is to concerns about disadvantage.[291] For example, the participation of representatives of unprivileged groups can enhance the political status of this particular faction.[292]

In contrast to the formalistic and descriptive view on representation, representation as 'acting for' focuses on 'the nature of the activity itself' – the substantive character of representation.[293] Representation in this sense is concerned with "[…] how well he acts to further the objectives of those he represents."[294] The conceptual problem inherent in this perspective of representation is the extent to which the representative should or must act independently from his constituents.[295] On the one hand, mandate theorists argue that a representative should

287 Schumpeter, Joseph Alois (1954). *Capitalism, socialism, and democracy*. London: Allen & Unwin, p. 269.

288 Pitkin, Hanna Fenichel (1972). *The concept of representation*. Berkeley: University of California Press, p. 60. Likewise, Albert Weale points out that "[…] in the representational model of democracy […] the emphasis is upon seeing the legislature as broadly representative of varieties of political opinion." Weale, Albert (2007). *Democracy*. Basingstoke: Palgrave Macmillan, p. 129.

289 Weale, Albert (2007). *Democracy*. Basingstoke: Palgrave Macmillan, pp. 145-147.

290 Pitkin, Hanna Fenichel (1972). *The concept of representation*. Berkeley: University of California Press, p. 71.

291 Weale, Albert (2007). *Democracy*. Basingstoke: Palgrave Macmillan, p. 151.

292 Phillips, Anne (1995). *The politics of presence*. Oxford; New York: Clarendon Press, p. 40.

293 Pitkin, Hanna Fenichel (1972). *The concept of representation*. Berkeley: University of California Press, p. 114.

294 Ibid., p. 116.

295 Birch, Anthony Harold (1971). *Representation*. London: Pall Mall Press, p. 15.

act only on explicit instructions. In this extreme sense, the representative is merely a tool without independent decision-making authority. On the other hand, at the other extreme the representative is acting completely independent of his constituents' views, for example, an oligarch. To find the right balance between these two endpoints is in part a function of what is to be represented. If, for example, interests are objective and impersonal, "[...] a representative is not to consult the wishes of his constituents; [or equally one could maintain that] it makes no sense for wise, superior men to take counsel with stupid inferior ones."[296] Similarly, based on Downsian analysis, Brennen and Hamlin argue that "[...] representation is required precisely because citizens have inadequate incentives to be informed."[297] At the other extreme stands the assertion that "[...] there is no one who knows what is in your interest, so well as yourself" which, however, renders representation as a substantive activity impossible as well.[298]

The aforementioned perspectives on representation can be combined into a comprehensive view on political representation which "[...] means acting in the interest of the represented, in a manner responsive to them. The representative must act independently; his action must involve discretion and judgment; he must be the one who acts. [...] The representative must act in such a way that there is no conflict, or if it occurs an explanation is called for."[299] The definition of political representation, in particular the requirement to justify one's decision, has clear intersections with the deliberative account of democracy. For example, Gutmann and Thompson point out that "[...] representatives are expected not only to deliberate among themselves but also to listen to, and communicate with, their constituents, who in turn should have many opportunities to hold them accountable."[300] In addition, Manin *et al.* point out that, since decisions are imposed on all, it requires deliberation of all "[...] but the existence of political parties is essential for deliberation."[301] Irrespective of any specific institutionalization of a representative system, the fundamental concerns that need to be con-

---

296 Pitkin, Hanna Fenichel (1972). *The concept of representation.* Berkeley: University of California Press, p. 170.

297 Brennan, Geoffrey and Hamlin, Alan (1999). *On Political Representation.* British Journal of Political Science. (29):1. 109-127, pp.114-115.

298 Pitkin, Hanna Fenichel (1972). *The concept of representation.* Berkeley: University of California Press, p. 199.

299 Ibid., pp. 209-210.

300 Gutmann, Amy and Thompson, Dennis (2004). *Why deliberative democracy?* Princeton, N.J.; Oxford: Princeton University Press, pp. 29-30.

301 Manin, Bernard, Stein, Elly and Mansbridge, Jane (1987). *On Legitimacy and Political Deliberation.* Political Theory. (15):3. 338-368, p. 357.

sidered are: in what way are representatives authorized, according to what criteria are they selected, and how can they be held accountable.[302]

The preceding discussion of the models of democracy revealed their strong interdependency. Participatory mechanisms are not sufficient if the decision-making process does not include deliberative elements. However, policy making at the transnational level limits the possibilities for direct participation; therefore some form of representation is needed. As a result, a legitimate account of transnational standard setting should include elements from participatory, deliberative and representative theories of democracy. These underlying principles constitute the procedural characteristics developed in chapter 3.3.

3.3 Procedural fairness characteristics

3.3.1 Effective participation

Effective participation provides an important standard against which to judge transnational collective decision-making procedures. If the two assumptions hold that: 'individuals are morally and legally equal' and 'equally capable of autonomy with respect to citizenship', Urbinati and Warren conclude that "[...] collective decisions affecting self-determination should include those affected."[303] Robert Salisbury refers to this as a 'legitimizing act' of political participation.[304] However, this does not prescribe any particular direct mode of participation nor participation only in terms of voting; it can very well refer to various forms of participation within representative systems. Albert Weale defines participation as "[...] taking part in the process of formulation, passage and implementation of public policies."[305] Whatever concrete form participation will take, to have the "[...] opportunity to take part in the decision-making process is one important element which results in a belief on the part of those involved that procedures are fair."[306] Irrespective of the final decision, a belief in the fairness of the procedure will increase the acceptance of the outcome.[307] Robert Dahl labels this procedural characteristic 'voice' which refers to the means by which those who are affected

302 Urbinati, Nadia and Warren, Mark E. (2008). *The Concept of Representation in Contemporary Democratic Theory*. Annual Review of Political Science. (11):387-412, p. 396.

303 Ibid., p. 395.

304 Salisbury, Robert H. (1975). *Research on Political Participation*. American Journal of Political Science. (19):2. 323-341, p. 326.

305 Weale, Albert (2007). *Democracy*. Basingstoke: Palgrave Macmillan, p. 104.

306 Tyler, Tom R. (2006). *Why people obey the law*. Princeton: Princeton University Press, p. 163.

307 Dahl, Robert Alan (1998). *On democracy*. New Haven; London: Yale University Press, p. 39.

or potentially affected by a decision have the opportunity to contribute to the decision-making process. This may either be directly or through some type of representation.[308] Conversely, "[...] if others do not have a voice in the making of a decision, it is too easy to assume that our decision will benefit them, especially if the decision benefits us."[309] Thus, decision-making procedures that link the public to policymakers and engage citizens in a dialogue can be used to create the sense of identity needed to establish a degree of democratic legitimacy.[310] As discussed in the previous chapter, participatory rights also have an instrumental value in that people can be directly responsible for the rules they ought to follow. Against this background, participation alleviates problems of accountability in terms of responsiveness of non-electoral representatives because citizens themselves now have some control over the final policy outcome. Finally, the opportunity to participate has another important psychological effect: decision makers taking the evidence presented by participants into account instills a sentiment of recognition as well as social standing, creating a belief of membership in the community.

3.3.2 Enlightened understanding

Enlightened understanding, according to Robert Dahl, is required to enable people to learn and understand what they want and to successfully communicate their preferences.[311] Gathering information and "[...] clarifying the issues under consideration is a simple but essential starting point for good governance. [...] Such a process tends to ensure that critical issues are identified and fully explored, a wide range of options are considered, all potential affected parties are notified, and a reasoned decision emerges."[312] Conversely, "[...] it would be hard to justify procedures that cut off or suppressed information, which, were it avail-

---

308 Ibid., p. 37.

309 Gutmann, Amy and Thompson, Dennis (2004). *Why deliberative democracy?* Princeton, N.J.; Oxford: Princeton University Press, p. 38.

310 Esty, Daniel C. (2006). *Good Governance at the Supranational Scale: Globalizing Administrative Law.* Yale Law Journal. (115):7. 1490-1562, p. 1516.

311 In Robert Dahl's words "[...] in order to express his or her preferences accurately, each citizen ought to have adequate and equal opportunities for discovering and validating, in the time permitted by the need for a decision, what his or her preferences are on the matter to be decided." Dahl, Robert Alan (1979). *Procedural Democracy. Philosophy, politics and society: fifth series: a collection.* Laslett, Peter and Fishkin, James S. Oxford: Blackwell, p. 104-105.

312 Esty, Daniel C. (2006). *Good Governance at the Supranational Scale: Globalizing Administrative Law.* Yale Law Journal. (115):7. 1490-1562, p. 1527-1528.

able, might well cause citizens to arrive at different decisions."[313] Gaining enlightened understanding is, therefore, closely connected to the deliberative conception of democracy. The two main features of deliberation are that it is firstly, a dialogical process which makes speakers answerable and accountable to one another; and secondly, it is public to the extent that it is a joint activity involving all citizens.[314] To have a real choice in the process of deliberation is an important aspect because it helps "[...] to prevent unfair outcomes, whereas the absence of choice omits this key line of defense against unfair outcomes."[315]

It goes without saying that a large information base (multiple viewpoints or ideas) gages the deliberative process. Therefore, and in order to keep the costs of gathering information at a reasonable level, it may be necessary to develop criteria for deciding which types of information constitute usable evidence. Against this background, Dolan *et al.* suggest the criterion of 'accurate information' that "[...] leads to decisions being made on the basis of evidence rather than personal bias or other vagaries of the decision-making process."[316] In a similar spirit to Dolan *et al.*, Gerald Leventhal defines accuracy of a decision as "[...] the ability of a procedure to reach solutions that are objectively of a high quality, and this depends on using accurate information and informed opinion."[317] In essence, the quality of deliberative processes can be ensured by placing a premium on rational argumentation instead of unfounded reasoning.

3.3.3 Representative rule

An individual's judgment of procedural fairness may also be based on a representativeness rule which prescribes that in all phases of the political process the concerns of important stakeholders must be reflected. In reference to the descriptive dimension of representation, Gerald Leventhal demands that "[...] deci-

---

313 Dahl, Robert Alan (1979). *Procedural Democracy. Philosophy, politics and society: fifth series: a collection.* Laslett, Peter and Fishkin, James S. Oxford: Blackwell, p. 105.

314 Bohman, James (2000). *Public deliberation: pluralism, complexity, and democracy.* Cambridge, Mass [u.a.]: MIT Press, p. 17.

315 Folger, Robert (1996). *Distributive and procedural justice: Multifaceted meanings and interrelations.* Social Justice Research. (9):4. 395-416, p. 403.

316 Dolan, Paul, Edlin, Richard , Tsuchiya, Aki and Wailoo, Allan (2007). *It ain't what you do, it's the way that you do it: Characteristics of procedural justice and their importance in social decision-making.* Journal of Economic Behavior & Organization. (64):1. 157-170, p. 160.

317 Leventhal, Gerald S. (1980). *What Should Be Done with Equity Theory? New Approches to the Study of Fairness in Social Relationships. Social exchange: advances in theory and research.* Gergen, Kenneth J., Greenberg, Martin S. and Willis, Richard H. New York; London: Plenum, p. 40.

sion-making bodies such as committees or legislatures should include representatives of important subgroups in the total population, perhaps in proportion to the subgroups' prestige and numerical size [in order that] the concerns of those affected should be represented in all phases of the allocation process."[318] Assaad Azzi argues that representation in decision-making bodies is a procedural resource because the "[...] degree of representation that a group receives relative to another group determines its degree of control over important distribution decisions and, ultimately, over its fate."[319]

The precise institutionalization of the representative rule in the descriptive sense may vary considerably depending on which subgroups are considered important. It goes without saying that a broad range of stakeholders increases the legitimacy of a decision-making process, but the relevant question is, however, who is to be included? Robert Dahl suggests that all individuals in a specific (geographical) area and subject to the respective laws have a *prima facie* right to representation.[320] Conversely, according to Albert Weale "[t]he burden of proof then lies with the person who wishes to disenfranchise any particular group of persons."[321]

In contrast, the substantive character of representation relates fundamentally to the mandate-independence controversy. Joel Wolfe describes a typical representative as one who "[...] articulates his followers' views, translates them into plans that can be effective, and helps obtain agreement on a single policy out of various alternatives."[322] Yet, at the other extreme the representative acts as a Trustee rather than as a delegate who does not take his constituents' view into account. Johnson and Solomon take up a middle position suggesting that "[...] the rule-making body act as a fiduciary in arbitrating disputes that may arise between the various interested parties, not as an agent of any party or group."[323] That the IASB should act as a mediator seems reasonable, although it regards investors as one of the key constituent groups, but it also aims to develop financial reporting standards in the public interest. Similarly, the IASB needs to mediate

318 Ibid., pp. 43-44.

319 Azzi, Assaad E. (1993). *Group representation and procedural justice in multigroup decision-making bodies*. Social Justice Research. (6):2. 195-218, p. 198.

320 Dahl, Robert Alan (1979). *Procedural Democracy. Philosophy, politics and society: fifth series: a collection*. Laslett, Peter and Fishkin, James S. Oxford: Blackwell, pp. 122-129.

321 Weale, Albert P. (1981). *Representation, Individualism, and Collectivism*. Ethics. (91):3. 457-465, p. 464.

322 Wolfe, Joel D. (1985). *A Defense of Participatory Democracy*. The Review of Politics. (47):3. 370-389, p. 381.

323 Johnson, Steven B. and Solomons, David (1984). *Institutional Legitimacy and the FASB*. Journal of Accounting & Public Policy. (3):3. 165-183, p. 173.

between different regional interests if it wants to credibly adhere to its international orientation.

In traditional government settings, the formalistic view on representation presumes that political agents are responsible to the people; if not, accountability (electoral defeat) is provided through the ballot box.[324] The regulatory shift in accounting standard setting towards a complex private-public decision-making process renders the use of such a traditional accountability model impossible. Instead, other control mechanisms are required,[325] which will be discussed in the subsequent chapter, in terms of procedural safeguards.

3.3.4 Procedural safeguards

Transparency

People not directly involved in collective decision-making processes require open and transparent procedures. If information about the process is retained, interested outsiders cannot "[...] infer what procedures are in use and whether procedural rules were followed [...]."[326] Therefore, the transparency of the decision-making process is an essential prerequisite and "[...] applies in almost all supranational policy-making contexts."[327]

Most importantly, if accountability mechanisms beyond voting need to be established, information about how the institution operates must be "(a) accessible at reasonable cost, (b) properly integrated and interpreted, and (c) directed to the accountability holders. Broad transparency is needed for critical revisability of the terms of accountability."[328] Like Buchanan and Keohane, Urbinati and Warren argue that accountability can be achieved "[...] not only through the direct mechanisms of voting but also through the gathering and exposure of information by groups and the media who claim (not always credibly) to act as repre-

---

324 Simms, Marian (1999). *Models of Political Accountability and Concepts of Australian Government.* Australian Journal of Public Administration. (58):1. 34-38, p. 35.

325 Freeman, Jody (1997). *Collaborative governance in the administrative state.* UCLA Law Review. (45):1. 1-98, p. 96.

326 Dolan, Paul, Edlin, Richard , Tsuchiya, Aki and Wailoo, Allan (2007). *It ain't what you do, it's the way that you do it: Characteristics of procedural justice and their importance in social decision-making.* Journal of Economic Behavior & Organization. (64):1. 157-170, p. 161.

327 Esty, Daniel C. (2006). *Good Governance at the Supranational Scale: Globalizing Administrative Law.* Yale Law Journal. (115):7. 1490-1562, p. 1530.

328 Buchanan, Allen and Keohane, Robert O. (2006). *The Legitimacy of Global Governance Institutions.* Ethics & International Affairs. (20):4. 405-437, pp. 427-428.

sentatives of the public."[329] David Esty further points out that "[...] a transparent decision-making process that provides opportunities for debate and political dialogue, with participation by those representing a broad range of views, is a key to legitimacy, substituting for the missing democratic legitimacy and accountability that elections provide."[330] Where traditional accountability mechanisms are absent, publicity must fill the gap. Finally, openness and transparency are also essential components of deliberative procedures, in order to determine whether particular arguments support policy proposals or not.[331]

Final control of the agenda

David Plotke points out that "[...] the opposite of representation is not participation. The opposite of representation is exclusion."[332] While decision makers can be responsive to a restricted audience, decision-making processes could equally be restricted by a narrow or closed agenda.[333] Emphasizing the importance of agenda items and priorities, the former chairman of the FASB pointed out that "I continue to believe that agenda setting is the single most important decision that we make at the FASB."[334] Therefore, it is necessary that affected stakeholders will have a say in which topics will be placed on the agenda. Otherwise any Board of decision makers can be "[...] fairly confident that the association will never act contrary to its interest, because it will never allow any proposal to be brought forward that would do so."[335]

Bias-suppression / neutrality

Gerald Leventhal highlights two specific biases that can occur in decision-making contexts. The first bias arises if the decision maker has a personal self-

---

329 Urbinati, Nadia and Warren, Mark E. (2008). *The Concept of Representation in Contemporary Democratic Theory*. Annual Review of Political Science. (11):387-412, p. 402.

330 Esty, Daniel C. (2006). *Good Governance at the Supranational Scale: Globalizing Administrative Law*. Yale Law Journal. (115):7. 1490-1562, pp. 1520-1521.

331 Buchanan, Allen and Keohane, Robert O. (2006). *The Legitimacy of Global Governance Institutions*. Ethics & International Affairs. (20):4. 405-437, p. 428.

332 Plotke, David (1997). *Representation is Democracy*. Constellations. (4):1. 19-34, p. 19.

333 See Robert Dahl who argues that there are two possible restrictions that invalidate legitimate decision-making processes: "[...] a narrow agenda, or [representatives] responsive to a highly exclusive demos, or both." Dahl, Robert Alan (1979). *Procedural Democracy. Philosophy, politics and society: fifth series: a collection*. Laslett, Peter and Fishkin, James S. Oxford: Blackwell, p. 105.

334 Beresford, Dennis R. (1993). Frustrations of a Standards Setter. Accounting HorizonsAmerican Accounting Association. 7. 70-76, p. 70.

335 Dahl, Robert Alan (1998). *On democracy*. New Haven; London: Yale University Press, p. 40.

interest in the final decision (outcome); the second type of bias occurs if the decision maker relies on narrow preconceptions rather than the arguments presented.[336] According to David Esty, "[...] nothing is more corrosive to governmental legitimacy than corrupt decision making."[337] To deal with the first kind of bias Fishkin suggests an 'insulation condition' by which he means that "[...] threats of bargains outside the political sphere should not decisively determine results within the political sphere."[338] This impartiality is important because many citizens lack the time and capacity to directly challenge political positions with which they disagree. Consequently, they want to know that their representatives can be trusted.[339] To infer whether or not representatives can be trusted has an important implication; in particular, people will deduce "[...] how authorities will act toward them in the future."[340] In addition, if trust is missing, people "[...] may define the relationship as more transactional, in which they assign less importance to intangible outcomes and more importance to tangible outcomes."[341]

The second kind of bias implicitly assumes that no one's point of view should have an *a priori* superior position in a policy debate. Rather, individuals should have about as good a chance at getting what they want from the process as everybody else. Viewed from this perspective, neutrality closely resembles the notion of political equality.[342]

Political equality may be applied to several procedural components, for example, participation, gaining enlightened understanding, and representation. For example, the possibility to participate in the process of decision making should be

---

336 Leventhal, Gerald S. (1980). *What Should Be Done with Equity Theory? New Approches to the Study of Fairness in Social Relationships. Social exchange: advances in theory and research.* Gergen, Kenneth J., Greenberg, Martin S. and Willis, Richard H. New York; London: Plenum, p. 43.

337 Esty, Daniel C. (2006). *Good Governance at the Supranational Scale: Globalizing Administrative Law.* Yale Law Journal. (115):7. 1490-1562, p. 1526.

338 Fishkin, James S. (1991). *Democracy and deliberation: new directions for democratic reform.* New Haven; London: Yale University Press, p. 32.

339 Gangl, Amy (2003). *Procedural Justice Theory and Evaluations of the Lawmaking Process.* Political Behavior. (25):2. 119-149, pp. 121-122, pp. 121-122.

340 Tyler, Tom R. (2006). *Why people obey the law.* Princeton: Princeton University Press, p. 164.

341 Brockner, Joel (2002). *Making Sense of Procedural Fairness: How High Procedural Fairness Can Reduce or Heighten the Influence of Outcome Favorability.* The Academy of Management Review. (27):1. 58-76, p. 63.

342 Taken together, both kinds of bias, in fact, their absence establishes institutional integrity. Buchanan, Allen and Keohane, Robert O. (2006). *The Legitimacy of Global Governance Institutions.* Ethics & International Affairs. (20):4. 405-437, pp. 422-424.

equally open to everyone.[343] In the light of political equality, Charles Beitz argues that "[...] the structural characteristics of political procedures do not so much matter because they conduce to acceptable outcomes as because they give public expression to each person's status as an equal citizen."[344] Conversely, "[...] if members are given greater opportunities than others for expressing their views, their policies are more likely to prevail, or, by curtailing opportunities for discussing the proposals on the agenda, a tiny minority of members might, in effect, determine the policies of the association"[345], a violation of the right to political equality. Albert Weale alleviates the equal qualification principle because not everyone is indeed equally qualified to advance policy proposals, but there is no reason to assume *prima facie* that someone is not equally capable of comprehending the relevant material "[...] provided they have adequate opportunities to learn about the matters [...] by inquiry, discussion and deliberation."[346] Empirical studies on procedural justice showed that a "[...] perception of unequal treatment is the single most important source of popular dissatisfaction with the American legal system."[347] Likewise, Solomons argues that "[...] nothing is more likely to undermine the credibility of financial reporting than the suspicion that the results reported were predetermined and that the accounting methods used were selected to produce the results desired by the preparers of the report."[348]

Finally, Gerald Leventhal's consistency rule is also closely related to political equality.[349] Consistent conduct, at least in the short term, should apply to the decision-making procedures: it therefore follows that the same decision-making criteria must be employed across a range of comparable decision contexts. The

343 Lane, Robert E. (1988). *Procedural goods in a democracy: How one is treated versus what one gets.* Social Justice Research. (2):3. 177-192, p. 185.

344 Beitz, Charles R. (1989). *Political equality: an essay in democratic theory.* Princeton: Princeton University Press, p. 92.

345 Dahl, Robert Alan (1998). *On democracy.* New Haven; London: Yale University Press, p. 39.

346 Weale, Albert (2007). *Democracy.* Basingstoke: Palgrave Macmillan, pp. 63-64.

347 Sarat, Austin (1977). *Studying American Legal Culture: An Assessment of Survey Evidence.* Law & Society Review. (11):3. 427-488, p. 434.

348 Solomons, David (1983). *The Political Implications of Accounting and Accounting Standard Setting.* Accounting & Business Research. (13):50. 107-118, p. 114, p. 114.

349 Leventhal, Gerald S. (1980). *What Should Be Done with Equity Theory? New Approches to the Study of Fairness in Social Relationships. Social exchange: advances in theory and research.* Gergen, Kenneth J., Greenberg, Martin S. and Willis, Richard H. New York; London: Plenum, p. 43.

consistency protocol calls for a universal treatment: to all current and potential constituents.[350]

Review / Changing Mechanism

To ensure accountability, democratic procedures should also provide the possibility for displeased individuals to repeal policy decisions. Correctability, in this sense, means the availability of procedures to voice appeals if a decision is made unfairly or results in unintended (negative) consequences.[351] The fallibility of human judgment does not imply that decisions should not be taken at all. Nevertheless, it might well be that the underlying assumptions that lead to a particular decision are mistaken.[352] Taking the process of deliberation seriously implies that "[...] decision makers must acknowledge the possibility that the reasonable views they reject may be shown to be correct in the future. [...] It imposes an obligation to continue to test their views, seeking forums in which they can be questioned, and keeping open the possibility of their revision."[353] Equally, if the deliberative process is brought to an end by means of voting, the "[...] decision reached by means of majority is, then, only the decision of the greatest number. By itself it does not confer any special privilege upon it [...] because majority will is not the equivalent of the will of all."[354] Moreover, if the nature of disagreement involves value judgments based on argumentation, the final decision will not necessarily result in a strict conclusion.[355] The opportunity to reverse policy decisions can then help to establish retrospective accountability in the absence of a "[...] fully functioning judicial system in the international realm [...]."[356] On this account, Gutmann and Thompson argue that "[...] even when prospective accountability fails, retrospective accountability [continuing delib-

350 Dolan, Paul, Edlin, Richard , Tsuchiya, Aki and Wailoo, Allan (2007). *It ain't what you do, it's the way that you do it: Characteristics of procedural justice and their importance in social decision-making.* Journal of Economic Behavior & Organization. (64):1. 157-170, p. 160.

351 Ibid., p. 160.

352 Weale, Albert (2007). *Democracy.* Basingstoke: Palgrave Macmillan, pp. 67-77 and p. 124.

353 Gutmann, Amy and Thompson, Dennis (2004). *Why deliberative democracy?* Princeton, N.J.; Oxford: Princeton University Press, p. 58.

354 Manin, Bernard, Stein, Elly and Mansbridge, Jane (1987). *On Legitimacy and Political Deliberation.* Political Theory. (15):3. 338-368, p. 360.

355 Ibid., p. 353.

356 Esty, Daniel C. (2006). *Good Governance at the Supranational Scale: Globalizing Administrative Law.* Yale Law Journal. (115):7. 1490-1562, p. 1536.

eration] may contribute to better decision making in the future, by calling a public official to critical account after the fact."[357]

Finally, review and alteration mechanisms apply, not simply to the content of policy outcomes, but also to the organizational structure responsible for developing these rules. Accordingly, institutional arrangements should "[...] allow for ongoing revisions over time [which, in turn,] may be some of the most important characteristics of successful international organizations during this time of change in the nature of global governance."[358]

3.4 Chapter summary

In general, democratic processes involve two consecutive steps. Firstly, the design of a process for decision making, and secondly, the actual decision making (voting).[359] All democratic conceptions of collective decision making share the premise that political decisions should be systematically related to the citizens that constitute the political community. David Easton defines democracy as "[...] government based on the consent of the governed, a consent that is contingent on popular demands being expressed and explicitly satisfied through the representative process."[360] Consent, as outlined earlier, is not directed to specific policy proposals or outcomes, rather the procedural characteristics to arrive at a collective decision must receive popular affirmation. Legitimate authority, defined in procedural terms, suggests that disagreements among persons on collective decisions should be solved by decision-making processes that are fair to the interests and opinions of each of the members constituting the community.

Democracy in its organizational manifestations is a highly complex phenomenon that can occur in various forms, sometimes intended to be alternatives, resting on distinct assumptions and principles. Likewise, the procedural characteristics for a legislative process, which are based on political theory, "[...] interact in complex ways – reinforcing and substituting for each other and sometimes

357 Gutmann, Amy and Thompson, Dennis (2004). *Why deliberative democracy?* Princeton, N.J.; Oxford: Princeton University Press, p. 45.

358 Livermore, Michael A. (2006). *Authority and Legitimacy in Global Governance: Deliberation, Institutional Differentiation, and the Codex Alimentarius.* New York University Law Review. (81):Available at: http://ssrn.com/abstract=903408. 766-801, p. 797.

359 Mueller, Dennis C. (1973). *Constitutional Democracy and Social Welfare.* The Quarterly Journal of Economics. (87):1. 60-80, p. 60.

360 For example, Easton, David (1975). *A Re-Assessment of the Concept of Political Support.* British Journal of Political Science. (5):4. 435-457, p. 439.

working at cross purposes."[361] Sigrid Quack notes that "[...] the criteria for evaluating legitimacy along these three dimensions [input/throughput/output] are not mutually exclusive."[362] As a consequence, finding the right balance between competing models of democracy is not only a technical matter, but also involves value judgments about relative priorities. From this follows that the institutional choice "[...] cannot be solved normatively *a priori*. Depending on the specific context, either form can be legitimate."[363] In addition, "[...] each procedural component in the perceiver's cognitive map may become the focus of a judgment process that evaluate[s] the fairness of that procedure."[364] Table 1 summarizes the discussions of chapter 3; in particular, it highlights the link between the models of democracy, the procedural characteristics and why these elements can provide a basis for legitimate authority (causal mechanisms). It also draws attention to potential research questions that need to be addressed in chapter 4.

Before proceeding with the institutional environment (actors and processes) responsible for the regulation of accounting in Europe, a prefatory remark is in order. Legitimacy conceptualized as fair procedures does not necessarily provide a benchmark against which to judge how unfair an institution must be to lack legitimacy.[365] While political institutions and procedures (political authority) are necessary, it is, at the same time, highly unlikely that they will "[...] achieve anything like perfect or ideal democracy."[366] Any evaluation of transnational governance modes employing normative ideals, therefore, needs to keep in mind that these criteria are goals toward which to strive, not reference points that can be fully met.

---

361 Esty, Daniel C. (2006). *Good Governance at the Supranational Scale: Globalizing Administrative Law*. Yale Law Journal. (115):7. 1490-1562, p. 1523.

362 Quack, Sigrid (2010). *Law, expertise and legitimacy in transnational economic governance: an introduction*. Socio-Economic Review. (8):1. 3-16, p. 7.

363 Vitale, Denise (2006). *Between deliberative and participatory democracy: A contribution on Habermas*. Philosophy & Social Criticism. (32):6. 739-766, p. 754.

364 Leventhal, Gerald S. (1980). *What Should Be Done with Equity Theory? New Approches to the Study of Fairness in Social Relationships. Social exchange: advances in theory and research.* Gergen, Kenneth J., Greenberg, Martin S. and Willis, Richard H. New York; London: Plenum, pp. 37-39.

365 Buchanan, Allen and Keohane, Robert O. (2006). *The Legitimacy of Global Governance Institutions*. Ethics & International Affairs. (20):4. 405-437, p. 425.

366 Dahl, Robert Alan (2006). *On political equality*. New Haven; London: Yale University Press, p. 10.

Models of Democracy	**Procedural characteristics**	**Causal mechanisms**	**Potential research questions**
Participatory Democracy	Participation	Self-development (social learning) Self-determination (social control)	How, when and where can constituents participate? How do those who are included in the decision-making process participate (mode of participation)? Are there different levels of participation?
Deliberative Democracy	Enlightened understanding	Self-development (social learning)	What deliberative elements do decision-making processes include? How do participants approach deliberations?
Representative Democracy	Representation	Self-determination through *indirect* participation	According to which criteria are stakeholders selected? What alternatives are available? Which mechanisms of ensuring accountability exist in a decision-making structure?
	Procedural safeguards • *Transparency* • *Final control of the agenda* • *Bias suppression / neutrality* • *Power-sharing* • *Review / Changing Mechanism*	Self-determination and trustworthiness	What information about the structure, content and current status of the decision-making process is made public? How and at what cost can those who may be affected inform themselves about decision-making processes? What possibilities exist to challenge rules? Are the criteria for agenda-setting interpreted (and equally weighted) the same way across all Board members?

Table 1: From democratic legitimacy to legitimization

Nevertheless, the previous discussion helped to clarify what is politically desirable and how it ought to be reflected in the arrangements of standard setting and governance. Therefore, the criterion of what is desirable can help to distinguish between better and worse institutional arrangements.[367] At the end, the discussion surrounding procedural legitimacy can only provide a standard for analyzing or comparing actual political arrangements while offering conceivable solutions that can close the 'reality-ideal' gap.[368]

---

367 Hamlin, Alan P. and Pettit, Philip (1989). *The Good polity: normative analysis of the state*. Oxford: Basil Blackwell, p. 10.

368 Dahl, Robert Alan (1998). *On democracy*. New Haven; London: Yale University Press, p. 29.

4 Accounting Regulation in Europe

4.1 The genesis of the IASC Foundation

4.1.1 A historical overview of the IASC Foundation

The IASC's status of global influence in corporate financial regulation remains unchallenged to this day. Nobes and Parker assert that, "[...] of the many bodies working for international standardization to be looked at [...], the IASC is perhaps the most important and most successful."[369] This chapter provides a brief historical overview of the IASC's evolution. A particular focus is placed on its achievements in gaining international acceptance as well as the recurring political pressures placed on its organizational structures. The historical development of the IASC / IASC-Foundation / IFRS Foundation[370] can be segmented into five different phases, which are depicted in Table 2.

Phase	Time Period	Major developments
(1)	1973 – 1988	Inauguration of the IASC and development of first standards
(2)	1989 – 1993	Development of conceptual framework and reduction of options
(3)	1994 – 2000	Recognition by IASCF by IOSCO, completion of core standards project
(4)	2001 – 2008	Reorganization and convergence with national accounting regulation
(5)	2008 – to present	Re-branding and recognition as global standard setter

Table 2: Historical overview of the IASC Foundation

369 Nobes, Christopher and Parker, Robert H. (2002). *Comparative international accounting.* Harlow: Financial Times/Prentice-Hall, p. 77.

370 According to the new Constitution, approved by the Trustees in January 2010 and effective from March 2010, the organization will be renamed to International Financial Reporting Standards Foundation (IFRS Foundation) and replace the name the International Accounting Standards Committee Foundation (IASC Foundation). IASC Foundation and IFRS Foundation are used interchangeably in this study.

Phase (1): 1973-1988: Inauguration and development of first standards

The International Accounting Standards Committee (IASC) was formed on June 29, 1973 with the objective of developing worldwide accounting standards. Decades before, other international bodies had already tinkered with the idea of harmonizing reporting standards. According to Botzem and Quack, the "[...] launching of the Marshall Plan in 1947 and the foundation of the Organization for Economic Cooperation and Development (OECD) in 1984 set the scene for intensified discussions among politicians and accounting professionals about national accounting harmonization."[371] At the company level, the Accountants' International Study Group (AISG) consisting of professional bodies from Canada, the UK and the US analyzed their divergence in accounting regulation.[372] The efforts to achieve increased harmonization, however, did not take place within a single entity, but rather by means of exchanging information and cooperation. This perspective on standardization changed however when, in 1972 at the Tenth International Congress of Accountants in Sydney, "Sir Henry Benson, invited professional bodies of six other nations to join in the initiative to set up an International Accounting Standards Committee (IASC)."[373] Eventually, the establishment of the IASC was a result of an agreement by accountancy bodies in ten countries (Australia, Canada, France, Germany, Japan, Mexico, the Netherlands, the United Kingdom, Ireland, and the United States), and these countries constituted the Board of IASC at that time. Zimmermann *et al.* explain the establishment of the IASC as "[...] a pre-emptive response of the private-Anglo-Saxon standard setters: the drafting of the Fourth Council Directive envisaged a strong role of the state as legislator, which would have considerably diminished the existing responsibilities of the professional organizations, particularly in the

371 Botzem, Sebastian and Quack, Sigrid (2008). *Contested rules and shifting boundaries: International standard-setting in accounting. Transnational governance: institutional dynamics of regulation.* Djelic, Marie-Laure and Sahlin-Andersson, KerstinCambridge University Press, p. 269.

372 Nobes, Christopher and Parker, Robert (2008). *Comparative international accounting.* Harlow: Financial Times/Prentice Hall, p. 81.

373 Botzem, Sebastian and Quack, Sigrid (2008). *Contested rules and shifting boundaries: International standard-setting in accounting. Transnational governance: institutional dynamics of regulation.* Djelic, Marie-Laure and Sahlin-Andersson, Kerstin. New York: Cambridge University Press, p. 273.

UK."[374] Equally, Nobes and Parker assert that the establishment can be regarded as a countervailing force.[375]

The activities of the accountancy bodies were organized under the International Federation of Accountants (IFAC), and Board membership was restricted to the founding accounting bodies.[376] Already in 1977 the IASCF adopted a revised constitution which stipulated an expansion of the Board to 11 countries whereby former 'associate' members became full members. From 1983, all members of the IFAC became members of the IASC. Accordingly, in its early days the IASC operated more like a representative body than an independent regulator. The relevant community was defined by membership and each member had a voting representative on the Council. The IASC's Board members agreed on the Committee's objectives to "[...] formulate and publish in the public interest, basic standards to be observed in the presentation of audited accounts and financial statements and to promote their worldwide acceptance."[377]

As early as 1974, the first exposure draft (ED) was published and subsequently IAS 1: Disclosure of Accounting Policies. Later on, between 1976 and 1982, the IASC Foundation progressively expanded its international activities: in 1976, the IASC started a working relationship with a group of ten bank governors on a project dealing with banks' financial statements. Three years later, the IASC met the Organization for European Economic Cooperation (OEEC) working group to discuss accounting standards for multinational enterprises[378]; made proposals on cooperation with the United Nations Intergovernmental Working Group on Accounting and Reporting; and started to visit national standard setters. In addition, financial analysts were granted Board membership in 1986, and contacts with business representatives were intensified.

The descriptive phase, as labeled by Thorell and Whittington, began with the inauguration of the IASC in 1973 and ended in 1988.[379] In the first phase, most of today's standards were developed: the IASC completed 31 accounting stan-

---

374 Zimmermann, Jochen, Werner, Jörg R. and Volmer, Philipp B. (2008). *Global governance in accounting: rebalancing public power and private commitment.* Basingstoke: Palgrave Macmillan, p. 58.

375 Nobes, Christopher and Parker, Robert (2008). *Comparative international accounting.* Harlow: Financial Times/Prentice Hall, p. 81.

376 First associate members were Belgium, India, Israel, New Zealand, Pakistan and Zimbabwe. In 1982, the Board was enlarged to a total of 17 members.

377 International Accounting Standards Committee Foundation (2010). Constitution, p. 103.

378 Hopwood, Anthony G. (1994). *Some reflections on 'The harmonization of accounting within the EU'.* European Accounting Review. (3):2. 241-254, p. 252.

379 Thorella, Per and Whittington, Geoffrey (1994). *The harmonization of accounting within the EU – Problems, perspectives and strategies.* European Accounting Review. (3):2. 215-240, p. 224.

dards by 1988. However, within this early phase, the IASC had to take into account various, often contrarian viewpoints by its constituents in the form of optional accounting treatments. This approach is labeled as descriptive because the IASC basically collected existing accounting methods that were used in developed countries. While Leonardo Martinez-Diaz argues that this situation resulted in the fact that the "[...] IASC had very little overall influence on reporting practices [...]"[380], Reginald Wallace emphasizes that a strategy of "[...] abrupt pursuit of harmonization would attract resistance and place the IASC in jeopardy."[381] Consequently, Nobes and Parker point out that "[a]lthough the standards have been criticized for allowing many options, this feature was probably essential to allow early progress, and it has been seriously addressed in the early 1990s."[382] Although the IASC did not achieve substantial harmonization across different accounting regimes, the end of the first phase is nevertheless described as a turning point with regard to the organizational development and international recognition. The IASC successfully established links with national standards setters or supervisory agencies, like the SEC or IOSCO. Subsequently, other relevant organizations joined the IASC Board or its advisory bodies, most notably the FASB in 1988.

Phase (2): 1989-1993: Development of conceptual framework and reduction of options

Although the IASC achieved considerable success in preparing standards in its early phase, it had also "[...] become clear that the substantial number of options in IASs were an obstacle to further enhancement of the status of the IASC's work."[383] Initiated by discussions with the IOSCO in the late 1980s, the IASC revised its strategy and started the Comparability and Improvements Project. The IOSCO, in turn, agreed to endorse IAS and advise its use by its members if the Comparability and Improvements Project promised to be successful. Accordingly, the new strategy considered the reduction of options as a priority, which

380 He further comments that "[t]he Committee's modest contribution was limited to helping small developing countries with no accounting standards of their own to develop accounting rules" Martinez-Diaz, Leonardo (2005). *Strategic Experts and Improvising Regulators: Explaining the IASC's Rise to Global Influence, 1973-2001*. Business and Politics. (7):3. 1-26, p. 1.

381 Wallace, Reginald Sylvanus Olusegun (1990). *Survival Strategies of a Global Organization: The Case of the International Accounting Standards Committee*. Accounting Horizons. (4):2. 1-22, pp. 4-5.

382 Nobes, Christopher and Parker, Robert (2008). *Comparative international accounting*. Harlow: Financial Times/Prentice Hall, p. 85.

383 Ibid., p. 82.

was reflected by the adoption in 1989 of E32: Comparability of financial statements.[384]

The contemporaneous development and completion of the conceptual framework (Framework for the Preparation and Presentation of Financial Statements) was an additional milestone for its subsequent work progress. The conceptual framework provided a benchmark for the future development of accounting standards as well as a basis for reducing the number of alternative accounting options.

Phase (3): 1994-2000: Recognition by IOSCO; completion of core standards project

In 1994 the IOSCO accepted 14 IASs but rejected a step-by-step endorsement of IASs. At this time, a new phase of the IASC history began, which focused on the development of a 'Core Set of Standards'. From now on, the idea was not to endorse individual standards but to develop standards which would fulfill the minimum requirements that the IOSCO posed on financial reporting. The comparability project was finished in December 1998 with the publication and approval of IAS 39 (Financial Instruments). Subsequently, in 1999, the IOSCO started its review of IASC core standards and advised its members in 2000 to allow IAS accounting standards for foreign listings at national stock exchanges.[385]

Between 1996 and 2000 the desire for harmonized international accounting standards received affirmation worldwide: in 1996 the US Congress asked for the "[...] establishment of a high quality comprehensive set of generally accepted international accounting standards [which] would greatly facilitate international financing activities and, most importantly, would enhance the ability of foreign corporations to access, and list in, the United States markets."[386] At the same time, the Australian Stock Exchange supported a program to harmonize Australian standards with IASs, the ministers at the World Trade Organisation (WTO) encouraged the successful completion of international standards, and the

384 Walton, Peter J., Haller, Axel and Raffournier, Bernard (1998). *International accounting* Internat. Thomson Business Press, pp. 32-33.

385 The European Commission supported the IASC/IOSCO agreement and the use of IASs by EU multinationals. Meanwhile, German companies reported under IASs for the first time back in 1995 already, and new laws in Belgium, France, Germany and Italy in 1998 allowed large companies to use IASs domestically.

386 U. S. Securities and Exchange Commission. (2000, http://www.sec.gov/rules/concept/34-42430.htm). *SEC Concept Release: International Accounting Standards*. Retrieved 10. January, 2010.

FEE urged European companies to adopt IASs. Moreover, in 1999, the G7 Finance Ministers[387] announced that they would support IASs in order to 'strengthen the international financial architecture'. Concurrently, the Eurasian Federation of Accountants and Auditors planned to approve the use of IASs in the Commonwealth of Independent States (CIS).[388] In 2000 then, the Basel Committee on Banking Supervision expressed its support for IASs and the idea of harmonizing accounting internationally. In Europe, the European Commission announced plans to require IASC standards for all EU listed companies from no later than 2005.

The years of global recognition and support were followed by a need to reconsider the existing structures of the IASC. In 1997, a 12-member Strategy Working Party (SWP) considered "[...] what strategy and structural reforms the IASC should undertake."[389] The 'Recommendations on Shaping IASC for the Future' included the following reasons for a change:[390]

(1) Limiting the direct influence of professional associations.
(2) Broadening the participation of countries and organizations, potentially as members of the Board.
(3) Intensifying the cooperation with national standard setters in order to increase worldwide convergence and acceptance of IAS.

The discussions on how to reform the IASC revealed a struggle between the Anglo-Saxon and continental European philosophy of standard setting.[391] Firstly, the European Commission emphasized the importance of 'political legitimacy' which involved a representative, constituency-based group empowered to select the IASC's Trustees. Secondly, the European Commission suggested that the Committee's members should be national standard setters rather than private-sector professionals. In contrast, the SEC emphasized the values of independence, professionalism and due process. Based on its domestic experience, the

387 The G7 is a group of seven industrialized nations. It was formed in 1976, when Canada joined the Group of Six: France, Germany, Italy, Japan, United Kingdom, and United States.

388 http://archive.iasb.org.uk/about/history.asp.

389 Martinez-Diaz, Leonardo (2005). *Strategic Experts and Improvising Regulators: Explaining the IASC's Rise to Global Influence, 1973-2001*. Business and Politics. (7):3. 1-26, p. 17.

390 Nobes, Christopher and Parker, Robert H. (2002). *Comparative international accounting*. Harlow: Financial Times/Prentice-Hall, p. 88. Botzem, Sebastian and Quack, Sigrid (2008). *Contested rules and shifting boundaries: International standard-setting in accounting. Transnational governance: institutional dynamics of regulation.* Djelic, Marie-Laure and Sahlin-Andersson, KerstinCambridge University Press, p. 277.

391 Ruder, David S., Canfield, Charles T. and Hollister, Hudson T. (2005). *Creation of World Wide Accounting Standards: Convergence and Independence*. Northwestern Journal of International Law & Business. (25):3. 513-588, p. 532.

SEC proposed a two-tiered body similar to the FASB. Powerful Trustees would be responsible for selecting Board members and ensuring a Board composed of full-time standard setters free from any commercial or political interests.[392] The negotiations over the IASC's restructuring were finalized in November 1999, when the SWP published its final report, and its recommendations were approved by the Board. In December, 1999, the Board voted in favor of discontinuing its operation.[393] Although the strategy paper of 1998 included a compromise in the form of a "[...] small technocratic Executive Board and a large representative Supervisory Board"[394], the final results of the the IASC restructuring negotiations indicate a strong Anglo-Saxon influence: "[p]owerful Trustees would appoint the IASC Board, which has sole responsibility for setting accounting standards. Board membership is based on technical expertise, not geographic representation. The more representative Consultative Group, which the Commission wanted strengthened, was renamed the Standards Advisory Council and left as a powerless forum for technical debate."[395]

Phase (4): 2001-2008: Reorganization and convergence with national accounting regulation

The finalized reform plans formed the basis for broad organizational restructuring, which resulted in the formal incorporation of the IASC Foundation, as a not-for-profit corporation incorporated in the State of Delaware, U.S., in March 2001. On April 1, 2001, the IASB assumed accounting standard-setting responsibilities from its predecessor, the IASC. The restructuring plans also touched upon the future strategy of how to achieve global accounting standards: previously, the IASC had tried to achieve consensus (by incorporating options) among various jurisdictional frameworks, whereas the IASB's approach was to develop international harmonized accounting standards.

As outlined in chapter 2.2, the European Union recognized the need for international accounting standards and passed the IAS Regulation to adopt IFRSs in 2002, which, according to Tony Porter, represents "[...] by far the most impor-

392 Camfferman, Kees and Zeff, Stephen (2007). *Financial Reporting and Global Capital Markets: a History of the International Accounting Standards Committee, 1973-2000*. Oxford: Oxford University Press, p. 469.

393 Nobes, Christopher and Parker, Robert (2008). *Comparative international accounting*. Harlow: Financial Times/Prentice Hall, p. 102.

394 Ibid., p. 102.

395 Martinez-Diaz, Leonardo (2005). *Strategic Experts and Improvising Regulators: Explaining the IASC's Rise to Global Influence, 1973-2001*. Business and Politics. (7):3. 1-26, p. 18.

tant boost for the IASB and its standards."[396] An equally significant change with regard to harmonization was a shift in the point of view of the relationship between US GAAP and the IFRS. After the Enron collapse in 2002, "[...] policy-makers increasingly expressed grave doubts about whether the 'rules-based' character of US GAAP, [...], had become dysfunctional."[397] Partly as a result of this negative experience, the FASB and the IASB decided to pursue closer cooperation in order to achieve convergence in accounting. In September 2002, the FASB and the IASB agreed within the scope of the 'Norwalk Agreement' to eliminate the existing differences between IFRS and US GAAP by 2005. On February 28, 2006, the Boards published 'A Roadmap for Convergence between IFRSs and US GAAP 2006-2008', the Memorandum of Understanding (MoU) between the IASB and the FASB. This document reaffirms the Boards' objective of developing high quality common accounting standards.

The ongoing success of the IASB once again spurred an interest in the organization's structure and governance arrangements. The voiced criticism, mainly pertaining to its exclusive membership, was lodged during the constitutional review that had been mandated when the IASB was established. In June 2005, further constitutional changes were approved by the Trustees. The IASC press release emphasized that decision making at the IASB remains "[...] appropriately protected from particular national or special interest pleading"[398], but highlights a number of changes, including improved transparency, consultation, and accountability. The release also drew attention to the greater involvement of public sector international and regional organizations in selecting Trustees, expanding the number of Trustees, including adding two new appointments from Asia/Oceania, explicitly noting the needs of small and medium firms, and a commitment to ensure inclusion on the IASB of members with practical experience.[399]

To summarize, the historical development of the IASC / IASCF / IFRS Foundation revealed that its continued success as a global standard setter concurrently placed great pressures on the organization, its Trustees responsible for the governance of the foundation, as well as the standard-setting processes itself. It becomes apparent that the more countries are using or planning to adopt IFRS, the greater pressure constituents from various jurisdictions will put on the standard-setting activities. As a result, the IASCF is forced to reconsider its institutional

396 Porter, Tony (2005). *Private Authority, Technical Authority, and the Globalization of Accounting Standards*. Business & Politics. (7):3. 1-30, p. 13.

397 Ibid., pp. 11-13.

398 International Accounting Standards Committee Foundation (2005). Trustees approve constitutional changes. Press Release (28 June 2005), p. 1.

399 Ibid., p. 1-2.

framework from time to time in order to gain or maintain support from its constituents. Hence, it is hardly surprising that a member of the International Monetary Fund (IMF) observed in 2008:

> "[...] that by the time of the next quinquinnial review, every major economy in the world would have either adopted or converged with IFRS and so, therefore, we need the constitutional review, to build a framework that allows for the expansion of adopters, without putting undue stress on people's assumptions or perceptions of appropriateness and representation, within the governance framework."[400]

In a similar spirit, the British Bankers' Association (BAA) affirmed the need to reassess the governance arrangements set out in the constitution which was approved in 2005:

> "[...] we welcome the Trustees' recognition that the governance structures and due process arrangements which were fit for a body producing financial reporting standards of an optional nature, are not fit for a body producing standards of fundamental importance to the health of global capital and financial markets."[401]

The organization has been subject to various changes over time. The second five-yearly review of the organization's constitutional arrangements initiated in 2008, however, resulted in some fundamental amendments. The proclaimed deficits pertaining to the organization's structure and ensuing changes to the constitution can be linked directly to the discussions of the models of democracy and procedural characteristics (see chapters 3.2 and 3.3), as will be detailed in the next chapter.

4.1.2 Constitutional review: Part one

In 2008, the Trustees initiated the second five-yearly review of the organization's constitutional arrangements, focusing on the appropriateness of the existing governance mechanisms. The IASCF was urged to quickly respond to the rising concerns of major jurisdictions that were applying IFRS. In particular, these countries criticized the foundation for its lack of public accountability, meaning the lack of direct accountability to national regulators that oversee the application of IFRS in their home jurisdictions. The constitutional review was therefore split into two phases, whereby the first part dealt with two major aspects: the creation of a Monitoring Group,[402] and the composition of the IASB.

---

400 Kenneth Sullivan, Senior Financial Sector Expert (IMF) (2008). Constitutional Review – Round-table meeting, Session 1 Part 1, p. 4.

401 Comment letter number 42 provided by the British Bankers' Association.

402 Monitoring Group and Monitoring Board are used interchangeably in this study.

Part one of the constitutional review started with publicly held round-table discussions on June 19, 2008, in London, where comments regarding the initial ideas developed by the Trustees were considered. In his opening statement, the Chairman of the IASCF Trustees, Gerrit Zalm, reiterated both the criticism of the existing governance arrangements and the need to establish a Monitoring Group (MG) to address the perceived lack of the organization's accountability:

> "I can understand members of parliament who are saying this is a private organization; it makes IFRSs, so we cannot change and we have to apply it, so they're actually setting law and there's no link to any democratic institution or public authority. So what we are trying to do in this proposal is make a link to the public authorities."[403]

Although it has been argued that the IASB issues 'soft' regulation, which means non-binding standards, Stig Enevoldsen, Chairman of the European Financial Reporting Advisory Group (EFRAG), emphasized that for Europe "[...] it looks like *de facto* legislation. Therefore it seems very important that there is this public oversight and public trust, for instance, for the European parliament, and other parliaments around the world."[404]

The opening statements of Gerrit Zalm as well as Stig Enevoldsen's observations clearly mirror the criticism expressed by the European Commission, the Financial Services Agency of Japan, the IOSCO and the US SEC. In a combined statement these bodies argue that:

> "International Financial Reporting Standards (IFRS) are becoming more widely used throughout the world. We have a common interest of ensuring continuing user confidence in the institutions responsible for the development of global accounting standards. A natural step in the institutional development of the IASB and the IASC Foundation would be to establish a means of accountability to those governmental authorities charged with protecting investors and regulating capital markets. We will work together to achieve these objectives."[405]

While accountability is one dimension of the concept of representation, the descriptive view of representation emphasizes the importance of the composition of the decision-making forum (see chapter 3.2.3). That being said, the IASCF/IASB

403 Zalm, Gerrit (Chairman, IASC Foundation). (2008). Constitutional Review – Round-table meeting, Session1 Part 1, p. 2.

404 Enevoldsen, Stig (Chairman, European Financial Reporting Advisory Group) (2008). Constitutional Review – Round-table meeting, Session 1 Part 2, p. 10.

405 International Organization of Securities Commissions (2007). Authorities Responsible for Capital Market Regulation Work to Enhance the Governance of the IASC Foundation. Richardson and Eberlein argue that "[...] in return for their endorsement or recognition of IFRS, the major securities and financial markets regulators demanded to reinforce the public interest oversight over the transnational accounting standard-setter." Richardson, Alan and Eberlein, Burkard (2011). *Legitimating Transnational Standard-Setting: The Case of the International Accounting Standards Board.* Journal of Business Ethics. (98):2. 217-245, p. 237.

was also objurgated for excluding key groups affected by its accounting standards. Previously, the IASCF had focused strongly on independent and technically competent staff for its standard-setting activities. Now it was urged to pay greater attention to geographical considerations. Accordingly, the composition and size of the IASB was addressed in this first phase as well. The Trustees believed that if IFRS were to become globally accepted, the composition and size of the IASB needed to be reconsidered to better reflect the users and their specific interests around the world. In addition, participants at the round-table discussions also stressed the mandate-independence controversy inherent in the concept of representation. One observer noted that "[...] if IFRS is to become the global standard, one of the things that we absolutely believe in is its independence. It must be independent. The Board cannot be influenced by any political process or national bias. It must be willing to hear differences of opinions. It must be there to listen to constituents and it must have an open due process that's available for everybody and anybody to participate in. However, to achieve the single set of high quality global accounting standards, the independence of the Board cannot be questioned."[406]

While being responsive to, but also independent of, others remains important, constituents were skeptical whether the IASB would and could continue to develop standards independent from any political pressure. Nevertheless, Christian Krohn, member of the Securities Industry and Financial Markets Association (SIFMA), stressed the relevance of the neutrality/bias suppression rule which should apply to the standard-setting process and argued that "[...] it's key for us that the IASB is and remains completely independent. Setting accounting standards and disclosure requirements for global capital markets must not be susceptible to interference from the political process, favored commercial interests, regional national bias or from any other form of vested interest."[407]

Following the round-table discussions, the proposal: *The review of the constitution – Public Accountability and the Composition of the IASB: Proposals for*

406 Gallagher, John (UBS – Global head of technical accounting). (2008). Constitutional Review – Round-table meeting, Session 2 Part 2. This statement clearly mirrors the comprehensive view on representation outlined in chapter 3.2.3: "[...] acting in the interest of the represented, in a manner responsive to them. The representative must act independently; his action must involve discretion and judgment; he must be the one who acts. [...]. The representative must act in such a way that there is no conflict, or if it occurs an explanation is called for." Pitkin, Hanna Fenichel (1972). *The concept of representation*. Berkeley: University of California Press, pp. 209-210.

407 Krohn, Christian (SIFMA) (2008). Constitutional Reveiw – Round-table meeting, Session 1 Part 1, p. 14.

Change was published in July 2008.[408] The policy proposal was accompanied by a questionnaire asking for comments in response to seven specific proposals.[409] The questions can be classified according to the analytical framework developed in chapter 3; however, the issues raised mainly deal with different aspects of representation.

Proposal	**Proposed constitutional change**	**Procedural characteristics**
1	Creation of a Monitoring Group.	Representation (accountability)
2	Membership in the Monitoring Group.	Representation (descriptive view)
3	The proposed mandate of the Monitoring Group.	Representation (substantive view)
4	Continued need of the Trustee Appointment Advisory Group.[410]	Not classified
5	Expansion of the IASB members from 14 to 16.	Representation (descriptive view)
6	Geographical formulation of the IASB suggested by the Trustees.	Representation (descriptive view)
7	Flexibility on part-time membership on the IASB.	Procedural safeguard: bias suppression

Table 3: Proposed constitutional changes: Constitutional review – Part One

In response to its questionnaire, the IASCF received 70 letters of comment which can be retrieved from its webpage. Table 4 illustrates the sample distribution in absolute numbers and percentage of the total population according to the specific questions raised. The answers were coded according to whether the proposal was approved (1); approved with qualifying remarks (0.5) or rejected (0). If respondents did not address a question, it was graded as missing.

408 International Accounting Standards Committee Foundation (2008). *Review of the Constitution: Public Accountability and the Public Accountability and the Composition of the IASB – Proposals for Change*

409 The questionnaire also included the possibility to indicate specific concerns not addressed by the seven questions.

410 Question 4 addresses the issue of whether there is a continued need for the Trustee Appointment Advisory Group (TAAG). Previously, the Trustees themselves were responsible for nominating and selecting new Trustees. Nevertheless, the Trustees were supported by the Trustee Appointment Advisory Group – a task which will be carried out by the Monitoring Group in future. Therefore, question 4 is excluded from further analysis.

Overall, the majority of respondents approved the policy proposals with an average approval of 0.71. More specifically, the proposed creation of a Monitoring Board (question 1), the expansion of IASB membership from 14 to 16 (question 5) and more flexibility on recruiting part-time members for the IASB (question 7) enjoyed great popularity among the respondents, with an average approval of 0.877, 0.736 and 0.845 respectively. Question two (membership in the Monitoring Group); question three (the proposed mandate of the Monitoring Group); question four (continued need for the TAAG) and question six (geographical formulation of the IASB suggested by the Trustees) proved to be the most controversial.[411]

Distribution of sample observations					
Question	**Approval**	**Approval (with qualifying remarks)**	**Dissent**	**Missing**	**Average approval**
1	54 (77.1%)	6 (8.5%)	5 (7.1%)	5 (7.1%)	0.877
2	25 (35.7%)	24 (34.2%)	9 (12.8%)	12 (17.1%)	0.638
3	24 (34.2%)	16 (22.8%)	8 (11.4%)	22 (31.4%)	0.667
4	26 (37.1%)	1 (1.4%)	26 (37.1%)	17 (24.2%)	0.500
5	38 (54.2%)	5 (7.1%)	12 (17.1%)	15 (21.4%)	0.736
6	32 (45.7%)	13 (18.5%)	12 (17.1%)	13 (18.5%)	0.675
7	43 (61.4%)	7 (10.0%)	5 (7.1%)	15 (21.4%)	0.845

Table 4: Comment letter analysis: Constitutional review – Part One

Respondents who approved the creation of the Monitoring Group (posited by question one) mostly referred to the criticism that the IASB in effect acts as a legislative body but does not provide an accountability mechanism in the traditional sense. For example, the Association of Chartered Certified Accountants

411 Whether a topic was deemed controversial or not is calculated (in percentage) as the number of Pro comments minus Dissent comments divided by the total number of comment letters received. Accordingly, the smaller the difference between the number of comments (pro or dissent) the clearer is the dividing line between opposing views. Question 2: 22.9%; question 3: 22.9%; question 4: 0.0%; question 6: 28.6%.

emphasized that "[…] the creation of a Monitoring Group ('Group') is a significant step in improving the overall governance of the IASC Foundation. [A]s the adoption of IFRS effectively means the surrender of sovereignty over accounting standards for a jurisdiction, an appropriate link between the Trustees and the Group will provide democratic oversight and therefore enhance public accountability."[412] Nevertheless, respondents who approved the creation of the Monitoring Board in general were concomitantly skeptical whether such a step could increase the risk of political pressure and reduce the independence of the standard setting process. For example, an approval with qualifying remarks is given by the Hong Kong Institute of CPAs: "[…] we generally support the creation of a Monitoring Group […] However, it is important to ensure that the proposed changes safeguard rather than undermine the independence of the standard-setting process […] and that neither the Monitoring Group nor the Trustees should, in their oversight, intervene in the IASB's standard setting process."[413] Dissenting opinions were mostly concerned with the potential benefits a Monitoring Board could provide since the Trustees themselves are primarily responsible for the governance of the Foundation and its operating bodies. Commentators who voted against the establishment of a Monitoring Board argued that overlapping authority and responsibility structures would "[…] needlessly usurp the authority and effective functioning of the Trustees and create unnecessary confusion. […] The formation of a Monitoring Group is likely to politicize the process needlessly and result in having formal representatives that may not possess the necessary and desired expertise."[414]

The creation of the Monitoring Board was less controversial compared to the proposed membership of the Monitoring Board (question two). Even respondents who approved the initial composition demanded that "[…] the Trustees [should] establish clear guidelines on the rationale for appointments and the maximum size of the Group."[415] Reservations about the initial composition were mainly based on the fact that a specific (in particular the respondent's) constituent group was excluded from the Monitoring Board. For example, the Committee of European Securities Regulators (CESR) argued "[…] directly involving CESR in the discussions would considerably reinforce the authority and legitimacy of the Monitoring Group as its composition would more effectively reflect the actual geographical spread of the use of the IFRS by listed companies. As a conse-

412 Comment letter number 53 provided by the Association of Chartered Certified Accountants (UK).

413 Comment letter number 69 provided by the Hong Kong Institute of CPAs (Hong Kong).

414 Comment letter number 50 provided by the International Corporate Governance Network.

415 Comment letter number 52 provided by the Institute of Chartered Accountants in England and Wales.

quence, it is essential to ensure adequate representation of the interests of the EU securities regulators. Therefore CESR proposes to amend the envisaged composition of the Monitoring Group to include a CESR representative."[416] On top of that, respondents who dissented with the composition of the Monitoring Board argued that all interested stakeholders should be represented, not just, for example, securities regulators.[417]

The mandate of the MG is dealt with in question three. According to the proposal, the responsibilities of the Monitoring Group would be to monitor and review the work of the Trustees to ensure that they are fulfilling their constitutional obligations. Moreover, the MG would be responsible for recommending and approving the selection of Trustees. Respondents who approved the proposed mandate specifically appreciated that the former mechanism of self-appointment would be abandoned.[418] Respondents who had qualifying remarks (or dissented) stressed that the Monitoring Board's mandate reached too far. For example, Deloitte Touch Tohmatsu is "[...] concerned about the proposal that the monitoring group should have direct access to the IASB Chairman to discuss 'any area of work' of the IASB and the 'proposed resolution of issues that the Monitoring Group has referred for timely consideration by the [...] IASB'."[419]

Questions five and six deal with the composition of the IASB. The proposed ideas relate to the descriptive view of representation which emphasizes the composition of the decision-making forum as a reflection of all its constituents. This perspective suggests the specific characteristics are decisive, and not what a representative does (see chapter 3.2.3). Question five initially asks if the IASB should expand from its current 14 members to 16. Similar to the proposed creation of the Monitoring Board, the idea of extending the IASB to 16 members enjoyed great popularity. Respondents who approved the proposal did so in light of the potential benefits provided by an expansion. For example, the Malaysian Accounting Standards Boards argued that the expansion of the IASB ensures "[...] diversity, representation and its ability to consult, liaise and communicate

416 Comment letter number 35 provided by Committee of European Securities Regulators (CESR).

417 The Ministry of Finance, Canada argued that "[w]e believe that the IASC should be accountable to all its stakeholders. Governance of the IASC should be on a broad basis with all interests represented. As proposed, the Monitoring Group would not represent all stakeholders nor would it be accountable to the public." Comment letter number 40 provided by the Ministry of Finance, Canada.

418 The Institut der Wirtschaftprüfer pointed out that "[...] especially, against the background of the numerous (European) calls for enhanced public accountability, we support that the Monitoring Group will approve the appointment of Trustees because in doing so the frequently expressed criticism pertaining to the current system of self-appointment is abolished." Comment letter number 2 provided by the Institut der Wirtschaftprüfer, Germany.

419 Comment letter number 22 provided by the Deloitte Touch Tohmatsu.

properly across the world."[420] Nevertheless, one of the 'Big Four' audit companies, KPMG, indicated the potential trade-offs which would come with such a step: "[…] a Board of 16 seems to be the maximum size for the organization to function effectively as a single group for standard setting. The transparency and credibility of the Board requires that not only its decision making but also its debate occurs in public meetings; too large a Board is likely to drive substantive discussions into informal working groups that meet outside of public meetings, with Board meetings becoming more a ratification of agreements reached privately. Such a move would be counterproductive for the Board's credibility and accountability."[421] Likewise, the International Actuarial Association pointed out that "[…] the Board should not become so large as to be unwieldy and slow its deliberations, impede effective discussions and decision making, or impose an undue burden on available funding."[422] Respondents who dissented from the proposal in question five mainly argued that the descriptive dimension of representation is not decisive; rather efficiency concerns and the quality of the process need to be considered. For example, the Canadian Accounting Standards Board disagrees that the "[…] legitimacy is enhanced by attempts to make the Board more representative. Rather we think that legitimacy results from the quality of the governance structures, the due process and, ultimately, the standards. The first is dependent on the Trustees, the latter two are dependent on the quality of the Board members – not on how many there are."[423]

To better reflect the geographical spread and use of IFRS around the world, the Trustees proposed in question six a new geographical formulation of the IASB. Respondents who approved the proposal believed that "[…] expansion will provide greater legitimacy to the IASB as those countries adopting IFRS see that representatives from their country or region participate in the standard-setting process at that level."[424] However, respondents with qualifying remarks placed a premium on the substantive dimension of representation and argued that as long as "[…] professional competence and practical experience remain paramount criteria, we believe that a more geographically diverse Board, reflecting the different cultural and professional backgrounds of countries that have adopted or are intending to adopt IFRS, certainly will help to ensure the legiti-

420 Comment letter number 21 provided by the Malaysian Accounting Standards Boards.

421 Comment letter number 70 provided by KPMG IFRG Limited.

422 Comment letter number 58 provided by the International Actuarial Association (Committee on Insurance Accounting).

423 Comment letter number 72 provided by the Canadian Accounting Standards Board / Accounting Standards Oversight Council's Strategy Committee.

424 Comment letter number 26 provided by UBS AG, Switzerland.

macy of the Board."[425] Dissenting opinions did not favor any geographical criteria. Instead, the French Institute of Chartered Accountants maintained that "[...] 'professional competence and practical experience should remain paramount'. [...] Consequently we do not favor geographical criteria and are of the opinion that sound principles should be maintained to select the IASB members", and further criticized the potential imbalance of the proposed composition: "[...] we do not agree with the proposal to have four members from North America, which raises issues with respect to one-country dominance in the Board composition."[426]

Question seven addresses the issue of whether the constitution should provide some flexibility on part-time membership on the IASB. Respondents approved the proposal on grounds of the potential practical implications of having part-time members on the IASB: "We believe that part-time members can serve a very useful function in bringing more current real world knowledge to the IASB's deliberations. We believe that the IASB has benefited significantly from the contribution of its part-time members."[427] Respondents with qualifying remarks or in disagreement argued that the independence of the standard-setting process would be undermined. For example, the National Association of State Boards of Accountancy refers to the US Sarbanes-Oxley Act (SOA) with its key provision that Board members must be full-time and independent from the profession. Section 101 (e) of the SOA states: "Each member of the Board shall serve on a full-time basis, and may not, concurrent with service on the Board, be employed by any other person or engage in any other professional or business International Accounting Standards Committee Foundation activity."[428] Similarly, the Centre for Financial Market Integrity placed much greater importance on independence than on recent or current practical experience: "[...] of much greater importance to us is that the IASB comprises full-time members with no remaining responsibilities or obligations to any other bodies or organizations and that it have adequate investor representation. Continued part-time employment of members may compromise the amount of time those members have to devote to the matters of the IASB. [...] IASB members have a significant work load, which is not conducive to part-time involvement. Furthermore, part-time members are by definition less independent than full-time members. The appearance

425 Comment letter number 53 provided by the Association of Chartered Certified Accountants (UK).

426 Comment letter number 25 provided by the French Body of statutory auditors (French Institute of Chartered Accountants).

427 Comment letter number 34 provided by Grant Thornton International.

428 Comment letter number 11 provided by National Association of State Boards of Accountancy, North America.

of independence, as well as independence in fact, will be a major determinant of the future success of IFRS as the single global financial reporting standard."[429]

Besides the specific comments made with regard to the questionnaire, the Trustees solicited other comments on topics not covered in the first part of the constitutional review. In general, additional comments were primarily concerned with procedural safeguards that should ensure an independent, high-quality due process. For example, EFRAG missed a discussion about how potential topics are added to the IASB's agenda. It emphasized that "[...] we have recently seen substantial changes being made to the scope of key IASB projects without any consultation taking place. Similarly, priorities can be changed without consultation. Adding projects to the agenda requires consultation with SAC, but not with the IASB's wider constituency. We think this is unacceptable; there needs to be much wider consultation."[430]

Another major concern to most constituents was found to be the current funding system of the IASCF which was not dealt with in Part 1 of the review. However, the funding regime and its importance with respect to bias suppression cannot be underestimated: "[...] we believe the structure and procedures of the accounting standard setter must provide for a secure, stable, and mandatory funding source for the standard setter. [...] We also believe that the key criterion for evaluating the appropriateness of a funding source for the GASB [Governmental Accounting Standards Board, US] or any other accounting standard setter is whether the source enhances rather than detracts from the independence of the standard setter."[431] Thornburg and Roberts highlight the relationship between funding and independence in politics. They argue that money in politics compromises the democratic process because "[...] special interest money can buy legislative favors and/or elective offices [and] if this is true, then interested money in politics undermines the equality ideal of pure democracy, where one person has one vote, and skews political representation towards the wealthy."[432] Accordingly, Andreas Fleckner argues that in order to "[...] avoid improper rule making, the process must be sheltered from outside influence by autonomous structures, independent funding, and self-government."[433]

---

429 Comment letter number 11 provided by CFA Institute – Centre for Financial Market Integrity.

430 Comment letter number 64 provided by the European Financial Reporting Advisory Group (EFRAG).

431 Comment letter number 62 provided by the Investors Technical Advisory Committee (ITAC).

432 Thornburg, Steven and Roberts, Robin W. (2008). *Money, politics, and the regulation of public accounting services: Evidence from the Sarbanes-Oxley Act of 2002*. Accounting, Organizations and Society. (33):2-3. 229-248, p. 231.

433 Fleckner, Andreas M. (2008). *FASB and IASB: Dependence Despite Independence*. Virginia Law & Business Review. (3):275-309, p. 277.

Bias or undue influence, however, is not only dependent on the funding regime. Political pressure can lead to undue political interference as well. Accordingly, the Council of Institutional Investors stressed the need to have an independent, neutral standard-setting process: "The governance structure and operating procedures should ensure that the technical decisions and judgments of the IASB are protected, as much as possible, from being overridden by governmental agencies and departments for reasons that are inconsistent with the development of high quality financial accounting and reporting standards that meet the needs of investors."[434]

Based on the support of its constituents, with an average approval of 71%, the IASCF incorporated all initially proposed constitutional changes. On January 15, 2009, the Trustees approved the ensuing changes to the constitutional review (Part one) to come into effect on February 1, 2009.

4.1.3 Constitutional review: Part two

In December 2008, the second part of the constitutional review started with a discussion document (DD) to identify issues that could or should have been addressed but were not considered in the first part of the review.[435] As a result of the initial discussions, the Trustees published the policy proposal: *Proposals for Enhanced Public Accountability* in September 2009, which was accompanied by a questionnaire asking for comments in response to 14 specific questions (see appendix Table 20).[436] From a governance perspective the questions four, five, seven, eight, 10, 11, 12 and 13 are of particular interest and can be classified according to the analytical framework developed in chapter 3 as depicted in Table 5. Whereas the creation of a Monitoring Board enjoyed great popularity (0.87) the exact composition (membership) and role was more controversial. Therefore, constituents urged the IASCF to reconsider and clarify issues related to the MB.

In response to its questionnaire, the IASCF received 63 comment letters. Table 6 illustrates the sample distribution in absolute numbers and percentages of the population according to the specific questions raised. Again, the answers were coded according to whether the proposal was approved (1); approved with qualifying remarks (0.5) or rejected (0). If respondents did not specifically address a particular question, it was graded as missing.

434 Comment letter number 57 provided by the Council of Institutional Investors.

435 International Accounting Standards Committee Foundation (2008). *Review of the Constitution – Identifying Issues for Part 2 of the Review.*

436 International Accounting Standards Committee Foundation (2009). – *Part 2 of the Constitution Review. Proposals for Enhanced Public Accountability.*

Question	Proposed constitutional change	Procedural characteristics
4	Reflecting the role of the Monitoring Board	Representation (accountability)
5	Recognizing the participation of Trustees from Africa and South America	Representation (descriptive) Participation
7	Continued emphasis on effective Trustee oversight	Representation (accountability)
8	Expanding the IASB's liaison activities with another or other organizations	Participation
10	The length of IFRS Board members' terms	Procedural safeguard: Bias suppression / neutrality
11	Accelerated due process	Deliberation
12	Encouraging greater input into the IASB's agenda-setting process	Participation Procedural safeguard: Final control of the agenda
13	Review of the Standards Advisory Council	Procedural safeguard

Table 5: Proposed constitutional changes: Constitutional review – Part Two

Overall, the majority of respondents approved the policy proposals (average approval: 0.826). More specifically, the proposed participation of Trustees from Africa and South America (question five) and the idea of expanding the IASB's liaison activities with another or other organizations (question eight) enjoyed great popularity among the respondents: 71.4% and 74.6% respectively approved the proposals. In contrast, question 11 (accelerated due process) provoked the most controversial discussion among the respondents and received little affirmation: 44.4% of the respondents disagreed with the proposed change.[437]

437 Whether a topic was deemed controversial or not is calculated (in percentage) as the number of Pro comments minus Dissent comments divided by the total number of comment letters received. Accordingly, the smaller the difference between the number of comments (pro or dissent) the clearer is the dividing line between opposing views. Question 11: 4.8%.

Distribution of Sample Observations					
Question	**Approval**	**Approval (with qualifying remarks)**	**Dissent**	**Missing**	**Average approval**
Q4	42 (66.7%)	8 (12.7%)	4 (6.3%)	9 (14.3%)	0.852
Q5	45 (71.4%)	6 (9.5%)	4 (6.3%)	8 (12.7%)	0.873
Q7	40 (63.5%)	2 (3.2%)	4 (6.3%)	17 (27.0%)	0.891
Q8	47 (74.6%)	2 (3.2%)	4 (6.3%)	10 (15.9%)	0.906
Q10	39 (61.9%)	3 (4.8%)	7 (11.1%)	14 (22.2%)	0.827
Q11	25 (39.7%)	7 (11.1%)	28 (44.4%)	3 (4.8%)	0.475
Q12	22 (34.9%)	25 (39.7%)	8 (12.7%)	8 (12.7%)	0.627
Q13	42 (66.7%)	2 (3.2%)	3 (4.8%)	16 (25.4%)	0.915

Table 6: Comment letter analysis: Constitutional review – Part Two

Question four deals with the accountability dimension of representation and reflects on the role of the Monitoring Board. In particular, the Trustees revisited the defining characteristics of the relationship between the Trustees and the MB. Commentators responded similarly to the first phase of the constitutional review. The majority of respondents approved the creation of the Monitoring Board in order to "[...] establish [...] democratic oversight and to enhance the credibility of both the IFRS Foundation and the IFRS Board."[438] More critical respondents emphasized the potential drawbacks associated with shared governance responsibilities between the Trustees and the MB, for example, overlapping authority structures and a subsequent diffusion of responsibilities.[439] Respondents who dis-

438 Comment letter number 4 provided by the Federation of European Accountants, Europe.

439 For example, the Association of British Insurers "[...] accepts that the institution of the Monitoring Board needs to be reflected in the Constitution. However, we consider that the governance of the IFRS Foundation should continue to rest solely with its Trustees. Any diffusion of responsibility, especially if it is ill-defined, does not accord with what we understand by good governance. We therefore do not support the inclusion of 'primarily' in section 3 of the Con-

approved the proposed role and relationship of the MB and Trustees argued that "[...] the Monitoring Board's responsibilities and activities should be narrowly confined to the education of, and communication with, representatives of public authorities about the benefits of independent private sector accounting standard setting that meet the needs of investors."[440]

Question five deals with the descriptive dimension of representation and asks if the specific recognition of participating Trustees from Africa and South America is appropriate. Although the majority of respondents approved the proposal (71.4%)[441], other respondents had clear objections to the proposal since it would impede the flexibility of selecting new Trustees[442] and, more importantly, eclipse other (and supposedly more valuable) skills required for developing accounting standards. For example, the Corporate Reporting Users' Forum argued in comment letter number 67 that "[...] the IFRS Board and the Trustees should be constituted of the individuals with the mix of skills best able to develop Financial Reporting Standards of the highest quality. We do not favor strict geographical quotas for membership such as those which are in place and are proposed."[443]

Question seven deals with the accountability dimension of representation and asks if the constitutional changes are needed to better enable (increase the effectiveness) the Trustees' oversight functions. Most respondents agreed (63.5%) that "[...] no amendments to the Constitution are needed in this regard."[444] Nevertheless, other respondents "[...] would welcome the Trustees playing a greater

stitution, nor the insertion of the reference to the Monitoring Board." Comment letter number 42 provided by the Association of British Insurers, United Kingdom.

440 Comment letter number 48 provided by the Council of Institutional Investors, North America.

441 See, for example, the comment of the Institute of Chartered Accountants of Scotland: "We believe that geographical balance should be the overriding principle in the composition of the Trustees. We acknowledge that Africa and South America are already represented among the Trustees but we have no objection to making that reference specific." Comment letter number provided by Institute of Chartered Accountants of Scotland (The Institute's Accounting Standards Committee), Scotland.

442 BDO International generally agreed that "[...] it is important for the geographic balance of the Trustees to reflect the broad range of constituencies that have adopted (or will soon adopt) IFRS. However, we believe that it is important for flexibility to be retained, in order that an appropriate balance of geographic representation, and technical and other attributes, is retained. [...] In addition, it would be helpful for an explanation to be given of how the geographic balance of representation has been reached, whether this is in the context of the actual use (or planned short term adoption) of IFRS or otherwise." Comment letter number 58 provided by BDO International, United Kingdom.

443 Comment letter number 67 provided by Corporate Reporting Users' Forum.

444 Comment letter number 13 provided by the Canadian Accounting Standards Oversight Council and the Accounting Standards Board, Canada.

role in assessing the IASB's effectiveness and in the agenda-setting processes, and they should demonstrate their review of the IASB's due processes in ensuring stakeholder input is duly considered."[445] On top of that, the Basel Committee on Banking Supervision suggested that the Trustees "[...] should ensure that due process is followed with respect to all aspects of standard setting. [...] The Committee acknowledges the creation of the Due Process Oversight Committee (DPOC), and considers this development to be an important step toward greater accountability of the IASB. The Committee recommends including the creation of the DPOC and detailing its responsibilities in the Constitution, as the DPOC will be instrumental in enhancing the accountability of the IASB."[446]

Question eight deals with the 'effective participation' criteria of procedural legitimacy. The Trustees solicited comments on whether the IASB should expand its liaison activities with other organizations. The suggestion was approved by a majority of 74.6%.[447] However, respondents also voiced the potential risk of increased liaison activities since "[...] it would give national standard setters additional, possibly excessive and undue influence on the standard-setting process compared with other interested parties."[448] On the other hand, the Association of British Insurers did not support "[...] the IASB liaising with the regulators to assist in the development of IFRSs in the way that the amendment proposed would seem to suggest."[449]

Question 10 deals with the retrospective-accountability dimension of representation. Most obviously, this dimension is constituted of electoral mechanisms, but the length of IFRS Board members' terms can play an important role as a procedural safeguard to ensure accountability and neutrality. In general, shorter

---

445 Comment letter number 41 provided by the Investment Management Association, United Kingdom.

446 Comment letter number 56 provided by the Basel Committee on Banking Supervision, Switzerland.

447 PricewaterhouseCoopers LLP argues that "[...] the IASB should continue to engage with all stakeholder organizations that are interested in high-quality international accounting standards. However, we suggest that more formalized arrangements for collaboration should be limited to those other standard-setting organisations that have achieved a reasonable level of maturity and development in relation to their own due process, governance and resourcing." Comment letter number 34 provided by PricewaterhouseCoopers LLP, United Kingdom.

448 Comment letter number 29 provided by the Roche Group, Switzerland. "We have observed this tendency in the Board's contacts with the FASB, paying less attention to the legitimate views of parties more directly involved in financial reporting." See also: "Nevertheless, we believe the Foundation should take measures to ensure transparency in relationships with some organizations, so that the independence of the Board would not be impaired and it would not suffer from political pressures." Comment letter number 20 provided by the Japanese Institute of Certified Public Accountants (JICP), Japan.

449 Comment letter number 42 provided by the Association of British Insurers, United Kingdom.

terms of office are associated with a smaller risk of power abuse and political capture. On the one hand, "[…] a shorter term might bring the associated risk of external influence, as the individual might otherwise look for a subsequent appointment with another organization shortly after being appointed to the IFRS Board. On balance, we support the proposals. It is appropriate for the initial term of appointment of an IFRS Board member to be of sufficient duration to ensure the independence of that individual."[450] Another potential downside of shorter terms of office might be a declining quality of IFRS because "[…] there is a lead time associated with learning about the standard-setting process. However, the Committee acknowledges that an infusion of new experience and practical knowledge within the IASB is necessary for high quality standard setting."[451] On the other hand, the Institute of Chartered Accountants in England and Wales is "[…] not convinced that this change would be beneficial, firstly as many major standard-setting projects take many years to complete, and secondly as we understand that it takes new Board members a substantial period of time to become familiar with the range of issues and considerations involved in relation to setting standards for the world. A ten year period of service is, in our view, about right."[452]

Question 11 deals with the deliberative (enlightened understanding) dimension of procedural legitimacy. In question 11, the Trustees asked if it is appropriate to introduce a 'fast-track' due process in exceptional circumstances. The proposed change provoked the most controversial discussion among the respondents and received little affirmation (39.7%). Even respondents who agreed on balance did so only on condition that "[…] some further acceleration may be appropriate in extremely rare circumstances [...] The ASRB is concerned however that: "There is no definition of 'exceptional circumstances'."[453] Furthermore, respondents believed that such a procedure "[…] brings with it associated difficulties, for example, perceived, and possibly actual, compromises to due process and quality if such a procedure is required, and difficulties for constituents in responding within the comment period."[454] Dissenting respondents pointed to the negative experience the IASB and its constituents made when a fast-track proce-

450 Comment letter number 58 provided by BDO International, United Kingdom.

451 Comment letter number 56 provided by Basel Committee on Banking Supervision. Switzerland.

452 Comment letter number 47 provided by Institute of Chartered Accountants in England and Wales, United Kingdom.

453 Comment letter number 9 provided by the Accounting Standards Review Board, New Zealand.

454 Comment letter number 23 provided by KPMG IFRG Limited, United Kingdom.

dure was applied.[455] Potential negative consequences of an accelerated due process can be: flawed decision outcomes, insufficient transparency and unrealistic translation, digestion, and feedback requirements on investors and preparers across multiple jurisdictions. More drastically, the Hermes Equity Ownership Services Limited argued that "[...] we do not see any practical difference between consultations shorter than 30 days and dispensing with consultation altogether – which the Foundation rightly frowns upon. We therefore oppose the proposed change to permit consultation periods shorter than 30 days."[456] In addition, the Life Insurance Association of Japan (LIAJ) emphasized "[...] accounting standards need to be developed according to the strict due process. It is important to ensure that all those affected globally are provided with sufficient time to review and comment on the IASB's proposals and that the IASB is never influenced by one region or party's opinions in particular. When amending existing IFRSs or adopting new guidance, we believe a shorter period of due process should not be allowed. It is in times of crisis that a deliberate and well-thought out approach is most needed. Hasty decisions are likely to exacerbate the problem, not fix it."[457]

Question 12 deals with two aspects of procedural legitimacy: participation and final control of the agenda (procedural control). The Trustees solicited views on encouraging greater input into the IASB's agenda-setting process. More precisely, the Trustees asked if the Constitution should "[...] expressly provide that the IASB must consult the Trustees and the SAC when developing its technical agenda."[458] Many commentators during the first part of the constitutional review indicated a desire to discuss this topic, in particular with respect to greater transparency and broader stakeholder input into determining which items and topics appear on the agenda. Consequently, the suggested amendments received strong approval ("[...] as rightly noted in the Consultation, concerns about agenda setting are most likely symptoms of concerns about whether the IASB is actually responsive towards stakeholder inputs or even transparent about its agenda-setting outcomes. Therefore, we strongly support any improvements in the con-

455 The CFA Institute Centre for Financial Market Integrity pointed out that "[t]he accounting standard changes that have occurred during recent months due to political pressure being exerted on both the IASB and Financial Accounting Standards Board (FASB) illustrate the risks of 'fast-track' standards. Clearly there have been undesirable consequences of accelerated due process." Comment letter number 54 provided by CFA Institute Centre for Financial Market Integrity.

456 Comment letter number 35 provided by Hermes Equity Ownership Services Limited, United Kingdom.

457 Comment letter number 32 provided by Life Insurance Association of Japan (LIAJ), Japan.

458 International Accounting Standards Committee Foundation (2009). – *Part 2 of the Constitution Review. Proposals for Enhanced Public Accountability*, p. 24.

sultative process, including consultation with the IASB Standards Advisory Council (SAC) and Trustees on agenda items. This will ensure that the IASB is responsive and accountable in appearance and in fact.)"[459] Respondents with qualifying remarks were actually in favor, but criticized that the proposed changes did not go far enough. For example, the Institute of Certified Public Accountants argued that "[...] whilst we can support the proposed modification by which the IASB will have to consult the Trustees and the SAC before drawing up its work program, we still consider it totally insufficient to reduce the opacity which continues to surround the current process. The IASB must effectively justify in these institutions why certain projects are taken onto its agenda or not and what level of priority they have. Much criticism has been made, and recently repeated at the Roundtables, about the lack of transparency in fixing the agenda. [...] The publication of the documents of the SAC does not seem likely to create a situation in which a proper debate on the work plan could take place; moreover we request a formal annual public consultation on the work plan and its priorities."[460] In contrast, dissenting views stressed the importance of independent decision making at the IASB: "[...] an independent accounting standard setter must have the ability to develop and pursue its own agenda. Requiring that the IASB consult with the Trustees (who clearly are not independent) about its agenda weakens the independence and, thus, the legitimacy of the standard-setting process."[461]

To summarize, the first part of the constitutional review focused on public accountability and the composition and size of the IASB – the representative dimension of procedural legitimacy. The Trustees approved the ensuing changes on January 25, 2009, to come into effect on February 1, 2009. In the first phase of the review, the Trustees mainly responded to the criticism of not having established public accountability mechanisms. To achieve external oversight (divided authority and accountability), the foundation established the Monitoring Board. Part two of the constitutional review mainly dealt with the standard-setting process – the participatory, deliberative and representative dimensions of procedural legitimacy. The Trustees approved the changes on January 26, 2010, to come into effect on March 1, 2010.

Most policy proposals of both parts of the constitutional review received strong approval or equally disaffirmation ('accelerated due process'); an indication that different dimensions of procedural legitimacy seem to be universally

459 Comment letter number 54 provided by the CFA Institute Centre for Financial Market Integrity.

460 Comment letter number 17 provided by Institute of Certified Public Accountants, Ireland.

461 Comment letter number 48 provided by the Council of Institutional Investors, North America.

acceptable. However, it also became evident that constituents around the world have quite different perceptions of the importance of governance issues or how to trade-off one dimension (descriptive representation) against the rational character (deliberation) of the due process (technical and practical competence).

4.2 Private standard setting

4.2.1 Monitoring Board

At a meeting in New Delhi, India, on January 15 and 16, 2009, the Trustees decided to enhance the organization's public accountability by establishing a link to a Monitoring Board (MB) consisting of public authorities (see also chapter 4.1.2.). The proposed initial composition of the MB was as follows:

(a) The responsible member of the European Commission.
(b) The chair of the IOSCO Emerging Markets Committee.
(c) The chair of the IOSCO Technical Committee (or vice-chair or designated securities commission chair in cases where either the chair of an EU securities regulator, commissioner of the Japan Financial Services Agency or chair of the US Securities and Exchange Commission is the chair of the IOSCO Technical Committee).
(d) The commissioner of the Japan Financial Services Agency.
(e) The chair of the US Securities and Exchange Commission.
(f) The chair of the Basel Committee on Banking Supervision (as an observer).

A Memorandum of Understanding (MoU)[462] explains the relations of the Monitoring Board with the Trustees. The MB is supposed to provide a formal link between the Trustees and national public authorities that have been responsible for overseeing national accounting standard setters in their home jurisdictions. As set out in the MoU:

> "The primary purpose of the IASCF Monitoring Board is to serve as a mechanism for formal interaction between capital markets authorities and the IASCF, thereby facilitating the ability of capital market authorities that allow or require the use of IFRS in their jurisdictions to effectively discharge their mandates relating to investor protection, market integrity and capital formation. The IASCF Monitoring Board will help ensure the public accountability of the IASCF by monitoring and reinforcing the public interest oversight function of the IASCF, as well as to promote the continued development of IFRS as a high-quality set of global accounting standards."[463]

462 See appendix: Figure 6.
463 See appendix: Figure , p. 3.

Accordingly, the MB's main responsibility is to ensure that the Trustees continue to discharge their duties as defined by the IASCF constitution, in particular with regard to the due process arrangements. In addition, members of the MB participate in the Trustee nomination process and are responsible for approving the appointment or reappointment of Trustees,[464] whereby all assessments have to be decided unanimously.[465] In order to execute its oversight duties, the MB is supposed to meet the Trustees at least once a year and provide a written report on its activities.

4.2.2 International Accounting Standards Committee Foundation

The organizational as well as governance structures described are the result of the constitutional review carried out between 2008 and 2010. The present constitution, effective from March 1, 2010, deals with the name and objectives of the institution and the governance of the IASC Foundation: the Trustees, the Monitoring Board, the IASB, the IFRS Interpretations Committee, the IFRS Advisory Council, as well as administrative issues.

The International Accounting Standards Committee Foundation (IASCF) is the organizational base of the privately organized standard setting institution, which operates as a not-for-profit corporation incorporated in the state of Delaware, USA. The IASC Foundation has two main bodies: the Trustees and the IASB (chapter 4.2.3), as well as the International Financial Reporting Interpretations Committee (IFRIC, see chapter 4.2.4) and a Standards Advisory Council (SAC, see chapter 4.2.5). The organization's objective is:

> "[…] to develop, in the public interest, a single set of high quality, understandable, enforceable and globally accepted financial reporting standards based upon clearly articulated principles. These standards should require high quality, transparent and comparable information in financial statements and other financial reporting to help investors, other participants in the world's capital markets and other users of financial information make economic decisions […]."[466]

The IASC Foundation's organizational set-up is shown in Figure 3.

464 International Accounting Standards Committee Foundation (2010). Constitution, p. 10.
465 Ibid., p. 11.
466 Ibid., p. 5.

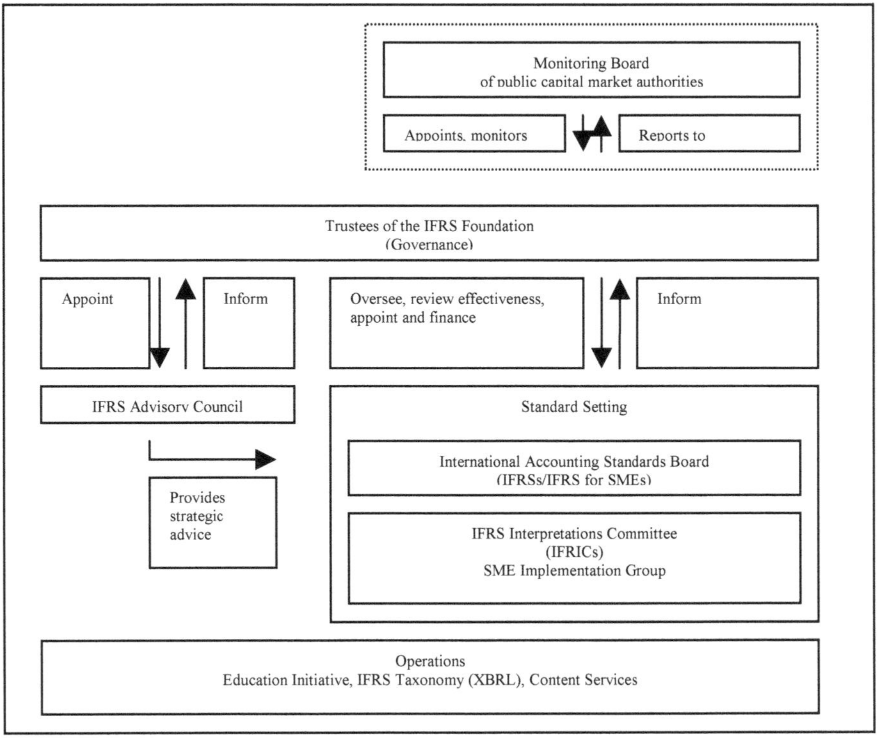

Figure 3: Structure of the IASC Foundation[467]

The IASCF is primarily governed by a Board of 22 Trustees. According to the IASC Foundation's constitution, the Trustees must:

> "[...] show a firm commitment to the IFRS Foundation and the IASB as a high quality global standard setter, to be financially knowledgeable, and to have an ability to meet the time commitment. Each Trustee shall have an understanding of, and be sensitive to, the challenges associated with the adoption and application of high quality global accounting standards developed for use in the world's capital markets and by other users."[468]

467 IFRS Foundation – International Accounting Standards Board (IASB): Who we are and what we do. Last revised: July 2010. Available at: http://www.ifrs.org/The+organisation/IASCF+and+IASB.htm.

468 International Accounting Standards Committee Foundation (2010). Constitution, p. 6.

The composition of the Trustees aims to ensure an overall geographical and professional balance. As required by the constitution, the geographical composition is as follows:[469]

Regional background of the IASC Foundation's Trustees (as required by the constitution)	
Asia/Oceania region	6 Trustees
Europe	6 Trustees
North America	6 Trustees
Africa	1 Trustee
South America	1 Trustee
Any area	2 Trustees, subject to maintaining overall geographical balance.

Table 7: Regional background of the IASC Foundation's Trustees

The intention of this geographical composition is to reflect, on the one hand, the world's most important capital markets while, on the other hand, ensuring a diversity of geographical backgrounds. Not only regional diversity but also differing professional backgrounds of the Trustees is considered important to guarantee a broad perspective on accounting matters. Table 8 provides an overview of the current Trustees, and their professional as well as regional backgrounds. In terms of past experience, the Trustees' professional backgrounds include auditors, preparers, users, academics, and officials serving the public interest.

Previously, the Trustees were not elected; instead they co-opted members when a vacancy arose. As a result of the constitutional review, the Monitoring Board (see also chapter 4.1.2 and chapter 4.2.1) is now responsible for the approval of all Trustee appointments and reappointments, which are normally for a term of three years, renewable once. In contrast, the termination of a Trustee appointment can only be executed by the Trustees themselves.[470]

The main duty of the IASCF's Trustees is to oversee and review the procedures of the foundation's operating bodies.[471] The Trustees are not responsible

469 Ibid., p. 6.

470 Ibid., p. 7.

471 The Trustees' work is supported by various committees, most notably the Finance Committee which approves the budget of the IASC Foundation and is responsible for fundraising, and the Audit Committee, which assists the Trustees in reviewing the financial reporting process, the system of internal control, the audit process, and the organization's mechanism for monitoring compliance with the laws and regulations in the jurisdictions in which it operates.

Name	Background / Constituency	Region
Gerrit Zalm, Chairman	Former Deputy Prime Minister and Finance Minister.	Europe: The Netherlands
Clemens Börsig	Chairman of the Supervisory Board, Deutsche Bank AG.	Europe: Germany
Oscar Fanjul	Vice Chairman, Omega Capita.	Europe: Spain
Alicja Kornasiewicz	CA IB Corporate Finance GmbH.	Europe: Poland
Sir Bryan Nicholson	Former Chairman of the Financial Reporting Council.	Europe: United Kingdom
Yves-Thibault de Silguy	Former member of the European Commission.	Europe: France
Luigi Spaventa	Commissione nazionale per le società e la borsa (CONSOB).	Europe: Italy
Antonio Vegezzi	Capital Italia Fund.	Europe: Switzerland
Samuel DiPiazza	Retired CEO, PricewaterhouseCoopers.	North America: United States
Scott Evans	TIAA-CREF Investment Management LLC.	North America: United States
Robert Glauber	Retired Chairman and Chief Executive Officer, NASD Regulation; former Under Secretary of the Treasury for Finance.	North America: United States
Harvey Goldschmid	Dwight Professor of Law, Columbia University; Former Commissioner of the US Securities and Exchange Commission.	North America: United States
David Sidwell	UBS, Board Member, Federal National Mortgage Association.	North America: United States
Paul Tellier	Former President and CEO, Bombardier and CN; former Clerk of the Privy Council and Secretary of the Cabinet; Director, Rio Tinto plc and Rio Tinto Ltd.; Director, McCain Foods and Chairman, Global Container Terminals (GCT).	North America: Canada
Marvin Cheung	Retired Chairman, KPMG Hong.	Asia/Oceania: People's Republic of China
Tsuguoki (Aki) Fujinuma	Former Chairman and President of the Japanese Institute of Certified Public Accountants (JICPA),	Asia/Oceania: Japan
Jeffrey Lucy AM	Chairman of the Australian Financial Reporting Council; former Chairman, Australian Securities and Investments Commission.	Asia/Oceania: Australia
T V Mohandas Pai	Director and member of the Board of Infosys Technologies Limited and Chairman, Infosys BPO Limited,	Asia/Oceania: India
Noriaki Shimazaki	Executive Vice President, Sumitomo Corporation.	Asia/Oceania: Japan
Liu Zhongli	President of the Chinese Institute of Certified Public Accountants; former Minister, Ministry of Finance.	Asia/Oceania: People's Republic of China
Pedro Malan	Former Chairman of the Board, Unibanco; former Finance Minister and President, Central Bank,	Other regions: Brazil
Jeff van Rooyen	CEO, Uranus Investment Holdings; member of the South African Financial Services Board.	Other regions: South Africa

Table 8: IASCF Trustee membership composition

for developing IFRS; that task rests solely with the IASB. However, the Trustees' Procedures Committee reviews the IASB's compliance with its due process procedures. In exercising their governance responsibilities, the Trustees can also change or amend the IASB's due process or recommend, for example, improvements to the IASB's liaison activities.

Moreover, the IASC Foundation Trustees appoint the members of the IASB, the IFRIC and the SAC.[472] Conversely, the Trustees may also "[...] terminate the appointment of a member of the IASB, the Interpretations Committee or the Advisory Council, on grounds of poor performance, misbehavior, incapacity or other failure to comply with contractual requirements [...]."[473] In addition, the Trustees' governance activities include: (1) an annual review of the strategy of the foundation and the IASB as well as its effectiveness;[474] (2) the responsibility for establishing and maintaining suitable financing arrangements[475]; (3) the publication of an annual report on the foundation's activities, including audited financial statements and priorities for the coming year.[476]

The Trustees of the IASC Foundation usually meet at least twice each year. During these meetings, the Trustees make their formal decisions by voting; generally by simple majority vote on matters other than termination of the appointment of a Trustee, amendments to the constitution, or minor variations made in the interest of feasibility of operations, in which cases a 75 per cent majority is required. All meetings of the Trustees, apart from administrative sessions, are held in public and webcast,[477] which also allows interested parties to access the recordings of past meetings in the 'Trustees meetings audio playback' section on the IASB webpage.

---

472 International Accounting Standards Committee Foundation (2010). Constitution, p. 8. In addition, the Trustees are in charge of developing adequate procedures for appointments to ensure that the IASB is seen to be, and is in fact independent.

473 Ibid., p. 9.

474 Ibid., p. 9. In November 2006, the Trustees approved a framework to guide and evaluate the effectiveness of their oversight function. As a result, the Trustees' effectiveness in exercising their functions is assessed by the Trustees' Due Process Oversight Committee (DPOC) which sets yearly objectives for the Trustees and makes regular progress reports. This report can be found in the annual report of the IASCF.

475 Ibid., p. 8.

476 Ibid., p. 8.

477 Ibid., p. 8.

4.2.3 International Accounting Standards Board

The IASB is the main operating body of the Foundation. It possesses full responsibility for preparing and issuing accounting standards and their non-binding precursors: the Exposure Drafts (ED).[478] The procedures for developing new or revised accounting standards are illustrated in chapter 4.2.6.

Presently, the Board consists of fourteen individuals, of which twelve are full-time and up to three part-time. Following a decision at the January 2009 Trustees' meeting; the IASB will be expanded to 16 members by July 2012. According to the constitution, the appointment as an IASB member is primarily based on professional competence and practical experience.[479] In compliance with the aforementioned requirements, the IASB is supposed to comprise "[...] a group of people representing, [...], the best available combination of technical expertise and diversity of international business and market experience in order to contribute to the development of high quality, global financial reporting standards."[480] The composition of the current Board members as well as their professional backgrounds is depicted in Table 9.

Member	Country	Background / Constituency
Sir David Tweedie	United Kingdom	Former Chairman, UK Accounting Standards Board.
Stephen Cooper	United Kingdom	Director and Head of Valuation and Accounting Research, UBS.
Philippe Danjou	France	Former Director of the accounting division, French securities regulator.
Jan Engström	Sweden	Former CFO Volvo Group and Chief Executive Officer, Volvo Bus Corporation.
Patrick Finnegan	North America	Former Director, Financial Reporting Policy Group, CFA Institute for Financial Market Integrity.
Robert P. Garnett	South Africa	Former Executive VP of Finance, Anglo American Plc.
Gilbert Gélard	France	Former Partner, KPMG France and member, French Accounting Standards Board.

478 The detailed responsibilities are set out in the IASCF Constitution with further reference to the Due Process Handbook.

479 International Accounting Standards Committee Foundation (2010). Constitution, p. 12. The criteria for qualifying as an IASB member are set out in the Annex to the IASCF Constitution (see also appendix: Table 21).

480 Ibid., p. 11.

Member	Country	Background / Constituency
Amaro Luiz de Olivera Gomes	Brazil	Former Head of Financial System Regulation Department, Central Bank of Brazil.
Prabhakar Kalavacherla	India/North America	Former Audit Partner, KPMG.
James J. Leisenring	North America	Former Vice-Chairman, US Financial Accounting Standards Board (FASB).
Patricia McConnell	North America	Former Senior Managing Director, Equity Research, Accounting and Tax Policy Analyst, Bear Stearns & Co.
Warren J. McGregor	Australia	Former CEO, Australian Accounting Research Foundation.
John T. Smith	North America	Former Partner, Deloitte & Touche, United States.
Tatsumi Yamada	Japan	Former Partner, PricewaterhouseCoopers.
Wei-Guo Zhang	China	Former Chief Accountant and Director General, Department of International Affairs at the China Securities Regulatory Commission.

Table 9: IASB membership composition

Once appointed, full-time members of the IASB have to cut all employment relationships and are enjoined from holding any position that could give rise to economic incentives. This requirement strives to ensure the independent judgment of Board members. Secondments and any rights to return to an employer are therefore not permitted.[481] Moreover, each full-time and part-time member of the IASB has to agree contractually to act in the public interest.[482] As a result of the constitutional review, the terms of office for IASB members have been changed, in particular the second term of office was shortened from five to three years.[483] In a manner consistent with the criteria for appointing IASB members (see appendix: Table 21) and in order to ensure a broad international basis, the following regional spread is required by July 1, 2012:

481 Part-time members of the IASB are not expected to sever all other employment arrangements. Ibid., p. 13.

482 Ibid., p. 12.

483 The Chair and the Vice-Chair of the Board are excluded from this provision; they "[...] may serve a second term of five years, but may not exceed ten years in total length of service as a member of the IASB." Ibid., p. 31.

Regional background of the IASB's members	
Asia/Oceania region	4 members
Europe	4 members
North America	4 members
Africa	1 member
South America	1 member
Any area	2 members, subject to maintaining overall geographical balance.

Table 10: Regional background of the IASB members

Nowadays, the regional composition of the IASB is in line with the one suggested and approved for the Trustees (second part of the constitutional review: question five). The first part of the constitutional review emphasized a geographical formulation for the Board members, in particular an explicit recognition of one member from Africa and South America.

To strengthen its outreach activities as well as to broaden participatory input, the IASB also established, in consultation with the Trustees, official liaison activities with national standard setters and other official bodies with an interest in financial reporting and the convergence of national accounting standards with IFRS.[484] The IASB's 'Statement of Best Practice' points out that "[...] forms of communicating views other than comment letters are increasingly important in gathering views, including forums on specific issues. Other accounting standard setters should use these forums as a mechanism for encouraging their constituents to participate in the IASB's standard-setting process. [In addition], other accounting standard setters can assist the IASB in identifying constituents who can be involved in round-table discussions and other forums and the issues of particular relevance to constituents. [Finally], other organizations, such as representative bodies with an interest in financial reporting, may also contribute to this process."[485]

IASB meetings are held at least once a month. These meetings are notified in a 'meetings diary' on the foundation's website, typically five days prior to the

484 Ibid., p. 12. See also International Accounting Standards Committee Foundation (2008). *Due Process Handbook for the International Accounting Standards Board (IASB)*, pp. 21-22. Typically, liaison activities take place along the whole due process. At its inauguration, the IASB set up official liaison relationships with standard setters in Australia and New Zealand, Canada, France, Germany, Japan, the United Kingdom and the United States.

485 International Accounting Standard Board (2006). Statement of Best Practice: Working Relationships between the IASB and other Accounting Standard-Setters. London: IASB. 1-16, p. 5.

date of the IASB. Similar to the Trustee conventions, all IASB meetings are held in public and webcast.[486] Interested parties can use the meetings diary to register as an observer or to view the agenda and observer notes[487] for a meeting.[488] In its meetings, the IASB discusses its technical work based on research by its staff; responses to the IASB's liaison activities; and in particular comment letters on consultative documents or other input provided by its advisory bodies.

4.2.4 IFRS Interpretations Committee

The IASB's interpretative body, the former IASC's Standing Interpretations Committee (SIC), was reconstituted in December 2001 as the International Financial Reporting Interpretations Committee (IFRIC). Subsequent to the last constitutional review, the committee was once more renamed, becoming the IFRS Interpretations Committee.[489] The IFRIC reviews, within the context of current IFRS and the IASB's conceptual framework, accounting issues that are likely to receive divergent or unacceptable treatment in the absence of explicit authoritative guidance. In developing interpretations, the IFRIC works closely with similar national committees; its final interpretations are published as 'authoritative literature'.

The IFRS Interpretations Committee comprises 14 voting members appointed by the Trustees of the IASC Foundation.[490] Predominantly appointed for their capability to discuss and decide on technical accounting issues, members of the IFRIC are drawn from a variety of countries and professional backgrounds.[491] In order to avoid divergent opinions regarding accounting matters, which mean to

---

486 International Accounting Standards Committee Foundation (2010). Constitution, p. 13. See also International Accounting Standards Committee Foundation (2008). *Review of the Constitution: Public Accountability and the Public Accountability and the Composition of the IASB – Proposals for Change*, p. 18.

487 Observer notes include background information on the issues considered by the IASB; relevant illustrations and examples given to the IASB as well as staff recommendations. International Accounting Standards Committee Foundation (2008). *Due Process Handbook for the International Accounting Standards Board (IASB)*, p. 19.

488 Past meetings are archived on the website. Soon after the meeting, the staff summarize the IASB's decisions, and a decision summary – IASB *Update* – is published. This publication, together with a webcast recording of the IASB meeting, is available from the website. Ibid., p. 19.

489 IFRIC and IFRS Interpretations Committee are used interchangeably in this study.

490 International Accounting Standards Committee Foundation (2010). Constitution, p. 15.

491 In December 2007, constitutional changes were announced, enlarging the IFRIC from 12-14 members and amending the quorum and voting requirements.

be consistent with accounting standards and their interpretations, the Interpretations Committee is chaired by a member of the IASB or a senior member of the IASB staff.[492] In addition, the Trustees, as they deem necessary, can appoint, as non-voting observers, representatives of regulatory organizations who are given the right to attend and speak at meetings.[493] Table 11 depicts the current composition of IFRIC members, and their professional as well as regional backgrounds.

Member	Professional background / Constituency	Region
Robert Garnett	Chairman, IFRS Interpretations Committee.	South Africa
Joanna Perry	Company Director and current Chair Financial Reporting Standards Board.	New Zealand
Luca Cencioni	Senior Accounting Manager Eni S.p.A.	Italy
Guido Fladt	Partner PricewaterhouseCoopers.	Germany
Jean Paré	Vice President Financial Reporting at Bombardier Inc.	Canada
Bernd Hacker	Professor for accounting.	Germany
Sara York Kenny	Former Principal Accounting Policy Advisor International Finance Corporation, World Bank Group	United States
Jean-Louis Lebrun	Partner Mazars & Guerard	France
Feilong Li	Controller, China National Offshore Oil Corporation	China
Takatsugu Ochi	General Manager Planning and Administration Department Sumitomo Corporation	Japan
Ruth Picker	Partner, Global IFRS – Ernst & Young	Australia
Laurence Rivat	Partner Deloitte & Associés	France
Margaret Smyth	Vice President, Controller United Technologies Corp	United States
Scott Taub	Managing Director of Financial Reporting Advisors, LLC.	United States
Andrew Vials	Partner KPMG LLP	United Kingdom

Table 11: IFRIC membership composition

In general, the IFRIC meets about every six weeks; its meetings are open to the public, "[…] but certain discussions (normally only about selection, appointment and other personnel issues) may be held in private at the Interpretations Com-

492 International Accounting Standards Committee Foundation (2010). Constitution, p. 15.
493 Ibid., p. 15.

mittee's discretion."[494] Nevertheless, all technical decisions are taken at sessions that are open to the public.

In January 2007, the Trustees approved a handbook laying out the procedures for the work of the IFRIC which are similar to those that are relevant for the IASB. The IFRS Interpretations Committee due process comprises seven stages: (1) identification of issues, (2) setting the agenda, (3) IFRS Interpretations Committee meetings and voting, (4) development of a draft interpretation, (5) the IASB's role in the issue of an Interpretation, (6) comment period and deliberation, and (7) the IASB's role in an Interpretation.

Each member of the IFRS Interpretations Committee has one vote, which should be based on their own independent, which means free from undue influence, views. The approval of a draft or a final interpretation requires that "[...] not more than four voting members vote against the draft or final interpretation."[495] Once the IFRS Interpretations Committee has reached a consensus on an interpretation, it is forwarded to the IASB for ratification (in a public meeting) before being published; an interpretation to be issued requires approval by at least nine IASB members. Approved interpretations are issued by the IASB.[496] However, if an interpretation is not endorsed, the IASB provides an analysis of the objections of those who voted against the interpretation. On the basis of this analysis, the IASB will decide whether the matter should be referred back to the IFRIC or added to the IASB's own agenda.

4.2.5 IFRS Advisory Council

The IFRS Advisory Council, formerly called the Standards Advisory Council (SAC), provides a discussion forum for organizations and individuals to participate in the development of corporate financial reporting.[497] According to the IASCF Constitution, the objectives of the Advisory Council are:[498]

(1) To give advice to the IASB on agenda decisions and priorities.
(2) To inform the IASB of the views of the organizations and individuals on the Advisory Council on major standard-setting projects.

494 Ibid., p. 15.
495 Ibid., p. 16.
496 Ibid., p. 16.
497 Standards Advisory Council (2005). *Terms of reference and operating procedures*, p. 1. This Charter was proposed by the SAC on July 7, 2004 and approved by the Trustees in March 2005. SAC and IFRS Advisory Council are used interchangeably in this study.
498 International Accounting Standards Committee Foundation (2010). Constitution, p. 17. See also Standards Advisory Council (2005). *Terms of reference and operating procedures*, p. 1.

(3) To advise on projects with reference to practical application and implementation issues that require evaluation by the IFRS Interpretations Committee.

In order to ensure the appropriateness of comments submitted to the IASB on specialized topics, the chairman of the IFRS Advisory Council may also establish subcommittees that, in turn, provide expert analysis. These subcommittees then report to the IFRS Advisory Council, which in turn presents its views to the IASB.[499] The two most prominent subcommittees are the Analyst Representative Group (ARG) and the Global Preparers Forum (GPF).[500]

The Trustees appoint members of the Advisory Council,[501] similarly to the composition of the IASB, so as to ensure that membership reflects a broad geographical spread and a range of functional backgrounds. Members are drawn from user groups, preparers, financial analysts, academics, auditors, regulators and professional accounting bodies. In addition, certain international organizations may be granted permanent seats on the SAC by the Trustees.[502]

Members of the Advisory Council are appointed for renewable terms of three years and required to serve as individuals, not as representatives of their respective employer or organization.[503] Although members of the Council are not remunerated for their time and effort, they are expected to express their individual views unless it is expressly stated that they are the opinions of the organizations they represent.[504] The IFRS Advisory Council has about 50 members, as depicted in Table 12.

---

499 Standards Advisory Council (2005). *Terms of reference and operating procedures*, p. 3.

500 The ARG consists of members with practical experience in analyzing financial information and diverse industry and geographical backgrounds. The ARG meets with IASB representatives three times a year. These meetings are held in public and usually take place in London. The GPF is an independent body that has been sponsored by a number of international or national preparer organizations to provide the IASB with input from the preparer community.

501 Likewise, the Chairman of the SAC is appointed by the Trustees from nominations submitted by the SAC. The term of office of the Chairman is three years renewable for up to three years, subject to a maximum of six years. Standards Advisory Council (2005). *Terms of reference and operating procedures*, p. 2.

502 Official observer status may also be granted to other bodies and organizations belonging to the global financial community. Ibid., p. 1.

503 International Accounting Standards Committee Foundation (2010). Constitution, p. 17. A maximum period of service of six years is permitted. Nevertheless, members of the SAC or the organizations they represent meet their own travel and accommodation costs.

504 Standards Advisory Council (2005). *Terms of reference and operating procedures*, p. 2.

Organization	Individual	Background
Brazilian Association of Listed Companies	Geraldo Toffanello	Accounting Director, GERDAU Group.
Accounting Standards Board	Ian Mackintosh	Chairman.
Associated Chambers of Commerce of India/ The Stock Exchange, Mumbai (BSE)	Narendra Sarda	Chairman, Deloitte Haskins & Sells.
Association of Banks in Singapore	Surya Subramanian	Director of the Financial Reporting Surveillance Division, Accounting and Corporate Regulatory Authority (ACRA).
Association of British Insurers/Investment Management Association (IMA)	Liz Murrall	Director of Corporate Governance and Reporting, IMA.
Basel Committee on Banking Supervision	Sylvie Matherat	Director, Financial Stability Directorate, Banque de France.
BDO International	Andrew Buchanan	IFRS Technical Partner.
CFA Institute	Dane Mott	Executive Director, JP Morgan Securities Inc.
Conseil National de la Comptabilité	Jean-François Lepetit	Chairman
Committee of European Securities Regulators	Richard Thorpe	Head of Capital Adequacy Policy Department and Accounting and Auditing Sector, UK Financial Services Authority.
Corporate Reporting Users' Forum (International)	Norbert Barth	Head of European Chemical Sector Research, WestLB.
Council of Institutional Investors (USA)	Gail Hanson	Deputy Executive Director, State of Wisconsin Investment Board.
Deloitte	Joel Osnoss	Partner-in-Charge of Global IFRS and Offerings Services.
DRSC e.V.	Liesel Knorr	President.
Ernst & Young	Leo van der Tas	Global Technical Director, IFRS.
European Central Bank	Mauro Grande	Director, Financial Stability and Supervision.
European Financial Reporting Advisory Group (EFRAG)	Françoise Flores	Chairman of EFRAG.
European Insurance and Reinsurance Federation (CEA)	Jacques Le Douit	Accounting Research and Development Director, AXA.
European Issuers/ European Round Table of Industrialists	Christoph Hütten	Chief Accounting Officer, SAP AG.

Organization	Individual	Background
Fédération Internationale des Experts-Comptables Francophones	Benoît Atangana Onana	Senior Partner and General Manager, African Consulting Enterprise.
Financial Executives International (Canada)	Karyn Brooks	SVP and Controller, Bell Canada Enterprises.
Financial Executives International (US)	Jamie Miller	Vice President and Controller General Electric Company.
Grant Thornton	April Mackenzie	Global Head of Public Policy.
Group of 100 (Australia)	Judith Downes	Chief Financial Officer, Alumina Limited.
Group of European national standard setters (France, Germany, Italy, and UK)	Piero di Salvo, Italy	Rotating annually among the standard setters of France, Germany, Italy, UK.
Group of North American Insurance Enterprises	Jerry de St. Paer	Executive Chairman GNAIE - Group of North American Insurance Enterprises.
Hong Kong Institute of Certified Public Accountants	P M Kam	Chief Executive Officer, Financial Reporting Council.
Institute of International Finance	Will Widdowson	Head of Group Accounting Policy and Group SOX Officer, UBS AG.
International Association for Accounting, Education & Research	Holly Ashbaugh Skaife	Associate Professor of Accounting, Wisconsin School of Business.
International Actuarial Association	Francis Ruygt	Deputy Chief Insurance Risk Officer and Group Actuary, ING Group.
International Association of Insurance Supervisors	Henning Goebel	Chief Accountant, Federal Financial Supervisory Authority.
International Corporate Governance Network	Gerben Everts	Compliance Officer, APG Investments.
International Federation of Accountants	Jim Sylph	Executive Director, Professional Standards.
International Monetary Fund	Kenneth Sullivan	Senior Financial Sector Expert.
International Organization of Securities Commissions (IOSCO)	One member each from a developed and emerging economy: Developed economy: Rotating between Sophie Baranger, Chief Accountant, AMF, France; and Christoph Ernst, Head of Accounting and Auditing Law Division, Federal Ministry of Justice, Germany Emerging economy: To be confirmed	

Organization	Individual	Background
Investment Company Institute (USA)	Donald J. Boteler	Vice President, Operations
Investors' Technical Advisory Committee (USA)	Neri Bukspan	Chief Quality Officer and Chief Accountant, Standard & Poor's.
Korea Accounting Standards Board	Chanhong Kim	Vice Chairman.
KPMG	Mark Vaessen	Head of IFRS, KPMG Europe LLP.
Ministry of Finance, People's Republic of China, China Accounting Standards Committee	Liu Yuting	Director-General of Accounting Regulatory Department of MOF, member of CASC.
Nippon Keidanren (Japan)	Shozo Yoneya	Corporate auditor, Itochu Corporation.
PricewaterhouseCoopers	John Hitchins	Global Chief Accountant.
Securities Analysts Association of Japan	Sei-Ichi Kaneko	Executive Vice President and Member of the Board.
South Africa Accounting Practices Board	Moses Kgosana	Chairman.
Securities and Exchange Commission of Brazil	Alexandro Broedel	
South Asian Federation of Accountants (SAFA)	Reyaz Mihular	Chairman, Accounting and Auditing Standards Committee.
World Bank	Charles McDonough	Vice President and Controller
Observer organizations: European Commission / Japan Financial Services Agency / US Securities and Exchange Commission		

Table 12: IFRS Advisory Council membership composition

The Advisory Council normally meets about three times a year. Generally, these meetings are held in public, webcast and typically take place in London. An Agenda Committee is responsible for preparing the agenda in consultation with the IASB secretariat. At the meeting, members are given the opportunity to discuss and comment on the questions raised by the IASB. Depending upon the issue, the chairman may also suggest a formal poll to demonstrate to the IASB the extent of support within the SAC for a particular discussion item. If the IASB nevertheless takes a different position on a particular issue, a feedback statement is normally given at the subsequent meetings of the SAC on the reasons for the IASB's decision.[505]

4.2.6 IASB working procedure: Due process

In March 2006, the IASCF's Trustees approved the IASB's Due Process Handbook,[506] which lays out the procedures by which IFRS are to be developed. The general requirements for the procedures to be followed are: (1) transparency and accessibility; (2) extensive consultation and responsiveness; and (3) accountability. Transparency and accessibility are indispensable requirements for the IASB once it thinks about adding topics to its agenda. Potential agenda items are discussed in open IASB meetings; observer notes, IASB's positions, letters of comment received as well as feedback statements are posted on the IASB's website.[507] Extensive consultation and responsiveness means that the IASB solicits, during its due process, views and suggestions through consultations with a wide range of interested parties. The formal due process involves inviting public comment on discussion papers and exposure drafts. If necessary, the IASB also conducts field visits,[508] arranges public hearings[509] or carries out impact analyses.[510] Additionally, IASB members appear at public events to exchange views with constituents. In general, the IASB has established the following consultation methods:

---

505 Ibid., p. 3.

506 Approved by the Trustees in March 2006, and amended in October 2008. It reflects the public consultation conducted by the IASB in 2004 and 2005 and enhancements made to the due process since then.

507 International Accounting Standards Committee Foundation (2008). *Due Process Handbook for the International Accounting Standards Board (IASB)*, pp. 6-7.

508 Ibid., pp. 24-25.

509 Ibid., p 25.

510 Ibid., pp. 25-26.

IASB consultation methods		
Formal	**Informal**	**Feedback**
Public exposure of proposals	One-to-one and small group meetings	Publication and wide-spread distribution of project summary and feedback statement
Round-table discussions	Live webcasts, including interactive Q&A sessions	Post-implementation review planned for 2011
Consultation with formal advisory bodies, including the IFRS Advisory Council and the Financial Crisis Advisory Group	Downloadable podcasts and recorded presentations	
Formation of expert panels to seek high quality practitioner input	Project-specific email alerts	
	Presentations at conferences around the world	

Table 13: IASB consultation methods[511]

After its consultation period the IASB evaluates and, "[...] where the IASB considers it appropriate, adopts suggestions received during the consultations."[512] Accountability of the IASB's due process is mainly assured by "[...] adopting the 'comply or explain' approach, which means that the IASB explains its reasons if it decides to omit any non-mandatory step of its consultative process as described in the constitution."[513]

In general, the IASB's standard-setting process comprises six stages:

At Stage one (setting the agenda) the IASB discusses and decides in public meetings which items to add to the agenda based on the perceived needs of financial statement users. The IASB evaluates whether there is a "[...] demand for

511 International Accounting Standards Committee Foundation (2009). Annual Report, p. 32.

512 International Accounting Standards Committee Foundation (2008). *Due Process Handbook for the International Accounting Standards Board (IASB)*, p. 7.

513 Ibid., p. 7. The following due process steps are mandatory: (1) developing and pursuing the IASB's technical agenda; (2) preparing and issuing IFRSs and publishing exposure drafts, each of which is to include any dissenting opinions; (3) establishing procedures for reviewing comments made within a reasonable period on documents published for comment; (4) consulting the SAC on major projects, agenda decisions and work priorities; (5) publishing bases for conclusions with IFRSs and exposure drafts (p. 27).

better quality information that is of value to all users of financial statements."[514] Additionally, agenda items are chosen in terms of relevance, and in terms of other considerations, like comments from the SAC or IFRIC.[515] The IASB's approval to add agenda items, as well as its decisions on their priority, is by a simple majority vote at an IASB meeting that is held in public.[516] Furthermore, the IASB is required to explain the factors considered in adding a topic to its agenda.

At Stage two (project planning) the IASB firstly decides whether to conduct a project alone or jointly with another standard setter. Subsequently, the project team, which may also include members of staff from other accounting standard setters, proposes the due process and presents the preliminary views of constituents. Depending on the nature of the issues and the level of interest among constituents, the IASB may also establish an additional working group at this stage: working groups provide the IASB with specialized input.[517] The Trustees' Due Process Oversight Committee reviews the proposed composition of each group to ensure that there is a satisfactory balance of perspectives. The resulting meetings of the working groups are announced in advance, open to the public, and chaired by an IASB member. Comments from group members are included in the materials for discussion in IASB meetings.

At Stage three (development and publication of a discussion paper) the IASB publishes a discussion paper as its first publication on any major new topic to explain the issue and solicit preliminary comment from constituents.[518] The publication of a discussion paper is not mandatory; however, if the IASB decides to omit this step, it will state its reasons. A discussion paper typically includes a comprehensive overview of the issue, possible approaches to dealing with the issue, preliminary views of the authors, and an invitation to comment.[519] Issues related to the discussion paper are discussed in IASB meetings (public sessions), and the publication of such a paper requires a simple majority vote by the IASB following a period of 120 days for comment.[520] Following the comment period,

514 Ibid., p. 8. Users include present and potential investors, employees, lenders, suppliers and other trade creditors, customers, governments and their agencies and the public. However, "[a]s investors are providers of risk capital to the entity, the provision of financial statements that meet their needs will also meet most of the needs of other users. The IASB therefore evaluates the merits of adding a potential item to its agenda mainly by reference to the needs of investors." (p. 8).

515 Ibid., p. 8.

516 Ibid., p. 9.

517 Ibid., p. 9.

518 Ibid., p. 10.

519 Ibid., p. 10.

520 Ibid., p. 10.

the project team evaluates the comment letters for further consideration. Comment letters are made public on the IASB's website.[521]

At Stage four (development and publication of an exposure draft)[522], an exposure draft (ED) sets out a specific proposal in the form of a proposed standard and an invitation to comment on the draft. The development of an ED begins with the IASB considering issues on the basis of staff research, as well as comments received on any discussion paper, and suggestions made by the SAC, working groups and other (national) accounting standard setters.[523] After the IASB has balloted the draft (nine votes in favor)[524], the ED is issued for public comment. The draft is accompanied by a basis for conclusions on the proposals and any alternative views of dissenting IASB members.[525] In general, the period for comment is 120 days. According to the revised constitution, however, the IASB "shall [...] in exceptional circumstances, and only after formally requesting and receiving prior approval from 75 per cent of the Trustees, reduce, but not dispense with, the period for public comment on an exposure draft below that described as the minimum in the Due Process Handbook."[526] Upon conclusion of the comment period, a project team analyzes the comments for further deliberation, and a summary of the comments is posted on the website as a part of IASB meeting observer notes.[527]

At Stage five (development and publication of an IFRS), the development of an IFRS is completed during IASB meetings, when the IASB considers the comments received on the ED. As it moves towards finalizing a new or revised standard, the IASB prepares a project summary and feedback statement. These documents "[...] give direct feedback to those who submitted comments on the exposure draft; identify the most significant matters raised in the comment process and explain how the IASB responded to those matters."[528] After resolving issues arising from the exposure draft, the IASB considers whether there is need to disclose its revised proposal for public comment.[529] Simultaneously, the IASB prepares an analysis of the likely effects, for example, implementation or com-

521 Ibid., p. 11.

522 Ibid., p. 11. The publication of an exposure draft is a mandatory due process step, whether or not the IASB has published a discussion paper.

523 Ibid., p. 11.

524 See Table 14: IASB balloting and drafting guidelines.

525 International Accounting Standards Committee Foundation (2008). *Due Process Handbook for the International Accounting Standards Board (IASB)*, p. 11.

526 International Accounting Standards Committee Foundation (2010). Constitution, p. 14.

527 International Accounting Standards Committee Foundation (2008). *Due Process Handbook for the International Accounting Standards Board (IASB)*, pp. 11-12.

528 Ibid., p. 12.

529 Ibid., p. 12.

pliance costs of the forthcoming standard. Finally, after the due process is completed and the IASB members have balloted in favor, the IFRS is issued. The voting requirements, as set out in the Due Process Handbook, are presented in Table 14. Each member of the IASB has one vote; however, in the case of a tied vote on a decision that is to be made by a simple majority of the IASB members, the Chair has an additional casting vote. The publication of an ED, an IFRS or an interpretation by the Interpretations Committee requires the approval of nine members of the IASB if there are fewer than sixteen members, or by ten members if there are sixteen members.

Voting requirements for IASB publication	
Simple majority of members in favor	**Nine votes in favor**
Agenda and topic decision	Exposure drafts (including revised proposals, and proposed amendments of IFRSs and the conceptual framework)
Discussion paper	IFRSs
Other discussion documents (such as those prepared by other standard setters)	Interpretations of IFRSs
Administrative decisions	

Table 14: IASB balloting and drafting guidelines[530]

At Stage six (procedures after an IFRS is issued), after the promulgation of an IFRS, the staff and the IASB members hold regular meetings with interested parties to review practical implementation issues. Following the constitutional review in 2005, the Trustees approved a proposal to require post-implementation reviews, which means that the IASB revises new IFRS, major amendments to existing standards, or major interpretations after two full years of implementation.[531]

530 Ibid., p. 20.

531 Ibid., p. 13. A review is also deemed necessary if general changes to the financial reporting environment occur, or comments from the SAC, the IFRIC, or other (national) standard setters indicate a declining quality of the IFRS. International Accounting Standards Committee Foundation (2008). *Due Process Handbook for the International Accounting Standards Board (IASB)*, p. 14.

4.3 Public rule making

4.3.1 European Financial Reporting Advisory Group

While discharging authority to the IASB, the European Union has recognized the risk of being faced with policy outcomes that could differ from the favored policy choice. To ensure some political oversight, the IAS Regulation established a screening mechanism. The measures necessary for the implementation of the IAS Regulation "[...] should be adopted in accordance with Council Decision 1999/468/EC of June 28, 1999 laying down the procedures for the exercise of implementing powers conferred on the Commission (1) and with due regard to the declaration made by the Commission in the European Parliament on February 5, 2002 concerning the implementation of financial services legislation."[532] Accordingly, each individual standard has to be endorsed by the European Commission in accordance with a specific committee procedure in order to become European law.

In general, the European Council (representing leaders of member states who make broad policy decisions) delegates the responsibility to enact legislative measures to the European Commission (comprising 27 members, appointed by member state governments), which is responsible for developing proposals for new laws and policies. To oversee and control the Commission's delegated implementation powers, the Council has established oversight committees.[533] The European Commission adopts more than 2,500 legal acts per year; "[...] assisted and controlled by 'comitology' committees composed of civil servants from the administrations of the Member States."[534] In general, four distinct comitology procedures exist: advisory procedure, management procedure, regulatory procedure and regulatory procedure with scrutiny which, to varying degrees, constrain

532 The Council decision of July 17, 2006 amended the decision 1999/468/EC laying down the procedures for the exercise of implementing powers conferred on the Commission (2006/512/EC), which resulted in an updated IAS Regulation. See regulation (EC) No 297/2008 of the European Parliament and of the Council of March 11, 2008, amending Regulation (EC) No 1606/2002 on the application of international accounting standards, as regards the implementing powers conferred on the Commission.

533 Ballmann, Alexander, Epstein, David and O'Halloran, Sharyn (2002). *Delegation, Comitology, and the Separation of Powers in the European Union.* International Organization. (56):3. 551-574, p. 553.

534 Neuhold, Christine (2008). *Taming the 'Trojan Horse' of Comitology? Accountability Issues of Comitology and the Role of the European Parliament.* European Integration Online Papers. (12):1. 1-18, p. 2.

the Commission's discretion.[535] Council decision 2006/512/EC[536] introduced the regulatory procedure with scrutiny, which enlarges the European Parliament's right considerably.[537]

The EU established a two-tier endorsement mechanism for adopting accounting standards. While the European Commission possesses the ultimate decision-making authority in adopting pronouncements, it initially receives input from two endorsement bodies: the European Financial Reporting Advisory Group (EFRAG)[538], and the Accounting Regulatory Committee (ARC).[539]

EFRAG, founded in 2001, is a private sector body which consists of organizations representing the European accounting profession, preparers, users and stock exchanges. A Supervisory Board, comprising 17 members, undertakes the governance tasks of EFRAG.[540] The European Commission and CESR act as official observers at the Supervisory Board meetings. In December, 2008, EFRAG issued the report: 'Strengthening the European Contribution to the International Standard-setting Process'. The resulting enhanced structure of EFRAG described in the report aims to effectively represent all European stakeholders in issues related to IFRS. Most importantly, the enhanced structure includes a substantial increase in the resources of the EFRAG Secretariat, and closer collaboration with the European national standard setters which, in turn, committed to contribute considerable resources and expertise to proactive projects.

---

535 Brandsma, Gijs Jan and Blom-Hansen, Jens (2010). *The EU comitology system: What role for the Commission?* Public Administration. (88):2. 496-512, p. 498 and p. 502. Regulatory procedures are the most constraining, whereas advisory procedures are the least.

536 Council of the European Communities (2006). *Council decision of July 17, 2006 amending Decision 1999/468/EC laying down the procedures for the exercise of implementing powers conferred on the Commission.*

537 Schusterschitz, Gregor and Kotz, Sabine (2007). *The Comitology Reform of 2006 Increasing the Powers of the European Parliament Without Changing the Treaties.* European Constitutional Law Review (EuConst). (3):01. 68-90, p. 68.

538 Article 3 of the IAS Regulation refers to the European Commission seeking advice from a technical committee prior to endorsing standards. EFRAG fulfils the role of that technical committee. Richardson and Eberlein ascribe the establishment of EFRAG to "[…] the restructuring of the IASC into the IASB [which subsequently] reduced the input of member states to the formal due process mechanisms and the role of initial members of IASB as liaisons to the largest national standard setters." Richardson, Alan and Eberlein, Burkard (2011). *Legitimating Transnational Standard-Setting: The Case of the International Accounting Standards Board.* Journal of Business Ethics. (98):2. 217-245, p. 227.

539 In addition to obtaining advice from EFRAG, the European Commission seeks advice from member states through the ARC, whereby EFRAG participates as an official observer.

540 Members of the Supervisory Board are selected to ensure a balance of professional backgrounds, and required to commit themselves formally to acting in the European public interest, independent of their professional or sector affiliation.

EFRAG's task is to assist the European Commission in the endorsement of IFRS, as issued by the IASB, by providing advice on the technical quality of IFRS. In March 2006, EFRAG's role was formalized in a working agreement with the European Commission, which states that "EFRAG will provide advice to the Commission on all issues relating to the application of IFRS in the EU."[541] In essence, however, EFRAG's role is a dual one: firstly, it delivers upstream technical input to influence the IASB, to create discussions and a better understanding of financial reporting issues in Europe, and, secondly, it gives endorsement advice to the European Commission. In order to do so, EFRAG conducts its own due process, however, primarily within its own consultative network. This includes the EFRAG sponsoring organizations and the national standard setters of Europe.

EFRAG's second objective is to provide endorsement advice to the European Commission within two months after an IFRS or an IFRIC is pronounced. The discussions that precede the final endorsement advice are held primarily within its own consultative network. The proposal that is finally sent to the European Commission indicates the nature of advice – positive or negative – and outlines the main reasons for its decision. In the case of negative advice, EFRAG outlines the potential (negative) consequences if companies of the EU were to be prohibited from complying.

The technical work is carried out by the Technical Expert Group (TEG). Members of the TEG are supposed to act in the European interest, rather than representing sectional or national interests. Accordingly, the 12 voting members of TEG are selected from throughout Europe and come from a variety of backgrounds. The European Commission and CESR are represented as observers at TEG meetings. The Chair of TEG is a full-time member, whereas the other voting members are supposed to devote 30 to 50% of their time to EFRAG's activities. All the members of the TEG, as well as the working groups, provide their time without charge to EFRAG. The members of TEG are appointed by the Supervisory Board, with the assistance of a nominating committee, following an open call for candidates. The Supervisory Board looks primarily to the qualifications of the TEG candidates in terms of knowledge and experience, and endeavors to ensure a broad geographical balance, together with experience from preparers, the accounting profession, users and academics.

In July 2006, the European Commission established a Standards Advice Review Group (SARG) comprised of experts and high-level representatives from

541 http://www.efrag.org/images/Efrag/EFRAG-EC%20Working%20Arrangement.pdf.

national standard setters.[542] The task of the group is to advise the European Commission on the endorsement process of IFRS and IFRIC to ensure that EFRAG's opinions are well-balanced.

4.3.2 Accounting Regulatory Committee

The Accounting Regulatory Committee (ARC) is set up according to the requirements of Article 6 of the IAS Regulation. The function of the Committee is a regulatory one (regulatory procedure with scrutiny). The ARC provides an opinion on Commission proposals to endorse an IFRS. This constitutes the formal part of the European Union's endorsement mechanism. With regard to the IAS Regulation, the ARC has drawn up its rules of procedures based on the standard rules of procedure adopted by the European Commission on January 31, 2002.[543] The ARC consists of representatives from the European member states' governments and is chaired by the European Commission, as depicted in Table 15.

Member	Composition
Austria	Bundesministerium für Justiz / Finanzministerium / Finanzmarktaufsicht
Belgium	Ministère des Affaires Economiques / Commission des Normes Comptables
Bulgaria	Ministry of Finance
Cyprus	Permanent Representation to the EU / Ministry of Finance
Czech Republic	Ministry of Finance
Denmark	Danish Financial Supervisory Authority / Danish Commerce and Companies Agency
Estonia	Ministry of Finance
Finland	Ministry of Finance / Ministry of Social Affairs and Health
France	Conseil National de la Comptabilité / Ministère de l'Economie, des Finances et de l'Industrie (trésor)
Germany	German Federal Ministry of Justice / Federal Ministry of Economics and Technology

542 Council of the European Communities (2006). *Commission decision of July 14, 2006 setting up a Standards Advice Review Group to advise the Commission on the objectivity and neutrality of the European Financial Reporting Advisory Group's (EFRAG's) opinions*, p. 1.

543 Council of the European Communities (2001). *Standard rules of procedure – Council decision 1999/468/EC: Rules of procedure for the ... committee.*

Member	Composition
Greece	Greek Accounting and Auditing Oversight Board / Ministry of Economy and Finance
Hungary	Ministry of Finance
Ireland	Institute of Chartered Accounts in Ireland / Department of Enterprise, Trade and Employment
Italy	CONSOB / ISVAP / Banca d'Italia / Ministry of Economy and Finance
Latvia	Ministry of Finance
Lithuania	Ministry of Finance / Accounting Institute
Luxembourg	Commission de Surveillance du Secteur Financier / Ministère de la Justice
Malta	Accounting Board / Ministry of Finance
Netherlands	Ministry of Justice / Ministry of Finance
Poland	Ministry of Finance
Portugal	CMVM / CNC / Ministry of Justice
Romania	Ministry of Public Finance
Slovakia	Ministry of Finance
Slovenia	Permanent Representation to the EU / Slovenian Institute of Auditors
Spain	Banco de España / ICAC
Sweden	Ministry of Justice
United Kingdom	Department of Trade and Industry
Observers	**Composition**
Iceland	Ministry of Finance
Norway	Financial Supervisory Authority / Ministry of Finance
European Central Bank Committee of European Insurance and	
Banking Advisory Committee (BAC)	
Committee of European Banking Supervisors (CEBS)	
Committee of European Security Regulators (CESR)	
Occupational Pensions Supervisors (CEIOPS)	
Chair and Secretariat	
European Commission	
Experts	
EFRAG (when invited)	

Table 15: ARC members and most frequent composition of delegation

In addition, the Committee may also create working groups, chaired by a representative of the Commission, to examine particular issues. Each member state delegation is considered to be one committee member and, with the Chairman's permission, the delegations may be accompanied by experts.[544] For example, if an international accounting standard for adoption is of particular importance for banks, insurance companies or other regulated markets, the chairman may invite a representative of the Banking Advisory Committee, and/or of the Insurance Committee, and/or of CESR, as an observer.[545]

The minutes of each meeting, drawn up under the auspices of the Chairman, typically contain the opinions expressed on the proposed standards. A summary report for the European Parliament will be prepared, briefly describing each agenda point and the result of the vote on the proposed measures submitted to the committee.[546] The ARC publishes its agenda items, a summary record and the final voting results. Yet, discussions, as well as the voting itself, are kept confidential and the individual positions of member states are not published. Non-European countries or organizations may be granted observer status, but they must withdraw when the committee moves to a vote.

4.3.3 European endorsement process

Once the IASB issues an IFRS, the endorsement process starts with the European Commission formally asking EFRAG for its view on whether an IFRS should be endorsed. Once the opinion of EFRAG has been received, the European Commission will draft a proposal for adoption of the standard. As outlined earlier, the Commission's work is assisted by a regulatory procedure with scrutiny.

The ARC receives the Commission's proposal to adopt or reject an IASB standard accompanied by EFRAG's technical assessment, and considers any political aspects, for example, whether a member state's government has any strong objections. In accordance with Article 7(2) of the IAS Regulation, the Commission must report to the ARC in a timely matter if it intends not to propose the adoption of a standard. For a standard to be endorsed by the ARC, a qualified majority vote (QMV) is required.[547] If the ARC accepts the Commission's endorsement proposal, the Commission sends the proposal to the European Parliament (EP) and the European Council (Council) for scrutiny. The EP and the Council have three months to react. Within these three months, the EP or the Council can oppose the adoption of the draft measures, justifying their opposi-

544 Accounting Regulatory Committee (2002). Rules of procedure for the Accounting Regulatory Committee, *Article 6*.

545 Ibid., *Article 8*.

546 Ibid., *Article 4*.

547 Ibid., *Article 5*.

tion by indicating that (1) the draft measures exceed the implementing powers, (2) the draft is not compatible with the aim or the content, or (3) the draft does not respect the principles of subsidiarity or proportionality. In that case, the proposal will not be adopted and the Commission may submit to the ARC an amended draft or present a legislative proposal on the basis of the Treaty. If neither the EP nor the Council has opposed the adoption of the proposed measure, it will be adopted by the Commission.

If the ARC changes or amends the Commission's endorsement proposal, the European Commission is required to submit its endorsement proposals to the European Council and to the European Parliament. The Council acts on the proposal by a qualified majority within two months from the date of referral. If, within that period, the Council opposes the proposed measures by a qualified majority, the measures will not be adopted. In that event, the Commission may submit to the Council an amended proposal. If the Council approves the amended proposal it will submit its opinion to the EP. Once the EP has received the opinion of the Council, it will give its opinion on endorsement to the Commission. The EP, acting by a majority of its component members within four months from the forwarding of the proposal, may oppose the adoption of the measures in question. In this case the proposal will not be adopted and the Commission is required to submit to the ARC an amended draft or present a legislative proposal on the basis of the Treaty. If the EP does not oppose the proposed measures, they will be adopted.

In case the EC is asked to submit a new proposal, it retains the power of initiative; which means the Commission will decide how to react in case of non-agreement by the Council or the EP with its proposal. Should the Commission decide to amend the proposed draft measures, the procedure to follow will depend on the complexity and substantiality of such an amendment. If there is a substantial change to the proposal, the ARC will need to discuss it again. Should the Commission decide to submit a legislative proposal on the basis of the Treaty establishing the European Community, the procedure to follow would be a standard legislative procedure according to the Treaty, in this case a co-decision procedure according to Art. 251. EFRAG would not need to be consulted, as EFRAG is an accounting technical committee which provides support and expertise to the EC in the assessment of international accounting standards (according to recital Nr. 10 of the preamble of the IAS Regulation – Regulation 1606/2002) and the Commission does not consult its endorsement regulation with EFRAG. The Commission's proposals for the endorsement of IFRS or their interpretations will then be discussed by the ECON, composed of EU Finance Ministers.

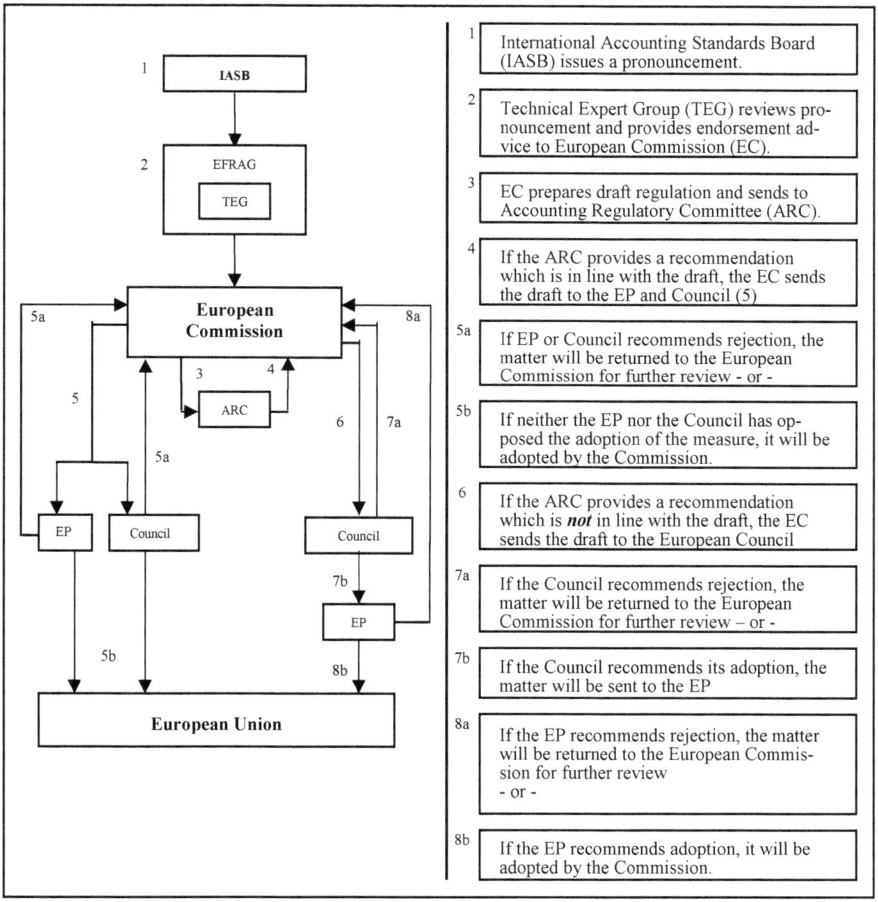

Figure 4: European endorsement process[548]

Once a standard has been adopted by the Commission, it is then published in full in each of the official languages of the Community as a Commission regulation in the Official Journal of the European Union. The standards thus become part of Community law, which also means that they will automatically come under the jurisdiction of the European Court of Justice.

548 Adopted from Luthardt, Ulf and Zimmermann, Jochen (2009). *A European view on the legitimacy of accounting procedures: Towards a deliberative-accountability framework for analysis*. Research in Accounting Regulation. (21):2. 79-88, p. 86.

4.4 The legitimacy of accounting procedures in Europe: An evaluation

In this chapter, the arrangements for standard setting and governance that provide the regulatory framework for financial reporting in Europe will be assessed against the (normative) procedural characteristics developed in chapter 3.3. Since this study is primarily concerned with collective decision making – the legislative process, the focus of the analysis will be placed on the private standard-setting procedures. However, the EU policy implementation step is considered important as well, but more in terms as an integral part (procedural safeguard) of the overall regulatory process. In addition, focusing on private standard setting seems to be adequate in the light of the potential elimination of the EU endorsement process. Charlie McCreevy, the European Commissioner for Internal Market and Services, pointed out that "[...] one of the cornerstones of my strategy is that we must be able to accept any future standards without any serious problems. The endorsement of accounting standards needs to disappear from the political limelight. It should not necessarily be a high profile political issue."[549]

Effective participation

Participatory mechanisms, as proposed, create a belief in the fairness of the procedure because they produce a sense of due ownership of the process. Although the final decision is not decisive to ensure compliance, it can be argued that meaningful participatory mechanisms reflecting a range of views also result in systematically better conclusions. Both features, in turn, increase the acceptance of the process and outcome.

From an organizational/structural perspective it is important to assess the opportunities to participate as well as the need to balance the ideal of direct involvement with other valuable/desirable procedural characteristics, for example, the quality or effectiveness of the accounting procedures. The descriptive analysis of the IASB, its structure and working procedures, illustrated ample opportunities to participate for individuals: either through active work in the SAC or other specialized working groups. At the aggregate level, the Memorandum of Understanding (MoU) on the role of national standard setters established formal links on their relationship with the IASB. Along this way, the IASB can incorpo-

549 McGreevy, Charlie (2007). EU-US cooperation on reporting standards audit oversight and regulation European Federation of Accountants' Conference on Audit Regulation. Brussels, November 27, 2007.

rate country-specific perspectives which are often considered to be impediments to the harmonization of accounting regulation.

In addition, the analysis revealed that many steps in developing a standard consist of inviting comments from interested parties, or conducting public hearings or field tests. A comment period of 120 days, in principle, allows constituents sufficient time to proffer their views.[550] In particular, a rather long comment period of 120 days enables other accounting standard setters to conduct a due process in their own jurisdictions. From an institutional 'supply-side' perspective, the IASB's extensive use of electronic and information technology as well as regional round-table discussions enables widespread participation, helping transnational decision making to replicate the participatory discussions that supposedly went on when nation-states themselves were responsible for standard setting. In 2009, the Due Process Oversight Committee surveyed all IASB working group members who supposedly have "[...] led to improvements in the IASB's practices to ensure that there is more effective dialogue and feedback between the IASB and its working groups."[551]

Overall, the institutional arrangements demonstrate the IASB's willingness to allow for widespread public participation. However, it must be stressed that research on political participation does not provide an unambiguous idea of stakeholder involvement. For example, Daniel Bodansky argues that "[...] expert decision making stands in sharp contrast to public participation."[552] This struggle between competing values is clearly visible in the IASB's proposition of a geographic formulation for the selection of Trustees and IASB members, while concomitantly emphasizing an independent, expert-based standard-setting process. In general, it seems reasonable to assume that decision-making structures based on expertise, in combination with inclusiveness, increase the acceptance (com-

550 While "[...] there is no restriction to the right to comment (non-exclusion principle)", Richardson and Eberlein point out that there "[...] there is no right to appear at open hearings." Richardson, Alan and Eberlein, Burkard (2011). *Legitimating Transnational Standard-Setting: The Case of the International Accounting Standards Board.* Journal of Business Ethics. (98):2. 217-245, p. 235.

551 International Accounting Standards Committee Foundation (2009). Annual Report, p. 10.

552 Bodansky, Daniel (1999). *The Legitimacy of International Governance: A Coming Challenge for International Environmental Law?* The American Journal of International Law. (93):3. 596-624, p. 620. In addition, it seems reasonable to balance opportunities to participate against other standards than the quality of deliberation. For example, procedural performance could also be negatively influenced by broad participation. If the IASB would be confronted with information overload or if participants strategically use information, board members may lose the ability to discuss accounting issues critically. Dahl, Robert Alan (1994). *A Democratic Dilemma: System Effectiveness versus Citizen Participation.* Political Science Quarterly. (109):1. 23-34.

pliance) as compared to those that rely only on expertise. Nevertheless, the quality of deliberation might decline if too many people are involved in decision making. Jim Rossi points out that "[w]hile participation encourages breadth in the agency decision-making process, deliberation is more concerned with depth."[553] Concerned with this balancing act between scope and quality of participation, constituents commented during the second phase of the constitutional review that "[...] if there are too many people, too many interests to be satisfied to get a standard out, [...] you run the risk that we've had in the past with some standards that options start creeping in, the standards become weaker and that would be a particular concern that we end up with standards that are not as good, not as high quality [...]."[554] Equally, Michael Livermore, analyzing an international food standard-setting body (the Codex Alimentarius) argues that "[...] greater authority has challenged the legitimacy [...] by subjecting the Codex to higher standards for public participation and democratic accountability and undermining the deliberative process that was at the heart of its successful functioning."[555]

The fundamental problem that underlies the continuing struggle between direct participation and other dimensions of procedural legitimacy is whether "[...] the Rousseauian assumption that any form of democracy that falls short of participation is not genuinely worthy of the name [...]" is true or not.[556] Depending on how one is willing to address this issue, the question whether it is valuable to increase the level of direct involvement within representative rule-making systems needs to be addressed. While this study argues that some form of representation is necessary due to the complexity of global accounting regulation, schol-

553 Rossi, Jim (1997). *Participation run amok: The costs of mass participation for deliberative agency decision-making.* Northwestern University Law Review. (92):1. 174-250, pp. 211-212.

554 Cearns, Kathryn (2008, Chairman of the Financial Reporting Committee (Institute of Chartered Accountants in England and Wales)). *Constitutional Review – Phase 1.* Round-table: Session 2 Part 2. (London, IASC Foundation):June. 1-24, pp. 12-13.

555 Livermore, Michael A. (2006). *Authority and Legitimacy in Global Governance: Deliberation, Institutional Differentiation, and the Codex Alimentarius.* New York University Law Review. (81):766-801, pp. 767-768.

556 Weale, Albert (2007). *Democracy.* Basingstoke: Palgrave Macmillan, pp. 105-106.

ars are nevertheless concerned with the level[557] or diversity[558] of participation and how it differs depending on the issue.[559]

Robert Larson, for example, commented on the lack of user participation in the written response stage, and many have criticized the IASB for failing to take account of their views.[560] As a result, there have been calls for greater user involvement in the standard-setting process but without any normative concern as to which participatory level is sufficient. Adequate user representation however, does not necessarily need to equate to direct involvement. Rather, the interests of users may be properly represented by other parties who are directly involved. Besides, it is pre-emptive to conclude that the mere presence of more actors results in an actual increase in the diversity of ideas. A different explanation for a low response rate is that it might just reflect the fact that a proposed standard is not at odds with the various interests of the financial community or that one may not wish to participate most of the time, but relies on procedures that ensure participatory means when the decisions taken become questionable.[561] From an economic perspective, Sutton's cost benefit model[562] showed that it is reasonable to remain silent, particularly if the costs of political action are relatively high. Instead, in this case, it could encourage people to become free riders rather than participants.[563] Such conclusions stem mainly from considering the outcome of the standard-setting process as a public good, whereby the benefits of a new standard are available to all – whether they contribute to the outcome or not.

To conclude, there is no general agreement with regard to the scope and quality of participation: "[...] it is not clear 'how much' participation (and how much

---

557 Schmidt, Matthias (2002). *On the legitimacy of accounting standard setting by privately organised institutions in Germany and Europe*. Schmalenbach Business Review (SBR). (54):2. 171-193.

558 Kaplan, David and Fender, Elizabeth A. (1998). *The Development of Comment Letters on FASB Proposals by the AICPA Accounting Standards Executive Committee*. Accounting Horizons. (12):2. 184-187.

559 Tandy, Paulette R. and Wilburn, Nancy L. (1992). *Constituent Participation in Standard-Setting: The FASB's First 100 Statements*. Accounting Horizons. (6):2. 47-58.

560 Larson, Robert K. (1997). *Corporate Lobbying of the International Accounting Standards Committee*. Journal of International Financial Management & Accounting. (8):3. 175-203, p. 187.

561 Warren, Mark E. (1996). *Deliberative democracy and authority*. American Political Science Review. (90):1. 46-60, p. 49.

562 Sutton's cost-benefit model is based on the Downsian voting model to analyze the characteristics of lobbyists. Sutton, Timothy G. (1984). *Lobbying of accounting standard-setting in the U.K. and the U.S.A.: A Downsian analysis*. Accounting, Organizations & Society. (9):1. 81-95, pp. 81-82.

563 Lindahl, Frederick W. (1987). *Accounting Standards and Olson's Theory of Collective Action*. Journal of Accounting & Public Policy. (6):1. 59-72, p. 60.

balance between constituencies) could be considered sufficient to establish legitimacy."[564] However, by giving interested individuals or groups the opportunity of voicing their ideas and objections with regard to a specific proposal, the IASB increases, at least in principle, the chance of finding a compromise that is acceptable to all parties.

Enlightened understanding

The procedural characteristic 'enlightened understanding' emphasizes the quality of collective decision making, which increases if the following conditions for an 'ideal speech situation' are met: non-exclusion, equal opportunities to participate, participants must mean what they say, elimination of any motivation/force except a desire for better decisions/reasons.[565] Conversely, institutions are closer to the non-deliberative end when "[...] an alternative is not contrasted effectively with its rivals, where arguments are not answered, and where the decision makers have little competence or factual background to evaluate the proposals offered to them."[566] From this follows that the formation of the policy outcome requires a diversity of viewpoints (covered by means of effective participation) and a process characterized by rationality because "[...] only the rational principle of deliberation can guarantee the legitimacy of the decisions."[567] Successful deliberation, in turn, "[...] promises to overcome the noted tension between participatory input and expertise-based output logic [because it] is about increasing the rationality of decision making by allowing different constituencies to submit their positions."[568] In this respect, deliberative theories strive "[...] to show how deliberation, as a more focused form of political participation, is the key to the fulfillment of democratic ideals in complex societies."[569]

---

564 Richardson, Alan and Eberlein, Burkard (2011). *Legitimating Transnational Standard-Setting: The Case of the International Accounting Standards Board*. Journal of Business Ethics. (98):2. 217-245, p. 223.

565 Richardson, Alan (2008). *Due Process and Standard-setting: An Analysis of Due Process in Three Canadian Accounting and Auditing Standard-setting Bodies*. Journal of Business Ethics. (81):3. 679-696, p. 683.

566 Fishkin, James S. (1991). *Democracy and deliberation: new directions for democratic reform*. New Haven; London: Yale University Press, p. 348.

567 Vitale, Denise (2006). *Between deliberative and participatory democracy: A contribution on Habermas*. Philosophy & Social Criticism. (32):6. 739-766, p. 756.

568 Richardson, Alan and Eberlein, Burkard (2011). *Legitimating Transnational Standard-Setting: The Case of the International Accounting Standards Board*. Journal of Business Ethics. (98):2. 217-245, p. 224.

569 Hauptmann, Emily (2001). *Can Less Be More? Leftist Deliberative Democrats' Critique of Participatory Democracy*. Polity. (33):3. 397-421, p. 420.

The IASB uses many steps in its consultation process to gain a better understanding of different accounting treatments and the potential impact of proposals on affected parties. In the light of its consultation, the IASB considers its position, and decides whether to modify its approach to standard-setting issues. The IASB also establishes feedback statements related to comments received throughout the consultation process. It therefore enables respondents and others to observe how the IASB deals with the comments received. The comply-or-explain rule in combination with notice and comment procedures helps to create a political environment for evidence-based reasoning. Ideally, however, a rigorous use of *ex ante* impact assessments of new standards would enhance still further the rational character of the due process and allow stakeholders to comment thereon during the consultation process.[570]

According to the Due Process Oversight Committee no "breach of the IASB's due process" commitments was found in 2009.[571] However, Richardson and Eberlein sharply observe that the Due Process Handbook "[...] makes extensive use of the adjective 'normally' in describing its procedures which signals that exceptions may arise and would allow variation in procedures without triggering the 'comply or explain' requirement."[572] In addition, the possibility to shorten the due process below the minimum required (30 days) stands in sharp contrast to the IASB's professed importance of a deliberative due process.

A further concern deals with the question of how the IASB processes the input it receives through its consultation activities. Stig Enevoldson argued during the first part of the constitutional review that "[...] the IASB's only legitimacy is its due process, otherwise it's just 14 wise guys. But it gets its legitimacy to issue standards because it has a due process. And therefore it's very important that the constituents are satisfied with the way the Board uses the input they get from the constituents."[573] A deliberative process requires leaders to provide reasons for their decisions which should, in principle, be comprehensible to all constituents. The Due Process Handbook notes that "[...] the IASB listens to, evaluates, and, where the IASB considers it to be appropriate, adopts suggestions received dur-

570 The Verband der Industrie- und Dienstleistungskonzerne argued during the constitutional review that "[i]n contrast to ex post review processes, a due process that includes intense field tests at preparers would produce relevant ex ante information on costs and benefits of a change in Financial Reporting Standards." Comment letter number 60 provided by the Verband der Industrie- und Dienstleistungskonzerne, Switzerland.

571 International Accounting Standards Committee Foundation (2009). Annual Report, p. 12.

572 Richardson, Alan and Eberlein, Burkard (2011). *Legitimating Transnational Standard-Setting: The Case of the International Accounting Standards Board.* Journal of Business Ethics. (98):2. 217-245, p. 232.

573 Enevoldsen, Stig (EFRAG) (2008). Constitutional Review – Round-table meeting, Session 1 Part 2, p. 13.

ing consultations."[574] While an independent standard setter needs to exercise professional discretion, Richardson and Eberlein criticize that "[...] it is not clear on which (evidential) basis the IASB comes to the conclusion that a given comment is 'appropriate' or not."[575] However, this is precisely what deliberation is about: the rational weighing of arguments in support of or against options for resolving disagreements. Its weakness, however, rests on the unresolved issue of how to exactly evaluate arguments in the light of value judgments. In this context, it is not possible to state whose arguments are 'appropriate' or 'better': rationality cannot guide the decision making because the 'force of the better argument' principle does not apply. At the very least, the IASB allows alternative solutions in the development of accounting standards and can claim that it has acted reasonably, which, in turn, meets the conditions of a deliberative procedure. Through an open and public due process the IASB tests its arguments and implements an additional element of procedural control.

Representation

The formalistic view of representation focused, on the one hand, on the 'pre-representation stage' (authorization) and, on the other hand, on the 'post-representation stage' (accountability mechanisms). Previously, the activities of the IASB and its predecessor were self-mandated without any direct governmental authorization. From a European perspective, this situation changed dramatically with the release of the IAS Regulation in 2002. Since this regulation prescribes the use of IAS, the European Commission at least indirectly transferred legislative competencies (authority) to the IASB. Before 2002, European member states already authorized IASB standards individually. Germany, for example, adopted the Capital Raising Facilitation Act (KapAEG) in 1998, which allowed listed companies to publish their consolidated financial statements according to IFRS or US GAAP.[576] Against this background, member states' legislative acts as well as the IAS Regulation constitute ex-post authorization. Accordingly, Larson and Street assert that the IASB gained greater legitimacy and stature through the IAS

574 International Accounting Standards Committee Foundation (2008). *Due Process Handbook for the International Accounting Standards Board (IASB)*, p. 4.

575 Richardson, Alan and Eberlein, Burkard (2011). *Legitimating Transnational Standard-Setting: The Case of the International Accounting Standards Board.* Journal of Business Ethics. (98):2. 217-245, p. 236.

576 Zimmermann, Jochen (2007). *The Role of the Nation-State in the Internationalization of Accounting Regimes. Transforming the golden-age nation state.* Hurrelmann, Achim, Leibfried, Stephan, Martens, Kerstin and Mayer, PeterPalgrave Macmillan, p. 53.

Regulation.[577] However, traditional accountability mechanisms – the other side of the story – are missing, which prompts Johnson and Solomons to argue that "[...] *de jure* authority of a particular nonmarket decision-making process is not, in general, sufficient to establish its legitimacy [...]."[578] For that reason, other control mechanisms at the 'post-representation' stage are required to ensure accountability. These will be discussed in terms of procedural safeguards.

The descriptive view of representation emphasizes the composition of the decision-making forum, which is supposed to mirror existing and potential constituents. Previously, the geographical background has been subject to criticism because Board members were mainly selected from 'Anglo-Saxon' countries. This, in turn, could impose the danger of an inadequate representation of geographical minorities. Examining the required geographical formulation in isolation for the selection of Trustees obscures the underlying 'accounting tradition'. North America, the United Kingdom, South Africa and Australia can be classified as belonging to the 'Anglo-Saxon' accounting tradition. Against this background, the current Trustee composition reveals an imbalance: 9 out of 22 (40%) Trustees represent one accounting tradition. Looking at the IASB members' geographical composition, this disproportion becomes even more problematic: 9 out of 15 Board members (60%) represent one particular accounting doctrine. The same holds true for the membership of the IFRS Interpretations Committee: 8 out of 14 (57%) voting members originate from countries with an 'Anglo-Saxon' accounting tradition. Although the selection of the Trustees as well as IASB members, as required by the constitution, should ensure an overall geographic balance, it becomes evident that one accounting tradition dominates.

Overall, however, different geographical and professional backgrounds in combination with the voting requirements prevent one country or region from dominating the standard-setting process. It also ensures that diverse perspectives feed into the deliberation process. Nevertheless, constituents from emerging economies criticized their underrepresentation during the second part of the constitutional review: "With respect to geographical allocation of Trustees, it seems necessary to incorporate some other measures in order to enhance diversity and fair opportunity. Under the current proposals, it is possible that only some leading countries take all of the seats while keeping the other countries from participation. If that is the case, one objective of the Constitution would not be

577 Larson, Robert K. and Street, Donna L. (2004). *Convergence with IFRS in an expanding Europe: progress and obstacles identified by large accounting firms' survey*. Journal of International Accounting, Auditing and Taxation. (13):2. 89-119, p. 90.

578 Johnson, Steven B. and Solomons, David (1984). *Institutional Legitimacy and the FASB*. Journal of Accounting & Public Policy. (3):3. 165-183, p. 171, p. 171.

achieved, which is to take account of emerging economies."[579] The objection by emerging economies reveals a more general criticism: clear criteria or principles that can be used to select Trustees or Board members are missing. While it is reasonable to broaden the geographical scope, underlying economic realities should not be neglected. IFRS are intended to help investors 'in the world's capital markets' to make economic decisions. In this respect, market capitalization in combination with an overall geographical and professional balance could provide objective standards for selecting new Trustees, Board members or candidates for the Monitoring Board. A purely geographical formulation (quota), in contrast, could result in candidates only acting as regional representatives, unable to develop international accounting standards.

In contrast to the formalistic and descriptive view on representation, representation as 'acting for' focuses on the substantive character of representation – the nature of the activity itself.[580] The conceptual problem inherent in this perspective of representation is the extent to which the representative should or must act independently from his constituents. In the introduction to the discussion document 'Review of the Constitution Public Accountability and the Composition of the IASB Proposals for Change', the IASC Foundation stressed that "[...] the new structure [of the IASB] was based on the operating premise that [...] the IASB [is] appropriately protected from particular national, sectoral or special interest pleading."[581] This exemplifies the problems that the IASB is having in reconciling responsiveness with independent standard setting. Again, political representation "[...] means acting in the interest of the represented, in a manner responsive to them. The representative must act independently; his action must involve discretion and judgment; he must be the one who acts. [...] The representative must act in such a way that there is no conflict, or if it occurs an explanation is called for."[582] The balancing act of private standard setters between independence and responsiveness is a highly controversial research object. Brown and Feroz point out that "[...] members of the FASB maintain that they consider these submissions to be important in their decision-making process [whereas] critics contend that FASB members do not consider the submissions at

579 Comment letter number 3 provided by the Korea Accounting Standards Board.

580 Pitkin, Hanna Fenichel (1972). *The concept of representation*. Berkeley: University of California Press, p. 114.

581 International Accounting Standards Committee Foundation (2008). *Review of the Constitution: Public Accountability and the Public Accountability and the Composition of the IASB – Proposals for Change*, p. 8.

582 Pitkin, Hanna Fenichel (1972). *The concept of representation*. Berkeley: University of California Press, pp. 209-210.

all in the standard-setting process [...]."[583] In the same way, one commentator emphasized during the constitutional review that "[t]he Board has won acclaim for its governance and due process system. However, a system is only as good as it is 'lived'. There is little to be gained from tweaking the system if the Board only pays it lip service and goes through the motions but then, for example, treats input from constituents in the due process dismissively."[584]

From an institutional 'supply-perspective' feedback statement, the comply-or-explain rule and a basis for conclusion explaining how the Board reached a decision has the potential to resolve the struggle between independence and responsiveness. At the very end, however, the substantive character of representation can only be assessed empirically.

Procedural safeguards

Transparency

The first procedural safeguard pertains to transparency requirements with regard to the scope and timeliness of publicly available information as well as the costs for acquiring the information. It has been argued that the well-functioning of decision-making processes depends, in part, on the degree of information available to stakeholders in order to limit the opportunities for politicians to engage in misbehavior. A study by Adsera Alicia shows that "[...] a well-informed electorate [...] explains between one-half and two-thirds of the variance in the levels of governmental performance and corruption."[585] The publication and recording of comments, observer notes etc., which can be reviewed from time to time, facilitates deliberation and "[...] protects against illegality, overreaching, and self-dealing by decision-makers. Thus, a structured fact-finding and option-evaluation process is at least partial compensation for the lack of direct electoral ties to the public."[586]

Publications and information related to the IASB's due process that are freely available on the organization's website are as follows: meeting schedules of the Trustees, the IASB, the SAC, public hearings and other public meetings; com-

---

583 Brown, Lawrence D. and Feroz, Ehsan H. (1992). *Does the FASB listen to corporations?* Journal of Business Finance & Accounting. (19):5. 715-731, p. 715.

584 Comment letter number 60 provided by the Verband der Industrie- und Dienstleistungskonzerne, Switzerland.

585 Alicia, Adsera (2003). *Are You Being Served? Political Accountability and Quality of Government.* Journal of Law Economics & Organization. (19):2. 445-490, p. 479.

586 Esty, Daniel C. (2006). *Good Governance at the Supranational Scale: Globalizing Administrative Law.* Yale Law Journal. (115):7. 1490-1562, p. 1532-1533.

ment letters and written submissions; discussion papers; exposure drafts of IFRSs and amendments; project summaries and feedback statements; effect analyses; comparisons of exposure drafts and current proposals of the IASB following IASB re-deliberations; post-implementation reviews. The extensive publication of relevant material thus serves to inform the public about the role interested parties play in the development of a standard (lobbying disclosure).[587] In addition, IASB meetings between outside parties and more than five members of the Board are open to the public, and all decisions are made in public meetings. Luthardt and Zimmermann conclude that "[...] these requirements make the IASB fairly transparent and enhance the credibility of IFRSs."[588] However, Gerhard Kurz criticizes that information (reasons) about appointments or refusals of Trustees or Board members are not made public.[589] However, it should be stressed that such contractual information is always confidential, whether it pertains to official agents or private persons. In this light, the publication of selection criteria for appointments seems to be sufficient to make inferences about the selection process.

Final control of the agenda

Robert Dahl points out that there are two possible restrictions that invalidate legitimate decision-making processes: "[...] a narrow agenda, or [representatives] responsive to a highly exclusive demos, or both."[590] Accordingly, the second procedural safeguard relates to how agenda items are selected and prioritized. The decision to add a topic to the IASB agenda and to commission a discussion paper is based on a simple majority vote, which allows issues to enter the standard-setting process fairly easily.[591] In addition, the Due Process Handbook established clear guidelines against which the IASB evaluates whether there is a

587 Richardson and Eberlein point out that due process norms can "[...] redirect lobbying from private meetings and indirect channels into a public forum." Richardson, Alan and Eberlein, Burkard (2011). *Legitimating Transnational Standard-Setting: The Case of the International Accounting Standards Board.* Journal of Business Ethics. (98):2. 217-245, p. 238.

588 Luthardt, Ulf and Zimmermann, Jochen (2009). *A European view on the legitimacy of accounting procedures: Towards a deliberative-accountability framework for analysis.* Research in Accounting Regulation. (21):2. 79-88, p. 82.

589 Kurz, Gerhard (2009). *Das IASB und die Regulierung der Rechnungslegung in der EU: eine Analyse von Legitimation und Lobbying.* Frankfurt: Peter Lang, p. 126.

590 Dahl, Robert Alan (1979). *Procedural Democracy. Philosophy, politics and society: fifth series: a collection.* Laslett, Peter and Fishkin, James S. Oxford: Blackwell, p. 105.

591 Richardson, Alan and Eberlein, Burkard (2011). *Legitimating Transnational Standard-Setting: The Case of the International Accounting Standards Board.* Journal of Business Ethics. (98):2. 217-245, p. 233.

"[...] demand for better quality information that is of value to all users of financial statements."[592] Before adding a topic to the agenda, the IASB assesses the relevance to users of the information, existing guidance available, the possibility of increasing convergence, the quality of the IFRS to be developed, and resource constraints.[593]

Bryan Howieson analyzed the agenda admittance criteria used by the FASB and concluded that there exists "[...] an apparent flexibility in the way FASB members may use these criteria."[594] A comparable study for the IASB and its agenda decisions does not exist. However, the second part of the constitutional review revealed that many stakeholders were concerned with the way agenda items are chosen, in particular who plays a role in the agenda-setting process. To meet this criticism, the constitutional review focused on encouraging greater input into the IASB's agenda-setting process. As a result, the IASB's technical agenda will be developed in accordance with a three-yearly public consultation starting in 2011.

Bias suppression / neutrality

Integrity, reputation and neutrality of the IASB are some of the most important factors for achieving legitimate authority. Bias suppression or neutrality of the standard-setting process can be achieved by systematic and sound rule making. A well structured process will promote rationality, legality and fairness resulting in "[...] systematically better results over time."[595] Against this background, the conceptual framework provides a benchmark against which future or revised standards will be developed. This, in turn, allows constituents to formulate expectations about future developments and to evaluate whether standards are formulated in the public interest. It therefore allows outsiders to assess whether Board members reached well-balanced judgments. William Bratton analyzed the FASB's use of the conceptual framework to import legitimacy and concludes that it "[...] did not achieve the stated goal, however. The Conceptual Frame-

592 International Accounting Standards Committee Foundation (2008). *Due Process Handbook for the International Accounting Standards Board (IASB)*, p. 8.

593 Ibid., p. 8.

594 Howieson, Bryan A. (2009). *Agenda formation and accounting standards setting: lessons from the standards setters*. Accounting & Finance. (49):3. 577-598, p. 594.

595 Furthermore, Rossi argues that more information enhances public understanding of policy proposals, and individuals "[...] become aware of others' perspectives, helping to forge understanding and consensus." Rossi, Jim (1997). *Participation run amok: The costs of mass participation for deliberative agency decision-making*. Northwestern University Law Review. (92):1. 174-250, pp. 185-186.

work neither determined nor justified the FASB's subsequent decisions, and the FASB, as a result, never realized the ideal in which agency legitimacy follows ineluctably from the combination of independence and expertise. But the Conceptual Framework nonetheless contributed to the FASB's institutional success by disavowing a neutral posture respecting the conflicting interests of its leading constituents, explicitly privileging the user interest over the preparer interest."[596] A comparable study for the IASB's use of its conceptual framework in developing standards does not exist.

Secondly, legitimate standard setting in terms of systematic and sound rule making is also achieved by clear procedural guidelines. The Due Process Handbook plainly lays down the procedural steps which have to be followed in the development of a new standard, resulting in a well-structured decision-making process. Due process is about rigor and as such "[...] it promises to counterbalance the arbitrariness of participation rules that results from the self-mandated character of private standard setting."[597] In addition, the Trustees and Board members' self-commitment to act in the public interest, as required by the constitution, compensates for the lack of formal accountability mechanism in this particular transnational governance context.

There is some risk, however, that participatory mechanisms during the due process consultations provide opportunities for special interest intervention. Empirical evidence shows that various interest groups participate in the standard-setting process and try to exert undue influence over the outcome.[598] However, even if it is acknowledged that respondent views on accounting issues correlate with policy outcomes[599], these studies did not demonstrate the influence of any

---

596 Bratton, William (2007). *Private standards, public governance: a new look at the Financial Accounting Standard Board.* Boston College Law Review. (48):1. 5-53, p. 9.

597 Richardson, Alan and Eberlein, Burkard (2011). *Legitimating Transnational Standard-Setting: The Case of the International Accounting Standards Board.* Journal of Business Ethics. (98):2. 217-245, p. 224.

598 Königsgruber, Roland (2009). *Lobbying bei der Rechnungslegungsstandardsetzung. Ein Literaturüberblick.* Zeitschrift für Betriebswirtschaft. (79):11. 1309-1329.

599 A report published by the US government concluded that the FASB was dominated by the big accounting firms and by the American Institute of Certified Public Accountants, and that these, in turn, were dominated by big corporate clients. Haring, John R. (1979). *Accounting Rules and 'The Accounting Establishment'.* Journal of Business. (52):4. 507-519, p. 508 Studies rejecting the hypothesis that the standard setter was influenced by sectoral interests are numerous. See, for example, Selto, Frank H. and Grove, Hugh D. (1982). *Voting Power Indices and the Setting of Financial Accounting Standards: Extensions.* Journal of Accounting Research. (20):2. 676-688, McKee Jr, A. James, Bell, Timothy B. and Boatsman, James R. (1984). *Management Preferences Over Accounting Standards: A Replication and Additional Tests.* Accounting Review. (59):4. 647-659, Buckmaster, Dale, Saniga, Erwin and Tadesse, Soloman (1994). *Meas-*

particular interest group if concomitantly accounting for other explanatory variables. In contrast to the often assumed negative influence of big audit firms or multinational companies, Kwok and Sharp show that "[...] the [standard-setting] process can be best characterized as a mixed power system where no party is accorded the absolute power potential to dictate IAS."[600] In addition, one can only speculate about the direction of influence from a correlation between interest and output. A positive association suggests that the standard setter was influenced by a certain group. Alternatively, one could argue that the standard setter convinces the business community through its deliberative process that its position was 'correct'. In the absence of a causal relation, a mere test for association cannot differentiate among different hypotheses. The fundamental problem pertains, in part, to the mandate-independence controversy as set forth in chapter 3.2.3. An evaluation of this issue depends on the specific perspective. On the one hand, the IASB is criticized for not being responsive enough, while lobbying theorists would argue that the IASB indeed listens to its stakeholders but only selectively.

Finally, numerous (lobbying) studies were designed as case studies.[601] In consequence, methodological difficulties arise if one wants to generalize the impact of interest group participation. In fact, it is mainly prominent one-off cases, e.g. IAS 39, that lead to the negative connotation of interest group participation. More importantly, the mere analysis of comment letters tends to obscure that

---

uring the lobbying influence using the Financial Accounting Standards Board public record. Journal of Economic & Social Measurement. (20):4. 331-356.

600 Kwok, Winston Chee Chiu and Sharp, David (2005). *Power and international accounting standard setting: Evidence from segment reporting and intangible assets projects.* Accounting, Auditing & Accountability Journal. (18):1. 74-99, p. 74.

601 Francis, Jere R. (1987). *Lobbying against proposed accounting standards: The case of employers' pension accounting.* Journal of Accounting and Public Policy. (6):1. 35-57, Deakin, Edward B. (1989). *Rational Economic Behavior and Lobbying on Accounting Issues: Evidence from the Oil and Gas Industry.* Accounting Review. (64):1. 137, Feroz, Ehsan Habib and Hagerman, Robert L. (1990). *Management Compensation, Insider Trading and Lobbying Choice: The Case of R&D.* Australian Journal of Management. (15):2. 297, Gorton, Donald E. (1991). *The SEC Decision Not to Support SFAS 19: A Case Study of the Effect of Lobbying on Standard Setting.* Accounting Horizons. (5):1. 29-41, McKee, James A., Williams, Paul F. and Frazier, Katherine Beal (1991). *A case study of accounting firm lobbying: Advice or consent.* Critical Perspectives on Accounting. (2):3. 273-294, Meier, Heidi Hylton, Alam, Pervaiz and Pearson, Michael A. (1993). *Auditor Lobbying for Accounting Standards: The Case of Banks and Savings and Loan Associations.* Accounting & Business Research. (23):92. 477-487, Klumpes, P. J. M. (1994). *The Politics of Rule Development: A Case Study of Australian Pension fund Accounting Rule-Making.* Abacus. (30):2. 140-159, Ryan, Christine and Dunstan, Keitha (1999). *Constituent participation in the Australian public sector accounting standard-setting process.* Financial Accountability & Management. (15):2. 173, Jupe, Robert E. (2000). *Self-referential lobbying of the Accounting Standards Board: The case of financial reporting standard No. 1.* Critical Perspectives on Accounting. (11):3. 337-359.

other factors may have a greater impact on regulatory outcomes. According to Luthardt and Zimmermann "[...] multi-issue/multi-period empirical studies did not demonstrate that the IASB is substantively influenced by any particular interest group to the disadvantage of another."[602]

A final point pertaining to bias suppression and neutrality relates to the funding regime of the IASCF. The general proposition is that monetary payments undermine the democratic process, creating dependency on major financial contributors. Larson and Kenny cite in their work a statement by the IASC Foundation from 1994, which might give rise to concerns about possible undue influence over the standard-setting process: "[...] each contributor is regularly contacted in order to provide input on the issues and principles being considered in current projects."[603] In this context, Alistair Brown characterized the milieu of the IASB as a "[...] cozy arrangement for a narrow band of stakeholders, but it does little to include other member groups of the global community that it purports to serve."[604] Equally, Tony Porter argues that the "[...] the role of accounting firms in funding the FASB has also raised concerns that this might provide undue leverage over standard setting, and this concern has been expressed with regard to the IASB as well."[605]

A report prepared by the European Commission asserts that "[...] the Trustees have successfully broadened the IASCF's geographic funding base; [...] the number of organizations contributing to the IASCF's funding has grown from less than 200 organizations in 2005 to several thousands in 2008, [but] the Foundation remains dependent on the major international audit networks for a significant part of its funding. Funding from some jurisdictions is also dominated by a specific stakeholder group, e.g. large financial institutions. This may give rise to continued concerns about the IASB's independence from key stakeholder groups."[606]

Indeed, the annual report of the IASC Foundation for 2009 shows a total budget of £ 16.583.544, of which £ 5.690.127 (about 34%) were contributed by

602 Luthardt, Ulf and Zimmermann, Jochen (2009). *A European view on the legitimacy of accounting procedures: Towards a deliberative-accountability framework for analysis.* Research in Accounting Regulation. (21):2. 79-88, p. 82.

603 Larson, Robert K. and Kenny, Sara York (2011). *The financing of the IASB: An analysis of donor diversity.* Journal of International Accounting, Auditing and Taxation. (20):1. 1-19, p. 5.

604 Brown, Alistair M. (2004). *The Milieu of the IASB.* Journal of American Academy of Business, Cambridge. (5):1/2. 385-390, p. 385.

605 Porter, Tony (2005). *Private Authority, Technical Authority, and the Globalization of Accounting Standards.* Business & Politics. (7):3. 1-30, p. 10.

606 European Commission (14 March 2008). Commission Services Working Paper on Governance Developments in the International Accounting Standards Board (IASB) and in the Intrernational Accounting Standards Committee Foundation (IASCF), 3rd Report, p. 6.

international accounting firms.[607] Nevertheless, whether financial contributions indeed bias the standard-setting activities is an unresolved issue, and any conclusions are speculative. Gerrit Zalm, chairman of the IASC Foundation pointed out that by voluntary contribution "[…] you can get the impression that companies say to you, if you are doing this nasty thing, I won't contribute to your organization any more, well in practice we haven't had it except once, from one company, so it is not a very heavy and serious impediment […]."[608] What should be of concern, however, is the reported funding gap since 2005, which results in part from the IASB's extensive outreach activities.[609] These activities can be expected to further increase in the future, thereby exerting more pressure on the IASC Foundation to secure a long-term, stable funding base which is independent of voluntary contributions.

Ideally, a funding regime should be established which is similar to that of the FASB. The Sarbanes-Oxley Act 2002 states in section 109 (annual accounting support fee for standard-setting body) that "[t]he annual accounting support fee for the standard-setting body […] shall be allocated in accordance with subsection (g), and assessed and collected against each issuer, on behalf of the standard-setting body, by 1 or more appropriate designated collection agents […] to provide for an independent, stable source of funding for such body, subject to review by the Commission […].[610] In general, the 'ideal' solution would be a levy system in every country which applies IFRS. However, the IASC Foundation does not possess that authority. Instead, national governments or standard setters should be urged to establish a broad-based compulsory funding regime.

A recent study by Larson and Kenny indicates several improvements with regard to the funding regime of the IASC Foundation. Firstly, they show that "[…] the number of donors tripled over the study period [1988-2008], and the IASB's donor base greatly increased in its stakeholder interest group and geographic diversity. While corporations continuously dominated the list of stakeholder interest group donors, the number of corporations making donations increased dramatically, thus decreasing the influence of any particular corporate donor."[611] Secondly, their results indicate that "[…] donations by country are now significantly correlated with measures of a country's economic and equity market size. In terms of the actual amount of donations, EU and Anglo-American contribu-

---

607 International Accounting Standards Committee Foundation (2009). Annual Report, pp. 46-50.

608 Zalm, Gerrit (Chairman, IASC Foundation). (2008). Constitutional Review – Round-table meeting, Session1 Part 1.

609 International Accounting Standards Committee Foundation (2009). Annual Report, p. 8.

610 Sarbanes-Oxley Act of 2002.

611 Larson, Robert K. and Kenny, Sara York (2011). *The financing of the IASB: An analysis of donor diversity*. Journal of International Accounting, Auditing and Taxation. (20):1. 1-19, p. 17.

tions are significant."[612] Thirdly, and most importantly, Larson and Kenny point out that "[...] the number and amount of mandatory contributions is increasing and the amount of voluntary contributions is declining. Since several countries, including Italy, South Africa, Sweden, and the U.K., are implementing mandatory broad-based payer financing systems [...]."[613]

Power sharing

The fourth procedural safeguard pertains to power sharing, which includes notions of divided authority and voting rules. Internally, divided authority is achieved through the IASCF-IASB divided role of oversight and standard-setting responsibilities but also due to the different professional and geographic backgrounds of the voting members. While the IASCF is responsible for establishing and maintaining appropriate financing arrangements, and ensuring the ongoing operation of the foundation and appointments, the IASB has sole authority in developing new standards. Externally, the establishment of the Monitoring Board adds a new layer of hierarchy and reporting above the Trustee level. In particular, the Monitoring Board's role in recommending and approving the selection of Trustees abandons the former mechanism of self-appointment, an often-raised concern: "[...] legitimacy is bound to remain contested unless the organization's stakeholders are given means, even indirect ones, to remove non-performing Trustees or to block questionable appointments. This problem persists even if the current Trustees are respected and the current appointments are sound."[614] While it is too early to comment on the precise functioning of the Monitoring Board and its implications for the standard-setting process[615], it is surprising from a conceptual perspective that, if the IASCF is the organization to be monitored, it simultaneously lays down in its own constitution governing the specific monitoring activities of the Monitoring Board. At this early stage, one might also be concerned about how the Monitoring Board fits into the overall structure of the IFRS Foundation and whether the stated objective of increased accountability can be achieved. This uncertainty with regard to the Monitoring Board's responsibilities might explain the European Commission's reluctance to sign the

612 Ibid., p. 17.

613 Ibid., p. 17.

614 Véron, Nicolas (2007). The Global Accounting Experiment. SERIES, BRUEGEL BLUEPRINT. Brussels: BRUEGEL. 2. 1-86, p. 50.

615 Güth, Simon and Zülch, Henning (2010). *Die neue Satzung der IASCF (IASCF-Constitution Review): Implikationen für den Standardsetzungsprozess und die zukünftige Ausrichtung der IFRS.* KoR – Fachzeitschrift für internationale und kapitalmarktorientierte Rechnungslegung. (10):4. 177-182, p. 182.

Memorandum of Understanding.[616] An excerpt of the MoU is provided in Figure 5.

E. From time to time, the IASCF Monitoring Board and the Trustees shall discuss the functioning of this MOU and discuss whether changes are appropriate. Changes must be approved by a consensus among all signatories to this MOU.

ARTICLE V: TERMINATION

11. The IASCF Monitoring Board or the Trustees may terminate this MOU upon 60 days written notice.

Signed in advance and ratified at London, this 1st day of April, 2009

Charlie McCreevy, Commissioner
For the European Commission

Gerrit Zalm, Chairman of the Trustees
For the International Accounting Standards Committee Foundation

Jane Diplock, Chairperson of the Executive Committee
For the International Organization of Securities Commissions

Takafumi Sato, Commissioner
For the Financial Services Agency of Japan

Christopher Cox, Chairman
For the United States Securities and Exchange Commission

Figure 5: Memorandum of Understanding (excerpt)

Supranational decision making, according to David Esty, should also "[…] include flexibility mechanisms to accommodate intense national political pressures. A provision that permits national governments to derogate from supranational policy prescriptions […] would promote good governance by transferring

616 Lanfermann, Georg (2009). *Steht das IASB durch die Finanzkrise vor einer Zerreißprobe?* Der Betrieb. (10):3. 1-5.

politically sensitive decisions to national officials with greater accountability."[617] Such a procedural safeguard (divided authority) exists in the form of the EU endorsement process, which constitutes an additional procedural safeguard because it limits the power transferred to the IASB; more specifically it acts as an outcome control element to ensure that the standards issued by the IASB are in Europe's interest. EFRAG's advisory function serves to represent European member states' interests by cooperating with, and pooling the wishes of, the national standard setters. The second main actor in the European screening mechanism is the ARC, which plays a major role due to its legal status. The Commission can enact a financial reporting standard only if the Committee supports the standard by a qualified majority vote (QMV), which ensures that minorities have to be taken into account. As a result, EFRAG and the ARC constitute an appropriate political interface for channeling the interests of the EU member states. To a certain extent, the organizational interaction between the IASB and the EU institutions mitigates Robert Dahl's criticism of international organizations' diversified constituency groups and distance from the electorate.[618] While standard setters with global reach "[...] are distant from their constituencies and less accountable to them"[619] the EU endorsement process provides at least a counterbalance to the notion of 'lost national sovereignty'.

In contrast, Richardson and Eberlein argue that legislative or administrative approval by public bodies is very limited because the standards "[...] are perceived to be 'take-or-leave' [which] leaves national authorities with limited options of amending or re-writing rules (carve-outs, exemptions or exceptions) if the commitment to IFRS within domestic borders is to be credible."[620] To the contrary, Roland Königsgruber argues that – due to the importance of the European Union as a major recipient of IFRS and due to various veto options by the European Commission, the ARC and the European Parliament – in the absence of any hierarchical order, the IASB is forced to anticipate preferences, and issues only standards that will not evoke disaffirmation by the European Union.[621]

617 Esty, Daniel C. (2006). *Good Governance at the Supranational Scale: Globalizing Administrative Law*. Yale Law Journal. (115):7. 1490-1562, p. 1536.

618 Dahl, Robert A. (1999). *Can International Organizations be Democratic? A Skeptic's View. Democracy's edges Contemporary political theory*. Shapiro, Ian. Cambridge [u.a.]: Cambridge Univ. Press, p. 23-26.

619 Fearnley, Stella and Sunder, Shyam (2006). *Global reporting standards: the Esperanto of accounting*. Accountancy. (137):1353. 26-26, p. 26.

620 Richardson, Alan and Eberlein, Burkard (2011). *Legitimating Transnational Standard-Setting: The Case of the International Accounting Standards Board*. Journal of Business Ethics. (98):2. 217-245, p. 220.

621 Königsgruber, Roland (2009). *Lobbying bei der Rechnungslegungsstandardsetzung. Ein Literaturüberblick*. Zeitschrift für Betriebswirtschaft. (79):11. 1309-1329, p. 1321.

Finally, appropriate voting rules can serve to safeguard the decision-making process. Without doubt, regulators must make decisions at some point, if consensus does not emerge from deliberative activities. This ultimately leads to the question of how should they decide or what decision rule to employ which, in turn, has important implications for perceptions of equality and fairness.[622] From this follows that power sharing as a procedural safeguard can be achieved through an appropriate voting rule. Ideally, a voting requirement should be a high-level requirement to enhance the reliability and acceptance of standards adopted. A supermajority voting rule, therefore, helps to alleviate some of the concerns of a bare majority of stakeholders imposing their views on the minority: it reduces "[...] the likelihood that any single perspective can dominate."[623]

Bearing in mind that at least five members of the IASB have a background as practising auditors and at least three as preparers, the IASB has been criticized that "[...] auditors and preparers can be confident that their concerns will be fully taken into consideration. However, this is not the case with the users."[624] As a consequence, it "raises the danger that the views of minorities will be overridden, with negative effects on the standard's acceptability."[625] This statement implicitly assumes that the interests of auditors and preparers are not in conflict, for a different perspective, see Georgia Saemann.[626] More importantly, the voting mechanism was changed in 2005. Currently, a vote of 9 of the 14 IASB members is required to approve an exposure draft, a final standard or interpretation. As such, preparers and auditors no longer have a qualifying majority.

Review / changing mechanism

The fifth and final procedural safeguard pertains to the existence of review or changing mechanisms. It has been argued that reversibility seems indispensable given that decision-making processes are imperfect; in the context of accounting regulation they involve value judgments and do not always result in strictly logical conclusions. To cope with this, the IASCF/IASB agreed that new IFRS, ma-

622 Fields, Thomas D. and King, Ronald R. (1996). *Voting Rules for the FASB*. Journal of Accounting, Auditing & Finance. (11):1. 99-117and Dahl, Robert Alan (1998). *On democracy*. New Haven; London: Yale University Press, p. 39.

623 Tweedie, David (2007). *IASB Chairman Addresses European Parliament*.

624 Flower, John (2004). *European financial reporting – Adapting to a changing world*. New York: Palgrave MacMillan, p. 148.

625 Ibid., p. 148.

626 For a different perspective see Saemann, Georgia (1999). *An Examination of Comment Letters Filed in the U.S. Financial Accounting Standard-Setting Process by Institutional Interest Groups*. Abacus. (35):1. 1-28, p. 6.

jor amendments to IFRS, and major interpretations will be subject to an *ex post* review after at least two full years of implementation to assess any unexpected costs or implementation problems encountered. Besides, the IASB can decide to re-disclose an ED if the comments by its stakeholders indicate strong opposition. This has been the case with the development of IFRS 3: Business Combinations.[627]

In addition, institutions that take the process of deliberation and the reconsideration of decisions seriously should "[…] also seek more flexible procedures for constitutional amendments […]."[628] In order to meet the claim to continued organizational flexibility, the IASCF reviews its constitution every 5 years, whereby changes must be subjected to a public review process. These basic requirements with regard to the final standard, as well as governance arrangement, provide reasonable means to challenge the organizational legitimacy of the IASB.

Table 16 contrasts the procedural characteristics of legitimate authority with the institutional features that were found in 'reality' and summarizes the evaluation of them.

627 Meier, André Rolf (2009). Abbildung von Unternehmensverbindungen im Konzernabschluss: eine Analyse der Business-Combinations-Projekte von IASB und FASB, Der Andere Verlag, p. 4.

628 Gutmann, Amy and Thompson, Dennis (2004). *Why deliberative democracy?* Princeton, N.J.; Oxford: Princeton University Press, pp. 59-60.

Procedural characteristics	Institutional features	Assessment
Effective participation	Broad input (participation) as part of the IASB's due process (comment letters, public hearings, field tests); Interpretations Committee; Advisory Council; liaison activities with national standard setters	+++
Enlightened understanding	Feedback statements, public hearings and field tests that ensure a dialogical process and evidence-based reasoning	++
Representation	Formalistic: *ex-ante*: IAS Regulation, *ex-post:* procedural safeguards	+++
	Descriptive: geographical and professional requirements for Trustees and IASB members	
	Substantive representation: feedback statements, comply-or-explain rule, basis for conclusion	
Procedural safeguards		
(1) Transparency	Publication of project time-tables, comment letters and discussions, public meetings	+++
(2) Final control of the agenda	Consultative process for agenda items and priorities	++
(3) Bias suppression / neutrality	Systematic and sound rule making; 'comply or explain' rule; self-commitment, funding rules and publication of funding sources	+++
(4) Power sharing / Divided authority	IASCF - IASB divided authority (responsibilities), voting rules, EU endorsement process, funding	+++
(5) Review / Changing mechanism	Possibility to re-disclose EDs, post-implementation review, mandated five-yearly constitutional review	+++

Table 16: Legitimacy assessment: +++ High / ++ Middle / + Low

5 Conclusion

Accounting standards are used for different purposes: tax, financial or managerial. Accordingly, accounting rules can and do change with the purpose, which makes a stable consensus about alternative accounting options impossible. From this follows that accounting standard setting is a political exercise because it reflects disagreement caused by diversity of condition and opinion. Without doubt, the differences among stakeholder groups increase if collective decision problems involve value judgments and/or are transposed to a broader audience, for example from national to international regulation. Previously, national governments were mainly responsible for setting accounting rules. Globalization trends, however, resulted in a shift of the institutional and organizational context of national rule making. In Europe, accounting standards are nowadays developed by a privately organized body – the IASB – and implemented into European law through a specific endorsement process. This alteration of responsibilities, shared among public and private actors, creates challenges to the idea of *legitimate* democratic decision making, most notably to the conception of participation and representation (accountability). However, it has been shown that the related criticism is strongly dependent on the context: the shift in actor involvement and their respective responsibilities need to be analyzed along the overall regulatory process. The structural analysis of the accounting procedures in Europe showed that the role and influence of nation states does not just dissolve, but shifts along the regulatory process, which ranges from agenda setting to promoting compliance and responding to noncompliance (enforcement).

The first objective of this study was to show how transnational governance modes characterized by non-state regulatory organizations can be linked to a democratic conception of legitimate political authority. Traditionally, research in accounting regulation employed an economic perspective and assumed that the acceptance of accounting rules is motivated by self-interest. In contrast, this study emphasizes the normative ideals which constitute legitimate rule making, and focuses on stakeholders' perceptions of fair procedures. Based on different models of democracy, more specifically, their underlying desirable properties, procedural characteristics were developed that allow the establishment of legitimate decision making beyond the nation-state. These procedural norms include: effective participation, deliberation and representation. Traditionally, accountability as one dimension of representation is provided through electoral mechanisms. The regulatory shift in accounting standard setting, however, does not allow the use of such an accountability model. Instead, procedural safeguards (transparency, final control of the agenda, bias suppression, power sharing and review mechanisms) were suggested in order to ensure accountability.

It has been argued that the IAS Regulation profoundly changed the regulatory landscape that governs the setting of accounting standards: from national to transnational, with a mix of private and public actors. Accordingly, the second objective of this study was to assess the institutional framework which emerged out of a need to harmonize accounting within Europe against the normative procedural characteristics. Any evaluation of governance modes employing normative ideals, however, needs to keep in mind that these criteria are goals toward which to strive, not standards that can be fully met. From an institutional 'supply-side' perspective, the analysis showed the IASC Foundation's achievements in establishing legitimate procedures: it provides ample opportunities to participate, emphasizes a deliberative due process, and strives to ensure an overall geographic and professional balance within its operating bodies. Overall, these institutional features are conducive to the public's confidence in the work of the IASB. The ongoing success of the IASB as a global standard setter can be seen as an indication that the organization has established legitimate collective decision-making structures. From a European perspective, the examination of private standard setting (IASCF-IASB) as well as public rule making (EU endorsement process) revealed that the EU is well positioned to develop legitimate accounting procedures. In particular, the European endorsement process can act as an additional procedural safeguard; it ensures that the standards prepared by the IASB will also be in Europe's interest. In addition, the endorsement process provides a counterbalance to the notion of 'lost national sovereignty'.

This study showed that democratic theory can guide the construction of a legitimate procedure. The picture nevertheless remains incomplete, because it attempts to answer the question of how people decide whether a procedure is fair *only* from a 'supply perspective'. The weakness of this approach is its exclusive focus on formal organizational structures and its inadequate recognition of the complementary need to observe the political system's actual performance: how does the IASB actually relate to its constituents, what role do deliberations in fact play in the development of a standard, or the substantive character of representation. The strategy of this study to partly circumvent this shortcoming was to analyze constituents' comment letters during the last constitutional review. In doing so, the analysis revealed how constituents evaluated the existing structures and processes, their limitations and potential improvements. Nevertheless, Botzem and Quack correctly observe that "[...] the successful diffusion of due process as a means of mediating contest and conflict within the international regulatory field of financial reporting deserves more detailed analysis."[629] The analysis of the constitutional review revealed that different procedural characteristics seem to be universally acceptable, but the importance constituents placed on various issues differed. Against this background, future research could focus on the diverse dimensions of a legitimate procedure and examine the importance and trade-offs of various procedural characteristics to the assessment of a fair procedure or the relationship of these procedural norms to one another.

Another question that arises for a democratic theory of legitimate authority is whether considerations of the justice or injustice of the outcome prevail over the fairness of the process of collective decision making. Charles Beitz makes it abundantly clear that no "[...] justification is likely to be persuasive if it excludes considerations about results entirely. The political outcomes to be expected from the operation of a set of procedures are simply too important to be left out of account."[630] In addition, Robert Folger notes that "[...], distributive and procedural justice tend to go together in people's minds (to be confounded) because people make inferences about the fairness of procedures based on the perceived fairness of outcomes."[631] To rephrase and reiterate, the fairness of a procedure is also linked to whether the procedures produce fair outcomes because if "[...] a procedure consistently produces unfair outcomes [it] will eventually be viewed as unfair itself."[632] Accordingly, distributive justice literature could be used to analyze the standard-setting process from an output perspective.

---

629 Botzem, Sebastian and Quack, Sigrid (2008). *Contested rules and shifting boundaries: International standard-setting in accounting. Transnational governance: institutional dynamics of regulation.* Djelic, Marie-Laure and Sahlin-Andersson, KerstinCambridge University Press, p. 284.

630 Beitz, Charles R. (1989). *Political equality: an essay in democratic theory.* Princeton: Princeton University Press, p. 95. It seems reasonable to assume the existence of an interaction effect of outcome favorability and procedural fairness. Joel Brockner elucidates the nature of interaction effect "[...] high procedural fairness reduces the effect of outcome favorability on people's support, relative to when procedural fairness is low." Brockner, Joel (2002). *Making Sense of Procedural Fairness: How High Procedural Fairness Can Reduce or Heighten the Influence of Outcome Favorability.* The Academy of Management Review. (27):1. 58-76, p. 60.

631 Folger, Robert (1996). *Distributive and procedural justice: Multifaceted meanings and interrelations.* Social Justice Research. (9):4. 395-416, p. 404.

632 Tyler, Tom R. (2006). *Why people obey the law.* Princeton: Princeton University Press, p. 164.

Appendix

Step	Date	Action
(1)	March – April 2008	Trustees developed preliminary proposals and document for Constitution Review
(2)	May – June 2008	Trustees met with interested parties to discuss proposals before publication of document on first part.
(3)	June 19, 2008	Trustees held round-table meeting in London to consult with interested parties prior to publication of consultation document.
(4)	June – August 2008	Publication of consultation document setting out the proposals concerning public accountability and IASB size/geographic diversity – Part 1 of the Constitution Review. Trustees to meet with interested parties to discuss proposals on Part 1. Comment period to end in August or September.
(5)	September 2008	Constitution Committee developed proposals to present to full Trustees, based upon analysis of comment letters and other input on Part 1 proposals.
(6)	October 2008	Trustees considered the proposed changes arising from Part 1 of the Constitution Review at their meeting in Beijing. Trustees agreed to consult further and consider the proposals at their meeting in January 2009.
(7)	December 2008	Trustees issued a discussion document seeking comments on the remainder of the Constitution, thereby commencing Part 2 of the Constitution Review. Comments were sought by March 31, 2009.
(8)	October 2008 – January 2009	Trustees met with interested parties to discuss Part 2 of the Constitution Review.
(9)	January 2009	Trustees reviewed the final comments received regarding Part 1 of the Constitution Review and approved the changes to the Constitution. Completion of Part 1 of the Constitution Review. All changes came into effect on February 1, 2009.

Table 17: Constitutional review: Part one timetable

Constitutional review: Part one questionnaire	
Q1	Do you support the creation of a link to a Monitoring Group in order to create a direct link of public accountability to official institutions?
Q2	The proposals contemplate a Monitoring Group comprising representatives of seven public authorities and international organizations with a link to public authorities. While recognizing that the Monitoring Group is an autonomous body, the Trustees would welcome comments regarding the Monitoring Group's membership and whether other organizations accountable to public authorities and with an interest in the functioning of capital and other financial markets should be considered for membership.
Q3	The Trustees will remain the body primarily responsible for the governance of the organization and the oversight of the IASB. Their responsibility to a Monitoring Group will enable regulatory and other authorities responsible for the adoption of IFRSs to review the Trustees' fulfillment of their constitutional duties. Does the formulation of the Monitoring Group's mandate and the Trustees' reporting responsibilities, as described in the proposed Section 19, appropriately provide that link, while maintaining the operational independence of the IASC Foundation and the IASB?
Q4	Given the proposed creation of a Monitoring Group, would there be a continued need for the Trustee Appointments Advisory Group in the selection of Trustees? If so, what should be the role and composition of the Trustees Appointments Advisory Group? The Trustees would welcome any additional comments related to the Monitoring Group proposal.
Q5	Do you support the principle behind expanding the IASB's membership to 16 members in order to ensure its diversity, its ability to consult, liaise and communicate properly across the world, and its legitimacy?
Q6	Do you agree with the geographical formulation suggested by the Trustees?
Q7	The Trustees are suggesting that the Constitution should provide flexibility on the matter of part-time membership. Do you support that proposal?

Table 18: Constitutional review: Part one questionnaire

Step	Date	Action
(1)	January – March 2010	Trustees confirmed the constitutional changes and announced the conclusion of the Constitutional Review. All changes came into effect from March 1, 2010. Completion of Part 2 of Constitution Review and publication of revised Constitution.
(2)	October – November 2009	Trustees consider the comments received at the consultation and round-table meetings. The Constitution Committee to draw up a report for the Trustees' consideration at their meeting in January 2010.
(3)	September – October 2009	Round tables to be held in London, New York and Tokyo. Trustees also meet interested parties to discuss the second part of the review.
(4)	August 2009	Part II Constitution Review consultation document to be published, with 90-day consultation period.
(5)	July 2009	Trustees consider the comments received following the December 2008 consultation and propose changes to the Constitution for consultation. The consultation document to be issued in August 2009.
(6)	March 31, 2009	Closing date for comments on the second part of the Constitution Review.

Table 19: Constitutional review: Part two timetable

Constitutional review: Part two questionnaire	
Q1	The Trustees seek views on the proposal to change the name of the organization to the 'International Financial Reporting Standards Foundation', which will be abbreviated to 'IFRS Foundation'. The Trustees also seek views on the proposal to mirror this change by renaming the International Accounting Standards Board (IASB) as the International Financial Reporting Standards Board, which will be abbreviated to 'IFRS Board'.
Q2	The Trustees seek views on the proposal to replace all references to 'accounting standards' with 'financial reporting standards' throughout the Constitution. This would accord with the name change of the Foundation, the Board and the formal standards developed by the IASB—International Financial Reporting Standards (IFRSs). Do you support this change?
Q3	The Trustees seek views on their proposal to change section 2 as follows: The objectives of the IASC IFRS Foundation are:
a	to develop, in the public interest, a single set of high quality, understandable, and enforceable and globally accepted accounting financial reporting standards that require high quality, transparent and comparable information in financial statements and other financial reporting to help participants in the world's capital markets and other users make economic decisions;
b	to promote the use and rigorous application of those standards;
c	in fulfilling the objectives associated with (a) and (b), to take account of emerging economies and, as appropriate, the special needs of small and medium-sized entities and emerging economies; and
d	to bring about convergence of national accounting standards and International Accounting Standards and International Financial Reporting Standards (IFRSs, being the standards and interpretations issued by the IFRS Board) to high quality solutions.
Q4	The governance of the IASC IFRS Foundation shall primarily rest with the Trustees and such other governing organs as may be appointed by the Trustees in accordance with the provisions of this Constitution. A Monitoring Board (described further in sections 18–23) shall provide a formal link between the Trustees and public authorities. The Trustees shall use their best endeavors to ensure that the requirements of this Constitution are observed; however, they are empowered to may make minor variations in the interest of feasibility of operation if such variations are agreed by 75 per cent of all the Trustees.

Constitutional review: Part two questionnaire	
Q5	The Trustees seek views on the proposal to amend section 6 of the Constitution as follows to include one Trustee from each of Africa and South America: All Trustees shall be required to show a firm commitment to the IFRS IASC Foundation and the IFRS Board IASB as a high quality global standard setter, to be financially knowledgeable, and to have an ability to meet the time commitment. Each Trustee shall have an understanding of, and be sensitive to, the challenges associated with the adoption and application of high quality global accounting financial reporting standards developed for use in the world's capital markets and by other users. The mix of Trustees shall broadly reflect the world's capital markets and diversity of geographical and professional backgrounds. The Trustees shall be required to commit themselves formally to acting in the public interest in all matters. In order to ensure a broad international basis, there shall be: (a) six Trustees appointed from the Asia/Oceania region; (b) six Trustees appointed from Europe; (c) six Trustees appointed from North America; and (d) one Trustee appointed from Africa; (e) one Trustee appointed from South America; and (f) two Trustees appointed from any area, subject to maintaining overall geographical balance.
Q6	The Trustees seek views on the proposal to amend section 10 of the Constitution as follows to allow up to two Trustees to be appointed as vice-chairmen of the Trustees. The Chairman of the Trustees, and up to two Vice-Chairmen, shall be appointed by the Trustees from among their own number, subject to the approval of the Monitoring Board. With the agreement of the Trustees, regardless of prior service as a Trustee, the appointee may serve as the Chairman or a Vice-Chairman for a term of three years, renewable once, from the date of appointment as Chairman or Vice-Chairman.
Q7	The Trustees seek views on the proposal to make no specific amendments to sections 13 and 15, but to address the valid and important concerns raised by commentators by way of enhanced accountability, consultation, reporting and ongoing internal due process improvements. (effectiveness of oversight activities)
Q8	Section 28 would be amended as follows: The IASB IFRS Board will, in consultation with the Trustees, be expected to establish and maintain liaison with national standard setters and other official bodies concerned with an interest in standard setting in order to assist in the development of IFRSs and to promote the convergence of national accounting standards and International Accounting Standards and International Financial Reporting Standards IFRSs.
Q9	The Trustees seek views on the proposal to amend section 30 of the Constitution as follows to permit the appointment of up to two Board members to act as vice chairmen of the IASB. The Trustees shall appoint one of the full-time members as Chairman of the IASB IFRS Board, who shall also be the Chief Executive of the IASC IFRS Foundation. Up to two of the full-time members of the IASB IFRS Board may also be designated by the Trustees as a Vice-Chairman, whose role shall be to chair meetings of the IASB IFRS Board in the absence of the Chairman or to represent the Chairman in external contacts in unusual

Constitutional review: Part two questionnaire	
	circumstances (such as illness). The appointment of the Chairman and the designation as Vice-Chairman shall be for such term as the Trustees decide. The title of Vice-Chairman would not imply that the individual member (or members) concerned is (or are) the Chairman-elect.
Q10	The Trustees seek views on the proposal to amend section 31 to allow for altered terms of appointment for IASB members appointed after July 2, 2009. The proposed amendment is to allow for Board members to be appointed initially for a term of five years, with the option for renewal for a further three-year term. This will not apply to the Chairman and Vice-Chairman, who may be appointed for a second five-year term. The Chairman or Vice-Chairman may not serve for longer than ten consecutive years. The proposed amendments to section 31 are as follows: Members of the IASB IFRS Board appointed before July 2, 2009 shall be appointed for a term of up to five years, renewable once for a further term of five years. Members of the IFRS Board appointed after July 2, 2009 shall be appointed initially for a term of up to five years. Terms are renewable once for a further term of three years, with the exception of the Chairman and a Vice-Chairman. The Chairman and a Vice-Chairman may serve a second term of five years, but may not exceed ten years in total length of service as a member of the IFRS Board.
Q11	The Trustees seek views on the proposal to insert in section 37 (to become section 38) of the Constitution an additional subsection as follows to allow the Trustees, in exceptional circumstances, to authorize a shorter due process period. Authority would be given only after the IASB had made a formal request. The due process periods could be reduced but never dispensed with completely. The IASB IFRS Board shall:
a	…
b	…
c	in exceptional circumstances, and only after formally requesting and receiving prior approval from the Trustees, reduce, but not eliminate, the period of public comment on an exposure draft below that described as the minimum in the Due Process Handbook.
Q12	The Trustees seek views on the proposal to amend section 37(d) (to become section 38) of the Constitution as follows to expressly provide that the IASB must consult the Trustees and the SAC when developing its technical agenda. The IASB IFRS Board shall: (d) have full discretion in developing and pursuing the technical agenda of the IASB IFRS Board, after consulting the Trustees (consistently with section 15(c)) and the SAC (consistently with section 44(a)), and over project assignments on technical matters: in organizing the conduct of its work, the IASB IFRS Board may outsource detailed research or other work to national standard setters or other organizations.

Constitutional review: Part two questionnaire	
Q13	Trustees seek views on the proposal to make no amendment to sections 44 and 45 (renumbered as 45 and 46), which are the provisions relating to the SAC, at this time.
Q14	The Trustees seek views on the proposal to amend section 48 by removing specific staff titles and replacing them with the term 'the senior staff management team'. Accordingly section 49 should be deleted. The Trustees also seek comment on the proposal to update the Constitution by removing all historical references that relate to when the organization was established in 2001.

Table 20: Constitutional review: Part two questionnaire

MEMORANDUM OF UNDERSTANDING TO STRENGTHEN THE INSTITUTIONAL FRAMEWORK OF THE INTERNATIONAL ACCOUNTING STANDARDS COMMITTEE FOUNDATION

PREAMBLE

The European Commission, the International Organization of Securities Commissions, the Financial Services Agency of Japan, and United States Securities and Exchange Commission (collectively referred to as "capital markets authorities" for the purposes of this Memorandum of Understanding), which together represent authorities responsible for setting the form and content of financial reporting in the majority of the world's capital markets, and the Trustees of the International Accounting Standards Committee Foundation ("IASCF"):

Considering that capital markets authorities are generally charged with the development and administration of accounting standards;

Considering that capital markets authorities historically have looked to private or stand-alone bodies to assist in establishing accounting standards;

Considering that capital markets authorities generally oversee national accounting standard setters to ensure that they are capable of improving the accuracy, transparency, comparability and effectiveness of financial reporting and the protection of investor interests;

Considering that accounting standard-setters should strive to keep their standards current to reflect changes in the business environment, as well as consider promptly emerging accounting issues and changing business practices;

Recognizing that the International Accounting Standards Board ("IASB") is a stand-alone international accounting standard-setter committed to developing, in the public interest, a single set of high quality, understandable and enforceable global standards, also known as International Financial Reporting Standards ("IFRS");

Recognizing that the IASB develops accounting standards for use by companies from developed and developing economies;

Recognizing that IFRS are increasingly used around the world, yet the IASCF has no formal relationship to capital markets authorities;

Asserting that establishing a formal relationship between capital markets authorities and the IASCF will facilitate the ability of these authorities to effectively discharge their mandates relating to investor protection, market integrity and capital formation;

Recognizing that the IASB is overseen by an independent body, the IASCF, which is charged with serving the public interest;

1

Desiring to further enhance the public accountability of the IASCF to support the increasing use of IFRS around the world;

Recognizing that the IASCF has changed its constitution to recognize the role of the IASCF Monitoring Board in reinforcing the public accountability of the IASCF Trustees;

Affirming and supporting the independence of the IASCF in setting high-quality accounting standards, through the IASB, for use around the world, and

Desiring to help strengthen this independence by supporting the establishment of a non-voluntary, transparent and stable funding platform for the IASCF;

Have reached the following understanding:

ARTICLE I: DEFINITIONS

For purposes of this Memorandum of Understanding ("MOU"),

1. "IASCF Monitoring Board" or "Monitoring Board" means a body established by agreement among its members, the mission and operation of which are described in its charter. Its relationship to the IASCF is described in this MOU. Its initial members are:

   - The European Commission;
   - The Emerging Markets Committee and the Technical Committee of the International Organization of Securities Commissions ("IOSCO");
   - The Financial Services Agency of Japan; and
   - The US Securities and Exchange Commission.

   The Basel Committee on Banking Supervision shall participate in the IASCF Monitoring Board as an observer with voice but no vote.

2. "IASCF Constitution" means the __________ 2009 Constitution of the IASCF, as amended from time to time.[1]

3. "Trustees" means the Trustees of the IASCF, whose roles are described in the IASCF Constitution.

[1] Located at www.iasb.gov.

ARTICLE II: GENERAL PROVISIONS

4. The IASCF Monitoring Board and the Trustees agree to collaborate in the manner specified in this MOU.

5. This MOU does not alter the terms of the relationship between the Trustees and the IASB. This MOU also does not alter the Trustees' responsibilities as described in the IASCF Constitution.

ARTICLE III: PURPOSE AND DUTIES OF THE IASCF MONITORING BOARD

6. **Purpose of the IASCF Monitoring Board**

   The primary purpose of the IASCF Monitoring Board is to serve as a mechanism for formal interaction between capital markets authorities and the IASCF, thereby facilitating the ability of capital market authorities that allow or require the use of IFRS in their jurisdictions to effectively discharge their mandates relating to investor protection, market integrity and capital formation. The IASCF Monitoring Board will help ensure the public accountability of the IASCF by monitoring and reinforcing the public interest oversight function of the IASCF, as well as to promote the continued development of IFRS as a high-quality set of global accounting standards.

7. **Duties of the IASCF Monitoring Board**

   The principal responsibilities of the IASCF Monitoring Board are to:

   i) Participate in the Trustee nominations process;

   ii) Approve Trustee nominees;

   iii) Review the adequacy and appropriateness of Trustee arrangements for financing the IASB;

   iv) Review the Trustees' oversight of the IASB's standard setting process, in particular with respect to its due process arrangements;

   v) Confer with the Trustees regarding their responsibilities, in particular in relation to the regulatory, legal and policy developments that are pertinent to the IASCF's oversight of the IASB; and

   vi) Refer matters of broad public interest related to financial reporting for consideration by the IASB through the IASCF.

8. Trustee Selection

A. Criteria for the selection or reappointment of a Trustee are those contained in the IASCF Constitution.

B. In accordance with paragraph 7 of the IASCF Constitution, the Trustees shall establish procedures to invite applications for Trustee positions, including advertising vacant positions. These procedures shall be agreed by the IASCF Monitoring Board. The selection process will be administered by the Trustees in a transparent manner.

C. The Trustees will propose a candidate for each open Trustee position. The Trustees shall provide the reasoning behind their choice of candidate. The IASCF Monitoring Board may submit names for the Trustees' consideration.

D. Each Trustee candidate must be approved by the IASCF Monitoring Board.

E. The Trustees will nominate a Chair from among their members, subject to the approval of the IASCF Monitoring Board.

9. IASB Oversight, Due Process and Funding

A. The IASCF Monitoring Board will confer with the Trustees regarding their oversight responsibilities in the following principal areas:

i. procedures relating to the due process and general oversight of the IASB;

ii. the IASB's agenda-setting process and work program, including the adequacy of the IASB's resources in the light of its work program;

iii. the adequacy of the IASB's procedures to ensure prompt and fair consideration of changes to IFRS accounting principles and standards so as to take into account emerging accounting issues and changing business practices;

iv. the IASB's due process, including the process for carrying out impact assessments and cost-benefit analyses;

v. the IASB's efforts to improve the accuracy and effectiveness of financial reporting and to protect investors; and

vi. the adequacy and appropriateness of the sources of funding and any other revenue arrangements of the IASCF, as well as the annual budget of the IASCF.

4

B. The IASCF Monitoring Board may refer accounting issues to, and will confer regarding these issues with, the Trustees and the IASB Chair.

i The Trustees will work with IASB to ensure these issues are addressed in a timely manner.

ii If the IASB determines that consideration of the issue(s) identified by the IASCF Monitoring Board is not advisable or that the issue(s) cannot be resolved within the time frame suggested by the Monitoring Board, the Trustees should:

1. call on the IASB to undertake all reasonable efforts to consider issue(s) in a manner that is consistent with the public interest, taking into account the protection of investors.
2. call on the IASB to explain its position through the Trustees regarding the IASB's position on the issue(s); and
3. promptly notify the IASCF Monitoring Board of the IASB's position.

ARTICLE IV: COMMUNICATION BETWEEN THE IASCF MONITORING BOARD AND THE TRUSTEES

10. The Trustees shall communicate with the IASCF Monitoring Board regarding their work, including in the following ways:

A. The Trustees shall report on the work of the IASCF annually in writing;

B. The Trustees shall meet regularly with the IASCF Monitoring Board to discuss its work. By common agreement of the two Chairpersons, other organizations with public policy responsibilities related to financial reporting may be invited to participate in these meetings on an *ad hoc* basis;

C. Upon request of the IASCF Monitoring Board, the Trustees, the Chairman of the Trustees, or the Chairpersons of the Trustees and the IASB shall meet with the IASCF Monitoring Board regarding any area of work of either the IASCF or the IASB. Without limitation, these discussions may cover the status of any matter that the IASCF Monitoring Board has referred for timely consideration by the IASCF and/or the IASB.

D. The IASCF Monitoring Board members shall update the IASCF and/or its staff on significant events in the regulatory environment (including those that relate to audit requirements and practices), or other areas to assist the IASCF in carrying out its responsibilities.

E. From time to time, the IASCF Monitoring Board and the Trustees shall discuss the functioning of this MOU and discuss whether changes are appropriate. Changes must be approved by a consensus among all signatories to this MOU.

ARTICLE V: TERMINATION

11. The IASCF Monitoring Board or the Trustees may terminate this MOU upon 60 days written notice.

in advance and ratified

Signed at London, this 1st day of April, 2009

Charlie McCreevy, Commissioner
For the European Commission

Gerrit Zalm, Chairman of the Trustees
For the International Accounting Standards Committee Foundation

Jane Diplock, Chairperson of the Executive Committee
For the International Organization of Securities Commissions

Takafumi Sato, Commissioner
For the Financial Services Agency of Japan

Christopher Cox, Chairman
For the United States Securities and Exchange Commission

Figure 6: Memorandum of Understanding

International Accounting Standards Committee Foundation: Criteria for IASB Members	
1	**Demonstrated technical competence and knowledge of financial accounting and reporting.** All members of the IASB, regardless of whether they are from the accounting profession, preparers, users or academics, should have demonstrated a high level of knowledge and technical competence in financial accounting and reporting. The credibility of the IASB and its individual members and the effectiveness and efficiency of the organization will be enhanced with members who have such knowledge and skills.
2	**Ability to analyze.** IASB members should have demonstrated the ability to analyze issues and consider the implications of that analysis for the decision-making process.
3	**Communication skills.** Effective oral and written communication skills are necessary. These skills include the ability to communicate effectively in private meetings with IASB members, in public meetings, and in written materials such as financial reporting standards, speeches, articles, memos and external correspondence. Communication skills also include the ability to listen to and consider the views of others. While a working knowledge of English is necessary, there should not be discrimination in selection against those for whom English is not their first language.
4	**Judicious decision making.** IASB members should be capable of considering varied viewpoints, weighing the evidence presented in an impartial fashion, and reaching well-reasoned and supportable decisions in a timely fashion.
5	**Awareness of the financial reporting environment.** High quality financial reporting will be affected by the financial, business and economic environment. IASB members should have an understanding of the global economic environment in which the IASB operates. This global awareness should include awareness of business and financial reporting issues that are relevant to, and affect the quality of, transparent financial reporting and disclosure in the various capital markets worldwide, including those using IFRSs.
6	**Ability to work in a collegial atmosphere.** Members should be able to show respect, tact and consideration for one another's views and those of third parties. Members must be able to work with one another in reaching consensus views based on the IASB's objective of

	International Accounting Standards Committee Foundation: Criteria for IASB Members
	developing high quality and transparent financial reporting. Members must be able to put the objective of the IASB above individual philosophies and interests.
7	**Integrity, objectivity and discipline**. The credibility of members should be demonstrated through their integrity and objectivity. This includes intellectual integrity as well as integrity in dealing with fellow IASB members and others. Members should demonstrate an ability to be objective in reaching decisions. Members also should demonstrate an ability to show rigorous discipline and carry a demanding workload.
8	**Commitment to the IFRS Foundation's mission and public interest**. Members should be committed to achieving the objective of the IFRS Foundation of establishing international financial reporting standards that are of high quality, comparable, and transparent. A candidate for the IASB should also be committed to serving the public interest through a private standard-setting process.

Table 21: ***Criteria for selecting IASB members***

References

Abbott, W. Kenneth and Snidal, Duncan (2009). *The Governance Triangle: Regulatory Standards Institutions and the Shadow of the State. The Politics of Global Regulation.* Mattli, Walter and Woods, Ngaire. Princeton: Princeton University Press.

Accounting Regulatory Committee (2002). Rules of procedure for the Accounting Regulatory Committee.

Alicia, Adsera (2003). *Are You Being Served? Political Accountability and Quality of Government.* Journal of Law Economics & Organization. (19):2. 445-490.

Arendt, Hannah (2006). *Between past and future: eight exercises in political thought.* New York ; London: Penguin Books.

Armstrong, Marshall S. (1977). *The politics of establishing accounting standards.* Journal of Accountancy. (143):2. 76-79.

Arrow, Kenneth Joseph (1970). *Social choice and individual values.* New Haven: Yale U. P.

Azzi, Assaad E. (1993). *Group representation and procedural justice in multigroup decision-making bodies.* Social Justice Research. (6):2. 195-218.

Ball, Ray (2006). *International Financial Reporting Standards (IFRS): pros and cons for investors.* Accounting & Business Research. (36):5-27.

Ballmann, Alexander, Epstein, David and O'Halloran, Sharyn (2002). *Delegation, Comitology, and the Separation of Powers in the European Union.* International Organization. (56):3. 551-574.

Beaver, William H. and Demski, Joel S. (1974). *The Nature of Financial Accounting Objectives: A Summary and Synthesis.* Journal of Accounting Research. (12):170-187.

Beetham, David (2002). *The Legitimation of Power.* Basingstoke: Palgrave Macmillan.

Beitz, Charles R. (1989). *Political equality: an essay in democratic theory.* Princeton: Princeton University Press.

Bennett, John G. (1979). *A Note on Locke's Theory of Tacit Consent.* The Philosophical Review. (88):2. 224-234.

Beresford, Dennis R. (1993). Frustrations of a Standards Setter. Accounting HorizonsAmerican Accounting Association. 7. 70-76.

Bernstein, Steven and Cashore, Benjamin (2007). *Can non-state global governance be legitimate? An analytical framework.* Regulation & Governance. (1):4. 347-371.

Bingham, Lisa Blomgren, Nabatchi, Tina and O'Leary, Rosemary (2005). *The New Governance: Practices and Processes for Stakeholder and Citizen Participation in the Work of Government.* Public Administration Review. (65):5. 547-558.

Birch, Anthony Harold (1971). *Representation.* London: Pall Mall Press.

Birch, Anthony Harold (1993). *The concepts and theories of modern democracy.* London: Routledge.

Black, Julia (2008). *Constructing and contesting legitimacy and accountability in polycentric regulatory regimes.* Regulation & Governance. (2):2. 137-164.

Bodansky, Daniel (1999). *The Legitimacy of International Governance: A Coming Challenge for International Environmental Law?* The American Journal of International Law. (93):3. 596-624.

Bohman, James (2000). *Public deliberation: pluralism, complexity, and democracy.* Cambridge, Mass [u.a.]: MIT Press.

Botzem, Sebastian and Quack, Sigrid (2008). *Contested rules and shifting boundaries: International standard-setting in accounting. Transnational governance: institutional dynamics of regulation.* Djelic, Marie-Laure and Sahlin-Andersson, Kerstin. New York: Cambridge University Press.

Botzem, Sebastian and Quack, Sigrid (2008). *Contested rules and shifting boundaries: International standard-setting in accounting. Transnational governance: institutional dynamics of regulation.* Djelic, Marie-Laure and Sahlin-Andersson, KerstinCambridge University Press.

Brackney, Kennard S. and Witmer, Philip R. (2005). *The European Union's Role in International Standards Setting – Will Bumps in the Road to Convergence affect the SEC's Plans?* CPA Journal. (75):11. 18-27.

Bradley, Curtis A. and Kelley, Judith G. (2008). *The Concept of International Delegation.* Law and Contemporary Problems. (71):1. 1-36.

Brandsma, Gijs Jan and Blom-Hansen, Jens (2010). *The EU comitology system: What role for the Commission?* Public Administration. (88):2. 496-512.

Bratton, William (2007). *Private standards, public governance: a new look at the Financial Accounting Standard Board.* Boston College Law Review. (48):1. 5-53.

Brennan, Geoffrey and Hamlin, Alan (1999). *On Political Representation.* British Journal of Political Science. (29):1. 109-127.

Brockner, Joel (2002). *Making Sense of Procedural Fairness: How High Procedural Fairness Can Reduce or Heighten the Influence of Outcome Favorability.* The Academy of Management Review. (27):1. 58-76.

Brown, Alistair M. (2004). *The Milieu of the IASB.* Journal of American Academy of Business, Cambridge. (5):1/2. 385-390.
Brown, Lawrence D. and Feroz, Ehsan H. (1992). *Does the FASB listen to corporations?* Journal of Business Finance & Accounting. (19):5. 715-731.
Buchanan, Allen and Keohane, Robert O. (2006). *The Legitimacy of Global Governance Institutions.* Ethics & International Affairs. (20):4. 405-437.
Buckmaster, Dale, Saniga, Erwin and Tadesse, Soloman (1994). *Measuring the lobbying influence using the Financial Accounting Standards Board public record.* Journal of Economic & Social Measurement. (20):4. 331-356.
Camfferman, Kees and Zeff, Stephen (2007). *Financial Reporting and Global Capital Markets: a History of the International Accounting Standards Committee, 1973-2000.* Oxford: Oxford University Press.
Cassinelli, C. W. (1961). *Political Authority: Its Exercise and Possession.* The Western Political Quarterly. (14):3. 635-646.
Cearns, Kathryn (2008, Chairman of the Financial Reporting Committee (Institute of Chartered Accountants in England and Wales)). *Constitutional Review – Phase 1.* Round-table: Session 2 Part 2. (London, IASC Foundation):June. 1-24.
Chiapello, Eve and Medjad, Karim (2009). *An unprecedented privatisation of mandatory standard-setting: The case of European accounting policy.* Critical Perspectives on Accounting. (20):4. 448-468.
Chua, Wai Fong and Taylor, Stephen L. *The rise and rise of IFRS: An examination of IFRS diffusion.* Journal of Accounting and Public Policy. (27):6. 462-473.
Chua, Wai Fong and Taylor, Stephen L. (2008). *The rise and rise of IFRS: An examination of IFRS diffusion.* Journal of Accounting and Public Policy. (27):6. 462-473.
Cohen, Joshua (1989). *Deliberation and Democratic Legitimacy. The good polity : Normative analysis of the state.* Hamlin, Alan P. Oxford: Blackwell.
Committe, Bruce Edward (1990). *The delegation and privatization of financial accounting rulemaking authority in the United States of America.* Critical Perspectives on Accounting. (1):2. 145-166.
Cooper, David J. and Robson, Keith (2006). *Accounting, professions and regulation: Locating the sites of professionalization.* Accounting, Organizations and Society. (31):4-5. 415-444.
Council of the European Communities (1978). *Fourth Council Directive 78/660/EEC of 25 July 1978 based on Article 54 (3) (g) of the Treaty on the annual accounts of certain types of companies.*

Council of the European Communities (1983). *Seventh Council Directive 83/349/EEC of 13 June 1983 based on the Article 54 (3) (g) of the Treaty on consolidated accounts.*
Council of the European Communities (2001). *Standard rules of procedure – Council decision 1999/468/EC: Rules of procedure for the ... committee.*
Council of the European Communities (2002). *Regulation (EC) No 1606/2002 of the European Parliament and of the Council of 19 July 2002 on the application of international accounting standards.*
Council of the European Communities (2006). *Commission decision of July 14, 2006 setting up a Standards Advice Review Group to advise the Commission on the objectivity and neutrality of the European Financial Reporting Advisory Group's (EFRAG's) opinions.*
Council of the European Communities (2006). *Council decision of July 17, 2006 amending Decision 1999/468/EC laying down the procedures for the exercise of implementing powers conferred on the Commission.*
Cushing, Barry E. (1977). *On the Possibility of Optimal Accounting Principles.* The Accounting Review. (52):2. 308-321.
Cutler, Claire A., Ed. (2002). *Private international regimes and interfirm cooperation.* Cambridge: Cambridge University Press.
D'Arcy, Anne (2001). *Accounting classification and the international harmonisation debate--an empirical investigation.* Accounting, Organizations & Society. (26):4/5. 327-349.
Dahl, Robert A. (1999). *Can International Organizations be Democratic? A Skeptic's View. Democracy's edges Contemporary political theory.* Shapiro, Ian. Cambridge [u.a.]: Cambridge Univ. Press.
Dahl, Robert Alan (1979). *Procedural Democracy. Philosophy, politics and society: fifth series: a collection.* Laslett, Peter and Fishkin, James S. Oxford: Blackwell.
Dahl, Robert Alan (1994). *A Democratic Dilemma: System Effectiveness versus Citizen Participation.* Political Science Quarterly. (109):1. 23-34.
Dahl, Robert Alan (1998). *On democracy.* New Haven ; London: Yale University Press.
Dahl, Robert Alan (2006). *On political equality.* New Haven ; London: Yale University Press.
Davis, Lane (1964). *The Cost of Realism: Contemporary Restatements of Democracy.* The Western Political Quarterly. (17):1. 37-46.
Deakin, Edward B. (1989). *Rational Economic Behavior and Lobbying on Accounting Issues: Evidence from the Oil and Gas Industry.* Accounting Review. (64):1. 137.

Demski, Joel S. (1973). *The General Impossibility of Normative Accounting Standards*. Accounting Review. (48):4. 718-723.
Demski, Joel S. (1974). *Choice among Financial Reporting Alternatives*. The Accounting Review. (49):2. 221-232.
Diggle, Graham and Nobes, Christopher (1994). *European Rule-making in The Seventh Directive as a Case Study*. Accounting & Business Research. (24):96. 319-333.
Dingwerth, Klaus (2007). *The new transnationalism: transnational governance and democratic legitimacy* Palgrave Macmillan.
Dolan, Paul, Edlin, Richard , Tsuchiya, Aki and Wailoo, Allan (2007). *It ain't what you do, it's the way that you do it: Characteristics of procedural justice and their importance in social decision-making*. Journal of Economic Behavior & Organization. (64):1. 157-170.
Dolan, Paul, Edlin, Richard , Tsuchiya, Aki and Wailoo, Allan (2007). *It ain't what you do, it's the way that you do it: Characteristics of procedural justice and their importance in social decision-making*. Journal of Economic Behavior & Organization. (64):157-170.
Doupnik, Timothy S. (1987). *Evidence of International Harmonization of Financial Reporting*. International Journal of Accounting. (23):1. 47-67.
Dye, Ronald A. and Sunder, Shyam (2001). *Why Not Allow FASB and IASB Standards to Compete in the U.S.?* Accounting Horizons. (15):3. 257-271.
Easton, David (1975). *A Re-Assessment of the Concept of Political Support*. British Journal of Political Science. (5):4. 435-457.
Edmundson, William A. (2008). *Consent and its Counterfeits*. Available at: http://papers.ssrn.com/sol3/papers.cfm?abstract_id=1222922. 1-33.
Enevoldsen, Stig (Chairman, European Financial Reporting Advisory Group) (2008). Constitutional Review – Round-table meeting, Session 1 Part 2.
Enevoldsen, Stig (EFRAG) (2008). Constitutional Review – Round-table meeting, Session 1 Part 2.
Estlund, David M. (2008). *Democratic authority: a philosophical framework* Princeton, N.J. ; Oxford : Princeton University Press.
Esty, Daniel C. (2006). *Good Governance at the Supranational Scale: Globalizing Administrative Law*. Yale Law Journal. (115):7. 1490-1562.
European Commission (14 March 2008). Commission Services Working Paper on Governance Developments in the International Accounting Standards Board (IASB) and in the Intrernational Accounting Standards Committee Foundation (IASCF), 3rd Report.
European Commission (1995). *Accounting Harmonisation: A new strategy vis-a-vis international harmonisation*.

European Commission (2000). *EU Financial Reporting Strategy: the way forward.*

European Commission ([EC] 2002). *Regulation on the application of international accounting standards.*

Fearnley, Stella and Sunder, Shyam (2006). *Global reporting standards: the Esperanto of accounting.* Accountancy. (137):1353. 26-26.

Feroz, Ehsan Habib and Hagerman, Robert L. (1990). *Management Compensation, Insider Trading and Lobbying Choice: The Case of R&D.* Australian Journal of Management. (15):2. 297.

Fields, Thomas D. and King, Ronald R. (1996). *Voting Rules for the FASB.* Journal of Accounting, Auditing & Finance. (11):1. 99-117.

Fields, Thomas D., Lys, Thomas Z. and Vincent, Linda (2001). *Empirical research on accounting choice.* Journal of Accounting and Economics. (31):1-3. 255-307.

Finnis, John M. (1990). *Authority.* Authority. Raz, Joseph. New York: New York University Press.

Fishkin, James S. (1991). *Democracy and deliberation: new directions for democratic reform.* New Haven ; London: Yale University Press.

Fleckner, Andreas M. (2008). *FASB and IASB: Dependence Despite Independence.* Virginia Law & Business Review. (3):275-309.

Flower, John (2004). *European financial reporting – Adapting to a changing world.* New York: Palgrave MacMillan.

Folger, Robert (1996). *Distributive and procedural justice: Multifaceted meanings and interrelations.* Social Justice Research. (9):4. 395-416.

Francis, Jere R. (1987). *Lobbying against proposed accounting standards: The case of employers' pension accounting.* Journal of Accounting and Public Policy. (6):1. 35-57.

Franklin, Julian H. (1996). *Allegiance and Jurisdiction in Locke's Doctrine of Tacit Consent.* Political Theory. (24):3. 407-422.

Freeman, Jody (1997). *Collaborative governance in the administrative state.* UCLA Law Review. (45):1. 1-98.

Friedman, R. B. (1990). *On the concept of Authority in Political Philosophy. Authority.* Raz, Joseph. New York: New York University Press.

Gallagher, John (UBS – Global head of technical accounting). (2008). Constitutional Review – Round-table meeting, Session 2 Part 2.

Gangl, Amy (2003). *Procedural Justice Theory and Evaluations of the Lawmaking Process.* Political Behavior. (25):2. 119-149.

Gerboth, Dale L. (1973). *Research, Intuition, and Politics in Accounting Inquiry.* The Accounting Review. (48):3. 475-482.

Gorton, Donald E. (1991). *The SEC Decision Not to Support SFAS 19: A Case Study of the Effect of Lobbying on Standard Setting.* Accounting Horizons. (5):1. 29-41.

Grant, Ruth W. and Keohane, Robert O. (2005). *Accountability and Abuses of Power in World Politics.* The American Political Science Review. (99):1. 29-43.

Gray, John, Ed. (1991). *Mill, John Stuart: On liberty and other essays. The world's classics.* Oxford: Oxford Univerity Press.

Green, Donald P. and Shapiro, Ian (1994). *Pathologies of rational choice theory : a critique of applications in political science.* New Haven ; London: Yale University Press.

Güth, Simon and Zülch, Henning (2010). *Die neue Satzung der IASCF (IASCF-Constitution Review): Implikationen für den Standardsetzungsprozess und die zukünftige Ausrichtung der IFRS.* KoR – Fachzeitschrift für internationale und kapitalmarktorientierte Rechnungslegung. (10):4. 177-182.

Gutmann, Amy and Thompson, Dennis (2004). *Why deliberative democracy?* Princeton, N.J. ; Oxford: Princeton University Press.

Habermas, Jürgen (1996). *Between facts and norms: contributions to a discourse theory of law and democracy.* Cambridge, Mass: MIT Press.

Hall, Rodney Bruce and Biersteker, Thomas J. (2002). *The emergence of private authority in global governance.* Cambridge: Cambridge University Press.

Hall, Rodney Bruce and Biersteker, Thomas J. (2002). *The emergence of private authority in the international system. The Emergence of Private Authority in Global Governance.* Hall, Rodney Bruce and Biersteker, Thomas J. Cambridge: Cambridge University Press.

Haller, Axel (2002). *Financial accounting developments in the European Union: past events and future prospects.* European Accounting Review. (11):1. 153-190.

Hamilton, Alexander and Fairfield, Roy P. (1966). *The Federalist papers: a collection of essays written in support of the Constitution of the United States.* Garden City, N.Y.,: Anchor Books.

Hamlin, Alan P. and Pettit, Philip (1989). *The Good polity : normative analysis of the state.* Oxford: Basil Blackwell.

Haring, John R. (1979). *Accounting Rules and 'The Accounting Establishment'.* Journal of Business. (52):4. 507-519.

Harris, Edward A. (1992). *From Social Contract to Hypothetical Agreement: Consent and the Obligation to Obey the Law.* Columbia Law Review. (92):3. 651-683.

Hartner, Martina, Rechberger, Silvia, Kirchler, Erich and Schabmann, Alfred (2008). *Procedural Fairness and Tax Compliance*. Economic Analysis & Policy. (38):1. 137-152.

Hauptmann, Emily (2001). *Can Less Be More? Leftist Deliberative Democrats' Critique of Participatory Democracy*. Polity. (33):3. 397-421.

Healy, Paul M. and Palepu, Krishna G. (2001). *Information asymmetry, corporate disclosure, and the capital markets: A review of the empirical disclosure literature*. Journal of Accounting and Economics. (31):1-3. 405-440.

Held, David (1995). *Democracy and the global order: from the modern state to cosmopolitan governance*. Cambridge: Polity.

Held, David (2006). *Models of democracy*. Cambridge: Polity.

Hibbing, John R. and Theiss-Morse, Elizabeth (2001). *Process Preferences and American Politics: What the People Want Government to Be*. The American Political Science Review. (95):1. 145-153.

Holthausen, Robert W. and Leftwich, Richard W. (1983). *The Economic Consequences of Accounting Choice*. Journal of Accounting and Economics. (5):2. 77-117.

Hopwood, Anthony G. (1994). *Some reflections on 'The harmonization of accounting within the EU'*. European Accounting Review. (3):2. 241-254.

Horngreen, Charles T. (1972). *Accounting principles: Private or public sector?* Journal of Accountancy. 37-41.

Howieson, Bryan A. (2009). *Agenda formation and accounting standards setting: lessons from the standards setters*. Accounting & Finance. (49):3. 577-598.

Hurrelmann, Achim, Schneider, Steffen and Steffek, Jens (2007). *Legitimacy in an age of global politics* Palgrave Macmillan.

Hyland, James L. (1995). *Democratic theory: the philosophical foundations*. Manchester: Manchester University Press.

International Accounting Standard Board (2006). Statement of Best Practice: Working Relationships between the IASB and other Accounting Standard-Setters. London: IASB. 1-16.

International Accounting Standards Committee Foundation (2005). Trustees approve constitutional changes. Press Release (28 June 2005).

International Accounting Standards Committee Foundation (2008). *Due Process Handbook for the International Accounting Standards Board (IASB)*.

International Accounting Standards Committee Foundation (2008). *Review of the Constitution – Identifying Issues for Part 2 of the Review*.

International Accounting Standards Committee Foundation (2008). *Review of the Constitution: Public Accountability and the Public Accountability and the Composition of the IASB – Proposals for Change*.

International Accounting Standards Committee Foundation (2009). Annual Report.
International Accounting Standards Committee Foundation (2009). – *Part 2 of the Constitution Review. Proposals for Enhanced Public Accountability.*
International Accounting Standards Committee Foundation (2010). Constitution.
International Organization of Securities Commissions (2007). Authorities Responsible for Capital Market Regulation Work to Enhance the Governance of the IASC Foundation.
Johnson, Steven B. and Solomons, David (1984). *Institutional Legitimacy and the FASB.* Journal of Accounting & Public Policy. (3):3. 165-183.
Jupe, Robert E. (2000). *Self-referential lobbying of the Accounting Standards Board: The case of financial reporting standard No. 1.* Critical Perspectives on Accounting. (11):3. 337-359.
Kaplan, David and Fender, Elizabeth A. (1998). *The Development of Comment Letters on FASB Proposals by the AICPA Accounting Standards Executive Committee.* Accounting Horizons. (12):2. 184-187.
Katz, Michael L. and Shapiro, Carl (1985). *Network Externalities, Competition, and Compatibility.* American Economic Review. (75):3. 424-440.
Kenneth Sullivan, Senior Financial Sector Expert (IMF) (2008). Constitutional Review – Round-table meeting, Session 1 Part 1.
Kingsbury, Benedict , Krisch, Nico, Stewart, Richard B. and Wiener, Jonathan B. (2005). *Global Governance as Administration – National and Transnational Approaches to Global Administrative Law.* Law and Contemporary Problems. (68):3/4. 1-13.
Klumpes, P. J. M. (1994). *The Politics of Rule Development: A Case Study of Australian Pension fund Accounting Rule-Making.* Abacus. (30):2. 140-159.
Königsgruber, Roland (2009). *Lobbying bei der Rechnungslegungsstandardsetzung. Ein Literaturüberblick.* Zeitschrift für Betriebswirtschaft. (79):11. 1309-1329.
Krohn, Christian (SIFMA) (2008). Constitutional Reveiw – Round-table meeting, Session 1 Part 1.
Kurz, Gerhard (2009). *Das IASB und die Regulierung der Rechnungslegung in der EU: eine Analyse von Legitimation und Lobbying.* Frankfurt: Peter Lang.
Kwok, Winston Chee Chiu and Sharp, David (2005). *Power and international accounting standard setting: Evidence from segment reporting and intangible assets projects.* Accounting, Auditing & Accountability Journal. (18):1. 74-99.
Lane, Robert E. (1988). *Procedural goods in a democracy: How one is treated versus what one gets.* Social Justice Research. (2):3. 177-192.

Lanfermann, Georg (2009). *Steht das IASB durch die Finanzkrise vor einer Zerreißprobe?* Der Betrieb. (10):3. 1-5.

Larson, Robert K. (1997). *Corporate Lobbying of the International Accounting Standards Committee.* Journal of International Financial Management & Accounting. (8):3. 175-203.

Larson, Robert K. (2002). *The IASC's search for legitimacy: An analysis of the IASC's standing interpretations committee.* Advances in International Accounting. (15):79-120.

Larson, Robert K. and Kenny, Sara York (2011). *The financing of the IASB: An analysis of donor diversity.* Journal of International Accounting, Auditing and Taxation. (20):1. 1-19.

Larson, Robert K. and Street, Donna L. (2004). *Convergence with IFRS in an expanding Europe: progress and obstacles identified by large accounting firms' survey.* Journal of International Accounting, Auditing and Taxation. (13):2. 89-119.

Laughlin, Richard C. and Puxty, Anthony G. (1983). *Accounting regulation: An alternative perspective.* Journal of Business Finance & Accounting. (10):3. 451-479.

Leventhal, Gerald S. (1980). *What Should Be Done with Equity Theory? New Approches to the Study of Fairness in Social Relationships. Social exchange: advances in theory and research.* Gergen, Kenneth J., Greenberg, Martin S. and Willis, Richard H. New York : London: Plenum.

Lewis, Thomas J. (1989). *On Using the Concept of Hypothetical Consent.* Canadian Journal of Political Science / Revue canadienne de science politique. (22):4. 793-807.

Lind, E. Allan, Kulik, Carol T., Ambrose, Maureen and Park, Maria V. de Vera (1993). *Individual and Corporate Dispute Resolution: Using Procedural Fairness as a Decision Heuristic.* Administrative Science Quarterly. (38):2. 224-251.

Lindahl, Frederick W. (1987). *Accounting Standards and Olson's Theory of Collective Action.* Journal of Accounting & Public Policy. (6):1. 59-72.

Livermore, Michael A. (2006). *Authority and Legitimacy in Global Governance: Deliberation, Institutional Differentiation, and the Codex Alimentarius.* New York University Law Review. (81):766-801.

Livermore, Michael A. (2006). *Authority and Legitimacy in Global Governance: Deliberation, Institutional Differentiation, and the Codex Alimentarius.* New York University Law Review. (81):Available at: http://ssrn.com/abstract=903408. 766-801.

Luthardt, Ulf and Zimmermann, Jochen (2009). *A European view on the legitimacy of accounting procedures: Towards a deliberative-accountability framework for analysis*. Research in Accounting Regulation. (21):2. 79-88.

Manin, Bernard, Stein, Elly and Mansbridge, Jane (1987). *On Legitimacy and Political Deliberation*. Political Theory. (15):3. 338-368.

Martinez-Diaz, Leonardo (2005). *Strategic Experts and Improvising Regulators: Explaining the IASC's Rise to Global Influence, 1973-2001*. Business and Politics. (7):3. 1-26.

Mattli, Walter and Buethe, Tim (2005). *Accountability in Accounting? The Politics of Private Rule-Making in the Public Interest*. Governance. (18):3. 399-429.

Mattli, Walter and Buethe, Tim (2005). *Global Private Governance: Lessons from a National Model of Setting Standards in Accounting*. Law and Contemporary Problems. (68):3/4. 225-262.

Mattli, Walter and Woods, Ngaire (2009). *The politics of global regulation*. Princeton: Princeton University Press.

May, Robert G. and Sundem, Gary L. (1976). *Research for Accounting Policy: An Overview*. Accounting Review. (51):4. 747-763.

McCreevy, Charlie (2009). *Keynote Address*. Financial Reporting in a Changing World, Brussels.

McGreevy, Charlie (2007). EU-US cooperation on reporting standards audit oversight and regulation European Federation of Accountants' Conference on Audit Regulation. Brussels, November 27, 2007.

McKee, James A., Williams, Paul F. and Frazier, Katherine Beal (1991). *A case study of accounting firm lobbying: Advice or consent*. Critical Perspectives on Accounting. (2):3. 273-294.

McKee Jr, A. James, Bell, Timothy B. and Boatsman, James R. (1984). *Management Preferences Over Accounting Standards: A Replication and Additional Tests*. Accounting Review. (59):4. 647-659.

Meier, André Rolf (2009). *Abbildung von Unternehmensverbindungen im Konzernabschluss: eine Analyse der Business-Combinations-Projekte von IASB und FASB*, Der Andere Verlag.

Meier, Heidi Hylton, Alam, Pervaiz and Pearson, Michael A. (1993). *Auditor Lobbying for Accounting Standards: The Case of Banks and Savings and Loan Associations*. Accounting & Business Research. (23):92. 477-487.

Mill, John Stuart (1861). *Considerations on representative government. On liberty and other essays*. Gray (ed.), John. Oxford: Oxford University Press, 2008.

Miller, David (2003). *Political philosophy a very short introduction*. Oxford: Oxford University Press.

Miller, Eugene F. (1987). *Hume, David: Essays: moral, political, and literary. Liberty classics*. New York: Liberty Fund.
Miller, J. D. B. (1962). *The nature of politics*. London: Duckworth.
Mueller, Dennis C. (1973). *Constitutional Democracy and Social Welfare*. The Quarterly Journal of Economics. (87):1. 60-80.
Mueller, Dennis C. (1976). *Public Choice: A Survey*. Journal of Economic Literature. (14):2. 395-433.
Mueller, Dennis C. (1991). *Public choice II: a revised edition of Public Choice* Cambridge Univ. Press.
Neuhold, Christine (2008). *Taming the 'Trojan Horse' of Comitology? Accountability Issues of Comitology and the Role of the European Parliament*. European Integration Online Papers. (12):1. 1-18.
Nobes, Christopher (2004). *On accounting classification and the international harmonisation debate*. Accounting, Organizations & Society. (29):2. 189-200.
Nobes, Christopher and Parker, Robert (2008). *Comparative international accounting*. Harlow: Financial Times/Prentice Hall.
Nobes, Christopher and Parker, Robert H. (2002). *Comparative international accounting*. Harlow: Financial Times/Prentice-Hall.
Nullmeier, Frank and Pritzlaff, Tanja (2010). *The Great Chain of legitimacy. Justifying Transnational Democracy*. TranState Working Papers. (No. 123): Bremen: Sfb 597 "Staatlichkeit im Wandel". 1-17.
Palmon, Dan, Peytcheva, Marietta and Yezegel, Ari (2011). *The Accounting Standards Setting Process in the U.S.: Examination of the SEC–FASB Relationship*. Group Decision and Negotiation. (20):2. 165-183.
Pateman, Carole (1970). *Participation and democratic theory*. Cambridge: University Press.
Pauly, Louis W., Ed. (2002). *Global finance, political authority, and the problem of legitimation*. Cambridge: Cambridge University Press.
Phillips, Anne (1995). *The politics of presence*. Oxford; New York: Clarendon Press.
Pink, Thomas (2004). *Free will: a very short introduction*. Oxford: Oxford Univerity Press.
Pitkin, Hanna (1965). *Obligation and Consent--I*. The American Political Science Review. (59):4. 990-999.
Pitkin, Hanna (1966). *Obligation and Consent--II*. The American Political Science Review. (60):1. 39-52.
Pitkin, Hanna Fenichel (1972). *The concept of representation*. Berkeley: University of California Press.
Plotke, David (1997). *Representation is Democracy*. Constellations. (4):1. 19-34.

Porter, Tony (2005). *Private Authority, Technical Authority, and the Globalization of Accounting Standards*. Business & Politics. (7):3. 1-30.
Powell, G. Bingham (2004). *The Chain of Responsiveness*. Journal of Democracy. (15):4.
Quack, Sigrid (2010). *Law, expertise and legitimacy in transnational economic governance: an introduction*. Socio-Economic Review. (8):1. 3-16.
Radwan, Alexander (2008). Report on International Financial Reporting Standards (IFRS) and the Governance of the International Accounting Standards Board (IASB), Committee on Economic and Monetary Affairs. European Parliament. 1-23.
Raz, Joseph (1990). *Authority and Justification. Authority*. Raz, Joseph. New York: New York University Press.
Raz, Joseph (1990). *Introduction. Authority*. Raz, Joseph. New York: New York University Press.
Reinicke, Wolfgang H. (1998). *Global public policy : governing without government?* Washington, D.C.: Brookings Institution Press.
Richardson, Alan (2008). *Due Process and Standard-setting: An Analysis of Due Process in Three Canadian Accounting and Auditing Standard-setting Bodies*. Journal of Business Ethics. (81):3. 679-696.
Richardson, Alan and Eberlein, Burkard (2011). *Legitimating Transnational Standard-Setting: The Case of the International Accounting Standards Board*. Journal of Business Ethics. (98):2. 217-245.
Risse, Thomas (2006). *Transnational Governance and Legitimacy, in: Governance and democracy: comparing national, European and international experiences*. London: Routledge.
Rogowski, Ronald (1981). *Representation in Political Theory and in Law*. Ethics. (91):3. 395-430.
Ronen, Joshua and Schiff, Michael (1978). *The setting of financial standards – private or public?* Journal of Accountancy. (145):3. 66-73.
Rossi, Jim (1997). *Participation run amok: The costs of mass participation for deliberative agency decision-making*. Northwestern University Law Review. (92):1. 174-250.
Rousseau, Jean-Jacques (2004). *The Social Contract*. London: Penguin; Revised Edition.
Ruder, David S., Canfield, Charles T. and Hollister, Hudson T. (2005). *Creation of World Wide Accounting Standards: Convergence and Independence*. Northwestern Journal of International Law & Business. (25):3. 513-588.
Ryan, Christine and Dunstan, Keitha (1999). *Constituent participation in the Australian public sector accounting standard-setting process*. Financial Accountability & Management. (15):2. 173.

Ryfe, David M. (2005). *Does deliberative democracy work?* Annual Review of Political Science. (8):1. 49-71.

Saemann, Georgia (1999). *An Examination of Comment Letters Filed in the U.S. Financial Accounting Standard-Setting Process by Institutional Interest Groups*. Abacus. (35):1. 1-28.

Salisbury, Robert H. (1975). *Research on Political Participation*. American Journal of Political Science. (19):2. 323-341.

Sarat, Austin (1977). *Studying American Legal Culture: An Assessment of Survey Evidence*. Law & Society Review. (11):3. 427-488.

Scharpf, Fritz W. (2004). *Legitimationskonzepte jenseits des Nationalstaats*. MPIfG Working Paper. (4):6. 1-31.

Schaub, Alexander (2005). *The Use of International Accounting Standards in the European Union*. Northwestern Journal of International Law & Business. (25):3. 609-629.

Schmidt, Matthias (2002). *On the legitimacy of accounting standard setting by privately organised institutions in Germany and Europe*. Schmalenbach Business Review (SBR). (54):2. 171-193.

Schoemaker, Paul J. H. (1982). *The Expected Utility Model: Its Variants, Purposes, Evidence and Limitations*. Journal of Economic Literature. (20):2. 529-563.

Schumpeter, Joseph Alois (1954). *Capitalism, socialism, and democracy*. London: Allen & Unwin.

Schusterschitz, Gregor and Kotz, Sabine (2007). *The Comitology Reform of 2006 Increasing the Powers of the European Parliament Without Changing the Treaties*. European Constitutional Law Review (EuConst). (3):01. 68-90.

Scott, Colin (2000). *Accountability in the Regulatory State*. Journal of Law and Society. (27):1. 38-60.

Scott, William R. (2009). *Financial accounting theory*. Toronto: Pearson Prentice Hall.

Selto, Frank H. and Grove, Hugh D. (1982). *Voting Power Indices and the Setting of Financial Accounting Standards: Extensions*. Journal of Accounting Research. (20):2. 676-688.

Simmons, A. John (1976). *Tacit Consent and Political Obligation*. Philosophy and Public Affairs. (5):3. 274-291.

Simms, Marian (1999). *Models of Political Accountability and Concepts of Australian Government*. Australian Journal of Public Administration. (58):1. 34-38.

Solomons, David (1983). *The Political Implications of Accounting and Accounting Standard Setting*. Accounting & Business Research. (13):50. 107-118.

Spencer, Martin E. (1970). *Weber on Legitimate Norms and Authority*. The British Journal of Sociology. (21):2. 123-134.
Standards Advisory Council (2005). *Terms of reference and operating procedures*.
Stark, Cynthia A. (2000). *Hypothetical Consent and Justification*. The Journal of Philosophy. (97):6. 313-334.
Stillman, Peter G. (1974). *The Concept of Legitimacy*. Polity. (7):1. 32-56.
Suchman, Mark C. (1995). *Managing legitimacy: Strategic and institutional approaches*. Academy of Management Review. (20):3. 571-610.
Sutton, Timothy G. (1984). *Lobbying of accounting standard-setting in the U.K. and the U.S.A.: A Downsian analysis*. Accounting, Organizations & Society. (9):1. 81-95.
Tandy, Paulette R. and Wilburn, Nancy L. (1992). *Constituent Participation in Standard-Setting: The FASB's First 100 Statements*. Accounting Horizons. (6):2. 47-58.
The Group of Twenty (G-20) (2009). *Declaration on strengthening the financial system – London summit, 2 April, 2009*. Available at: http://g20london.wordpress.com/2009/04/02/g20-london-summit-declaration.
Thorell, Per and Whittington, Geoffrey (1994). *The harmonization of accounting within the EU -- Problems, perspectives and strategies*. European Accounting Review. (3):2. 215-240.
Thorella, Per and Whittington, Geoffrey (1994). *The harmonization of accounting within the EU – Problems, perspectives and strategies*. European Accounting Review. (3):2. 215-240.
Thornburg, Steven and Roberts, Robin W. (2008). *Money, politics, and the regulation of public accounting services: Evidence from the Sarbanes-Oxley Act of 2002*. Accounting, Organizations and Society. (33):2-3. 229-248.
Tuck, Richard (1997). *Hobbes, Thomas: Leviathan. Cambridge texts in the history of political thought*. Cambridge: Cambridge University Press.
Tweedie, David (2007). *IASB Chairman Addresses European Parliament*.
Tyler, Tom R. (2006). *Why people obey the law*. Princeton: Princeton University Press.
U.S. Securities and Exchange Commission. (2000, http://www.sec.gov/rules/concept/34-42430.htm). *SEC Concept Release: International Accounting Standards*. Retrieved 10. January, 2010.
U.S. Securities and Exchange Commission (2008). *SEC Proposes Roadmap Toward Global Accounting Standards to Help Investors Compare Financial Information More Easily*. Press Release, Washington, D.C., Available at: http://www.sec.gov/news/press/2008/2008-184.htm.

Urbinati, Nadia and Warren, Mark E. (2008). *The Concept of Representation in Contemporary Democratic Theory*. Annual Review of Political Science. (11):387-412.
van Hulle, Karel (1992). *Harmonization of accounting standards: A view from the European community*. European Accounting Review. (1):1. 161-172.
van Hulle, Karel (1993). *Harmonization of accounting standards in the EC – Is it the beginning or is it the end?* European Accounting Review. (2):2. 387-396.
Véron, Nicolas (2007). The Global Accounting Experiment. SERIES, BRUEGEL BLUEPRINT. Brussels: BRUEGEL. 2. 1-86.
Vitale, Denise (2006). *Between deliberative and participatory democracy: A contribution on Habermas*. Philosophy & Social Criticism. (32):6. 739-766.
Wallace, Reginald Sylvanus Olusegun (1990). *Survival Strategies of a Global Organization: The Case of the International Accounting Standards Committee*. Accounting Horizons. (4):2. 1-22.
Walton, Peter J., Haller, Axel and Raffournier, Bernard (1998). *International accounting* Internat. Thomson Business Press.
Warren, Mark E. (1993). *Can Participatory Democracy Produce Better Selves? Psychological Dimensions of Habermas's Discursive Model of Democracy*. Political Psychology. (14):2. 209-234.
Warren, Mark E. (1996). *Deliberative democracy and authority*. American Political Science Review. (90):1. 46-60.
Watts, Ross L. and Zimmerman, Jerold L. (1986). *Positive accounting theory*. Englewood Cliffs, New Jersey: Prentice-Hall.
Weale, Albert (2007). *Democracy*. Basingstoke: Palgrave Macmillan.
Weale, Albert P. (1981). *Representation, Individualism, and Collectivism*. Ethics. (91):3. 457-465.
Weber, Max (1947). *The theory of social and economic organization*. New York: Oxford University Press.
Werner, Jörg Richard and Zimmermann, Jochen (2009). *Internationaler Vergleich von Rechnungslegungssystemen*. Die Betriebswirtschaft. (61):1. 85-106.
Whittington, Geoffrey (2005). *The adoption of International Accounting Standards in the European Union*. European Accounting Review. (14):1. 127-153.
Wolfe, Joel D. (1985). *A Defense of Participatory Democracy*. The Review of Politics. (47):3. 370-389.
Wolff, Jonathan (2006). *An introduction to political philosophy*. Oxford: Oxford University Press.
Zalm, Gerrit (Chairman, IASC Foundation). (2008). Constitutional Review – Round-table meeting, Session1 Part 1.

Zeff, Stephen A. (2007). *Some obstacles to global financial reporting comparability and convergence at a high level of quality*. The British Accounting Review. (39):4. 290-302.
Zimmermann, Jochen (2002). *Ordnungspolitische Fragen zur Unternehmenspublizität nach der Enron-Insolvenz*. Wirtschaftsdienst. (82):5. 303-312.
Zimmermann, Jochen (2007). *The Role of the Nation-State in the Internationalization of Accounting Regimes. Transforming the golden-age nation state*. Hurrelmann, Achim, Leibfried, Stephan, Martens, Kerstin and Mayer, Peter-Palgrave Macmillan.
Zimmermann, Jochen (2008). *The Role of the Nation State in the Internationalization of Accounting Regimes. Transforming the Golden-Age Nation State*. Leibfried, Stephan, Martens, Kerstin and Mayer, Peter. Basingstoke: Palgrave Macmillan.
Zimmermann, Jochen (2010). *EU Federalism and the Governance of Financial Reporting*. Publius: The Journal of Federalism. (40):1. 200-225.
Zimmermann, Jochen, Werner, Jörg R. and Volmer, Philipp B. (2008). *Global governance in accounting: rebalancing public power and private commitment*. Basingstoke: Palgrave Macmillan.

Peter Lang · Internationaler Verlag der Wissenschaften

Christian Reisloh

Influence of National Culture on IFRS Practice

An Empirical Study in France, Germany and the United Kingdom

Frankfurt am Main, Berlin, Bern, Bruxelles, New York, Oxford, Wien, 2011.
XXXI, 400 pp., num. fig. and tab.
Münsteraner Schriften zur Internationalen Unternehmensrechnung.
Edited by Peter Kajüter. Vol. 4
ISBN 978-3-631-62052-6 · hb. € 74,80*

The adoption of IFRS for group accounts of capital market oriented EU companies in 2005 was a milestone in European and international accounting harmonization. The benefits of a harmonized EU capital market, however, might be jeopardized by the inconsistent application of IFRS due to remaining national peculiarities. This study investigates IFRS measurement and disclosure practices in the leading EU economies of France, Germany and the UK. The empirical results show that differences in IFRS application are associated with national cultural differences. The findings of the study lead to several implications for IFRS accounting research and practice.

Content: Field study on IFRS measurement and disclosure practice in France, Germany and the UK · Theory guided analysis of the association between national culture and IFRS practice

Frankfurt am Main · Berlin · Bern · Bruxelles · New York · Oxford · Wien
Distribution: Verlag Peter Lang AG
Moosstr. 1, CH-2542 Pieterlen
Telefax 00 41 (0) 32 / 376 17 27

*The €-price includes German tax rate
Prices are subject to change without notice

Homepage http://www.peterlang.de

www.ingramcontent.com/pod-product-compliance
Ingram Content Group UK Ltd.
Pitfield, Milton Keynes, MK11 3LW, UK
UKHW021014120926
8556IPUK00040B/1136

9 783631 621264